# RUSSIAN AVANT-GARDE
# ART AND ARCHITECTURE

# RUSSIAN AVANT-GARDE

# ART AND ARCHITECTURE

## GUEST-EDITED BY CATHERINE COOKE

## CONTENTS

**Editor/Publisher**
Dr Andreas C Papadakis

This AD Profile was edited and designed by Frank Russell in association with Kelly Crossman and Richard Cheatle

*Front Cover*
Iakov Chernikhov, architectural fiction, Composition No 28, from *Architectural Fictions 101 Compositions*, 1933.

*Back Cover*
Liubov Popova, *Painterly Architectonics*, c 1918–1919. (Costakis Collection)

*Inside Front Cover*
Iakov Chernikhov: theatrical set. A unified dynamic composition of curved cylindrical bodies, planes, slogans and signs. Colouring: bright cold green and white with orange accents. Construction No 7 from *The Construction of Architectural and Machine Forms*, 1931.

*Page 1*
Antonina Sofronova, untitled composition, nd. (Costakis Collection)

*Frontispiece:*
Axonometric representation of an architectural composition in volume and plan. A manifestly constructive amalgamation of extended elements in a structure of verticals and horizontals. Fantasy B, from *Architectural Fictions 101 Compositions*, 1933.

First published in Great Britain in 1983 by Academy Editions and Architectural Design, 7 Holland Street, London W8

AD Profile 47 is published as part of Architectural Design Volume 53 5/6–1983

Distributed in the United States of America by St Martin's Press, 175 Fifth Avenue, New York, NY10010, USA

Library of Congress Catalogue Card Number 83–50700
ISBN 0 312 69612 4 (USA only)

Printed and bound by Garden House Press, London

Lindsey Hughes

# RUSSIA'S FIRST ARCHITECTURAL BOOKS: A CHAPTER IN PETER THE GREAT'S CULTURAL REVOLUTION

1

1  Peter the Great in his shipwright's clothes.
2  Contemporary popular woodcut depicting Peter the Great, right, as the barber of his noblemen's beards. A beard could only be worn after a tax was paid, for which a special 'seal' or token was attached to the beard as proof of payment to legalise it.
3  A coat of blue velour from Peter's wardrobe, typical of the many 'modern', 'efficient' clothes he purchased from Europe.

Architecture was one of the many areas profoundly affected by the cultural and political changes in eighteenth-century Russia known as the 'Petrine Revolution'. What more appropriate symbol can there be of Peter the Great's efforts to modernise his backward and introspective country than the new capital city of St Petersburg, founded in 1703 on land newly conquered from Sweden, its face firmly turned towards Europe and its chief buildings designed by foreign architects?

The character of St Petersburg, Peter's 'window on the West', was a consistent extension of earlier moves towards absorbing Western culture made by Peter. Having ascended the Russian throne in 1682 at the age of ten, he spent much of his rather wild and free adolescence in the company of Europeans from the so-called 'German colony' where Russia's technical and commercial advisors were forced to live, ghetto-like, outside the Moscow city walls. Then in 1697–8 he set off on a pioneering tour of Northern Europe – the first Russian Tsar ever to venture abroad in this way. Indulging his passion for science and technology he studied navigation, shipbuilding and all manner of practical crafts, working with his own hands – where possible incognito – in the yards of Amsterdam and London. Deptford's 'Czar Street' still records his visit, and John Evelyn, the diarist, was to rue the day he lent him his house. Throughout the travels of his so-called Great Embassy, Peter was recruiting technical and scientific experts who would come and work for him in Russia.[1]

The tour was cut short by a rebellion of the conservative Moscow guards regiment, the *streltsy*, which Peter suppressed with characteristic cruelty; shortly afterwards different victims, the nobility, were subjected to an assault which although symbolic, must have seemed equally cruel. Russian courtiers were forced to shave off their long beards, hitherto regarded as attributes of godliness, in order to become 'decent beardless Europeans'. A series of decrees starting in January 1700 ordered the nobility, government officials and men of property throughout the Empire to discard their long, flowing Russian robes in favour of 'practical' Western dress of the kind Peter himself had bought extensively in his European travels. Upper class women were encouraged to leave the seclusion to which they had been condemned in traditional Russian society.

In January 1700 Peter also adopted the Western Julian calendar in preference to Old Russian computation of the year from the Creation, and in the same year the Patriarch, the head of the Orthodox Church, died and was not replaced: both indications that the strong official Muscovite orientation towards religion was changing. That same year Russia went to war with Sweden, a war which was to end formally 21 years later with Russia triumphant and newly prominent in European affairs. In the midst of that, however, the cultural innovations and transformations on which he was determined proceeded unabated at home, the architectural changes conspicuous amongst them.

The *streltsy* uprising had been one more demonstration, after many bloody Kremlin events observed in his childhood, of the medieval obscurantism that Peter associated with Moscow. Petersburg started with requirements for a northern defence point against Sweden, to hold land newly won. Once transformed in concept into a new city, its architectural character reflected from the first Peter's own simple tastes and practical priorities: a Dutch simplicity and domesticity was not surprising. But the architects he imported to turn it into a capital city

4 Peter sails a small Dutch-built sloop on the River Neva amidst the early buildings of St Petersburg. Behind him lies the North bank of the Great Neva, just downstream of the Peter and Paul Fortress. His wife Catherine, the future Empress Catherine the First, sits in the stern. (Part of a panoramic engraving by A F Zubov, of 1716).

5 Gatehouse church of the Transfiguration in the Novo-devichy monastery, Moscow, 1687. A balance of traditional composition with certain classical elements already imported in the fifteenth century, and 'new' classical elements characteristic of the Naryshkin Baroque. *For further illustrations of this period see page 78.*

of the Enlightenment were mainly French, German and Italian. They became the basis of a new architectural profession in Russia that was grounded in the classical rules, and the founders of formal architectural education. Their activity was supported by a programme of translation and publication of the great Western handbooks of classical design which was directly initiated and supervised by Peter himself, most notably a series of editions of Vignola's *Rules of the Five Orders*.

As I shall show later, various components of classical architecture were already to be found in Russian architecture: a partial assimilation of elements of the Orders and some knowledge of the important publications predated Peter's reforms by several decades. This however was the first attempt to introduce Russia to the classical canons, to the whole classical system whence those elements had previously been borrowed, and rather freely – indeed inventively – reworked into combination with Russian compositional and formal prototypes. Now, these rule systems formed an important and conscious aspect of the wider 'Petrine Revolution', and in two respects particularly. Firstly, architecture, especially in the new capital, provided one of the most visible signs of Westernisation. As the Soviet architectural historian N A Evsina has recently observed: 'It was through the perception of architecture that changes in the artistic outlook of people in the Petrine era, in their tastes, values and notions of the 'free sciences' and 'arts' were most clearly manifested.'[2] Secondly, the translation, publication and acquisition of works of technical literature were important channels of reform. The fact that Peter himself took a close personal interest in both architecture and publishing adds to the attraction of the subject. At first sight, however, this promising combination provides disappointing fare since only one

translated work on architecture actually appeared in print for 'mass' distribution during Peter's reign. But, as we shall see, works on architecture in the strictest sense of the word were only one part of the story.

**Foreign influences before Peter**

For the Westerner to whom an exotic structure like the sixteenth century St Basil's Cathedral may be the only familiar image, Russian architecture before Peter the Great may be perceived as something entirely remote from that of Western Europe.[3] Long before Peter's time however, Russian architecture had been influenced by periodic injections of foreign styles and expertise, so that this isolation was far from complete. The first churches in newly Christianised Kiev of the tenth century were based on Byzantine models, whilst in the eleventh and twelfth centuries Northern Russia saw something akin to the Romanesque. Builders in the city-state of Novgorod acquired a number of stylistic ideas through trade with Northern Europe. In 1237–40, however, Russia was conquered by Mongols, invading from the East, and the Mongol 'yoke', formally lifted only in 1480, effectively curtailed major building projects and significant artistic links with the outside world for over two centuries. The Gothic made no inroads into Russia proper, although it penetrated close neighbours such as Byelorussia and Lithuania. Russian builders clung to indigenous traditions and the well established Byzantine canons. Interestingly enough, Ivan III (1462–1505), the Tsar who finally ended the Mongol occupation, sought the aid of Western architects. Determined that the architecture of Moscow should reflect the city's status as ecclesiastical and political capital, he invited Italians to construct cathedrals, palaces and fortifications. Such visitations remained the exception

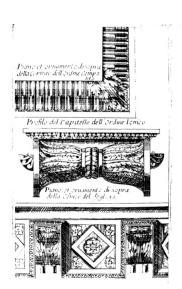

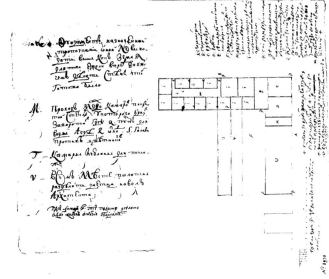

6,7 Two pages from the first Russian edition of Vignola, 1709. The first page of the text, on 'How to build foundations', at this stage still engraved, and illustrations, in Italian, still taken direct from the original.

8 Annotated drawing by Peter himself, 1721, relating to a proposed building in the Summer Park, St Petersburg.

however. The building which was erected by his successor as final celebration of that Mongol defeat was St Basil's – erected in 1555. It has a surprisingly Italianate, symmetrical ground-plan, but the feast of cupolas and tapered *shatëory* erected from it was programmatically and nationalistically Russian.

Throughout this sixteenth century, Muscovite architecture remained largely isolated from current Western trends. Brick and stone were reserved almost exclusively for fortifications and churches, the latter designed according to strict conventions. The one main innovation, the tent-shaped *shatër*, owed little to foreign influence. Practically everything else, including civic buildings and the dwellings of nobles and peasants alike, was built of wood, the ancient traditions of which were unreceptive to outside influence. The results were often pleasing and picturesque, but there was comparatively little room for independent creative design, except in decorative details. Russian stone masons received their basic skills from their fathers and had no need of theoretical works or even literacy to guide them. The art of precise architectural drawing was unknown (it has been argued that most buildings were constructed without the aid of plans at all); indeed, architectural design was scarcely perceived on an intellectual level, and although echoes of the Renaissance reached Russia there was little awareness of the original classical models.

Significant changes took place in the seventeenth century, as Russia drew nearer to the West both physically and mentally.[4] Contacts increased through wars, trade and diplomacy, and foreigners entered Muscovite service in their hundreds to impart much-needed skills in the military arts, engineering, mining and other practical fields. In 1652, an area of Moscow, the 'German Colony', was allocated to them, and Western architecture started to arrive 'in the flesh' as the immigrants built their own houses and churches. It was here the younger Peter had spent much of his time.

At this stage the Muscovite court of his parents, however, did not express any *explicit* desire to acquire the latest in Western artistic styles. Until Peter's own reign, the attitude to secular art was to remain ambiguous because of pressures from the Orthodox church, which hitherto had maintained a virtual monopoly on such culture as existed. Yet foreign artefacts – furniture, fabrics, clocks, mirrors, engravings – were imported, and a handful of foreign artists entered the Tsar's artistic workshops, the Moscow 'Armoury', where they began to produce the first portraits from life – hitherto considered sacriligious images – canvases on secular themes, and introduced the art of precise engraving.[5]

In architecture, the most vigorous product of this seventeenth century 'Renaissance' was the Moscow Baroque style, alternately called the Naryshkin Baroque, which flourished in the 1680s and 1690s.[6] The Naryshkin's were Peter's mother's family – she was Natalia Kirilovna Naryshkina – and prominent members of that family were patrons of several of the style's greatest masterpieces, such as the churches of the Intercession at Fili and of the Trinity at Troitse-Lykovo, on their estates then adjacent to Moscow City. Generally playing deep red brick against richly carved white stone details, the style was characterised in church-building by dynamic superimpositions of octagonal tiers upon square ones. Many of the overall designs were traditional, or bore the influence of Russian and Ukrainian wooden architectures. The articulation of facades though, and much of the decorative stonework, was clearly derived from Western sources: here were elements of the Classical Orders: broken pediments, twisted and carved columns, great volutes. These motifs, added by Russian craftsmen who could have had no direct knowledge of Western architecture (generally only diplomats and certain merchants could travel outside Russia), were almost certainly inspired by imported architectural manuals and other illustrated books.[7] Peter's father Tsar Aleksei Mikhailovich, for example, who lived till 1676, owned a work illustrating 'the stone buildings of all German states' and another with drawings of Holland. His elder son, Fedor, who ruled from 1676–82, had a book on the construction of palaces and a description of Rome in his library.

The most extensive collection of foreign books belonged at this time to the Foreign Chancellery, the *Posol'skii prikaz*, in the Kremlin, which alongside the conventional duties of diplomatic relations maintained artistic and architectural workshops, and carried out numerous projects in the Moscow Baroque style during the 1680s and 1690s. It is recorded, for example, that in 1683–4 Prince Vasily Golitsyn, then Director of the Chancellery and an active patron of architecture, borrowed seventeen books 'with models for gardens, palaces and

Second Russian edition of Vignola, 1712, produced in pocket format for students.

9  Flyleaf announcing: 'By command of the Great Tsar Peter Alekseivich, autocrat of all the Russias, is prepared and printed in Moscow this architectural book, in the year of our Lord 1712, September.'

10  Title page, with portrait of Vignola

11  Page 1, 'How to build foundations', now printed in the new alphabet (cf 1709 edition, above).

12  Page 10: 'On modules', and on 'The Doric Order'.

13  Page 17: 'The method of setting out an Ionic capital.'

14  Page 18: Illustration on the Ionic capital.

15  Page 61: Russian terms for parts of the building.

16  Page 73: 'The theatre or square in front of St Peters by architect Bernini'.

17  Page 92: The proportions of a window.

# ПОВЕЛѢНІЕМЪ

### Велікаго Государя Царя,
### и велікаго Князя

# ПЕТРА АЛЕѮІЕВІЧА

### Самодержца всероссійскаго.

Грыдорована и Печатана сія Архітектурная книга въ МОСКВѢ, лѣта отъ рождества Хрістова 1712, Сентября въ день.

9

10

## ФУНДАМЕНТЪ
### КАКЪ СТРОИТЬ.

Еже ли глина, то добро, ежелижъ твердои песокъ помѣшанъ съ каменьемъ. [какъ въ рѣкѣ на днѣ.] и то добро, сіи два лутче суть, по плитахъ, и въ таковыхъ мѣстахъ надлежітъ копать только три локтя, еже ли безъ погреба, [а погребъ еже ли дѣлать, то по изволенію и высотѣ оной, которои глубіна такова надлежітъ быть чтобъ своды были съ землею равны ради ходу. Своды наименше полъ локтя толстотою] такожъ подобаетъ знать, что фундаментъ въ земли. Еже ли добраи грунтъ, какъ выше опісано] два раза толще надлежітъ быть стѣнъ, которая сверхъ земли: и надлежітъ вынересенной фундаментъ отъ испода къ верху отмсь вести, уже пока изъ земли выдетъ малымъ чѣмъ ширъ стѣнъ, такожъ надлежітъ двѣ доли снаружи, а третьюю внутрь пустіть, какъ видѣть мочно.

Учели

11

## О МОДУЛЯХЪ.

Модули [какъ всѣ называютъ] или части, которыми ордіны разбвляются, тоскана, і дорика, которыя каждую модуль надлежітъ въ двѣнатцать частицъ раздѣлить.
А Іонику, корінту, и композіту надлежітъ осмнатцать частеи каждую модуль.

## ОРДОНА ДОРІКА.

Базаменто подъ педесталомъ 10 частеи отъ модуля.
Самои педесталъ 4 модуля, цымаза надъ педесталомъ полъ модуля. [или 6 частеи] база подъ колумною 1 модуль. Колумна 14 модулеи, капітель одінъ модуль, архітравъ, 1 модуль. фрісъ подъ 2 модуля, гзымзъ полъ 2. всего высоты 25 1/3 модулеи.

Педестала и база 2 модуля, и 10 частеи. Цымаза свѣсится полъ модуля, колумну раздѣлить, на три равныя доли въ высоту, въ нізу 2 модуля толстоты.

Въ

12

1:

## СПОСОБЪ СОЧІНІТЬ КАПІТЕЛЬ ІОНІКИ

Хотя и на семъ лістѣ начерчено съ планомъ и профілемъ, однакожъ для яснѣйшаго выразумленія надлежітъ протянуть 2 лінеи перпендікулярно или прямо отъ линеи до лінеи 2 модуля, которые проідутъ чрезъ центръ, или точки отъ средіны шныркали [или волуты] имѣеть быть 16 частеи отъ модуля высота 8 ихъ останутца надъ репьемъ, которая есть 2 частеи; а досталныя 6 останутся внізу репья, а какімъ способомъ дѣлаются шныркали назначено въ другомъ лісту и краткое о ономъ опісаніе, [какою шіротою] оныя дѣлать объявлено.

13

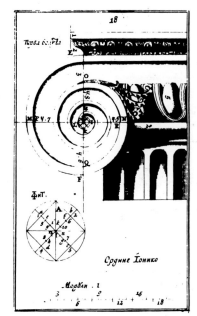

14

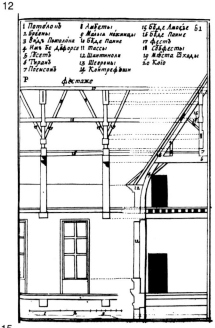

15

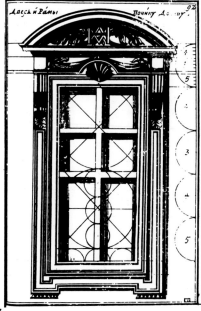

16

17

7

town-planning, carving and fountains and sculptures' from the library there. Other government departments which owned architectural books included the Artillery Chancellery and the Armoury, both of which employed foreign personnel. In addition to works specifically devoted to architecture and allied crafts, there were many others which were lavishly illustrated, including atlases, cosmographies and the 'Piscator' bible, whose influence on Russian painting has been well attested. Foreign prints and broadsheets also were sold in markets. Unfortunately, seventeenth-century Russian scribes rarely recorded bibliographical details of foreign books, so a certain amount of guesswork is required to establish precise titles from descriptions in library and other records. Soviet scholars have suggested that works by Palladio, Dietterlin, Furtenbach and Vignola, amongst others, were available in seventeenth-century Moscow in the original Italian and German editions. At this stage though it is likely that such materials were consulted mainly for decorative ideas. Both the structural designs of the Moscow Baroque and levels of literacy and intellectual awareness suggest that the wider theoretical and philosophical implications of Classical architecture were still not appreciated.

Peter had come to the throne as a boy of ten after Fedor's death in 1682, but his active reign began only after his mother's death in 1694 and, more precisely, after his visit to Western Europe during 1697–8. After this, architecture, like so many other things, became a state concern. Peter himself was deeply interested in it, and in the translation and publication of secular, practical works.

## Peter's publishing programme

That architecture was one of the fields envisaged in Peter's early programme for secular publications in Russian is indicated in a decree issued to Amsterdam printer Jan Tessing in February 1700, authorising him to publish in Russian 'pictures and charts of European, Asiatic and American lands and seas, all manner of printed sheets and portraits and books on army and navy personnel, on mathematical, architectural (*arkhitekturskie*), town-planning and other artistic topics.'[8] *Arkhitekturskie* may be interpreted here in the wider sense current in the early eighteenth century, to include fortification and even 'naval architecture'. Despite this instruction, architecture did not figure among the subjects of books recorded as being published in Russian in Amsterdam between 1699 and 1702. Nor does it appear amongst secular works issued by the Moscow press before the introduction of the new 'civil script' in 1708.

This new, simplified alphabet was itself a dimension of Peter's revolution, of his attempt to liberate areas of Russian life from the Church's conservatism and cultural monopoly. Religious works, hitherto virtually the only reading matter published in Russia, continued to appear in the older, more florid alphabet and type-faces, but the introduction of this new, more accessible Russian alphabet onto the Moscow Printing Press made 1708 a key year for secular publishing in Russia.

The publications that ensued, many guided through the press by the Tsar himself, highlighted the practical, military orientation of Peter's reforms – here were works on artillery, fortification, mathematics, navigation, weaponry. The prominence of architecture amongst Peter's concerns is testified by the appearance of the first architectural manual to be published in Russia in the very next year.

The year 1709 thus saw a new departure for both Russian architecture and printing, marked by the publication in Moscow of *Pravilo o piati chinekh arkhitektury Iakova Barotsiia devignola*.[9] This was a translation of Vignola's treatise *Regnola delli cinque ordini d'architettura* – Rules of the Five Orders of Architecture – first published in Rome in 1562.

## The Russian Vignola: the first architectural book

The original for the first Russian edition of Vignola has not been positively identified. The work was still available in numerous editions and languages at the beginning of the eighteenth century, and it is

18,19 First Russian book on etiquette: title page, and page on the new alphabet, from *The Honourable Mirror of Youth*, published by order of Peter, in 1717, as part of his attempt to civilise the next generation. It told the young gentleman such things as how to eat boiled eggs, and not to tread on ladies' toes in dancing.
20 One of Tressini's model designs for the development of Petersburg's outskirts. According to the inscription, middle right, signed 'Iuvenit D. Trezzini, St. P. Burg', 'He who chooses to build a suburban house in accordance with this plan may alter the gateways and pavilions . . . And he who has good natural woodlands behind his site may clear it up but not cut it down.'

possible that the text and engravings of Peter's edition were selected from different sources. A practical note is struck by the opening page of text, *Fundament kak stroit'* – How to build foundations – which is followed by equally practice-oriented sections on walls and modules. The overall emphasis however is firmly on the engravings, 102 of them, which form the bulk of the book.

Peter was personally involved in the preparation of this work for the press, and extracts from its publishing history throw interesting light upon Peter's minute attention to these affairs.[10]

The best authenticated references to the last stages of preparation relate to correspondence, in August – October 1709, between the Tsar and his close associate Prince M P Gagarin. On August 18, Gagarin informed Peter that he was sending by courier a 'small book on architecture' (*kniga malaia arkhitekturnaia*) and asked for instructions on possible corrections and on the number of copies to be printed.[11] On September 14, Peter acknowledged receipt of the book and sent a number of corrections, which he asked should be revised by the Italian architect G M Fontana, in conjunction 'with somebody Russian who knows at least something about architecture' (*s kem-nibud russkim kotoryi by khotia nemnogo znal arkhitekturu*). The revised version was to be printed in a hundred copies and samples sent for Peter's further inspection. The list of corrections referred to bad positioning of captions, some obscurities and the omission of numbers in keys to the engravings.[12] Gagarin later sent three corrected copies to Peter.[13]

This exchange, and many others like it, show that in the midst of apparently more pressing problems of foreign and domestic policy Peter insisted upon supervising publishing matters, in fields he considered central to his overall plans. His knowledge of architecture was, like many of his other accomplishments, on an amateur level, but it was good enough for him to make his own designs and sketches for many building operations in Petersburg, for such important developments as parts of the Peter and Paul Fortress amongst others. It was also good enough for him to refer with some confidence to stylistic technicalities, as for example in a letter of January, 13, 1709, in which he refers to a gallery in St Petersburg designed 'after the Corinthian Order' (*ordonom korinti*).[14] As the famous Russian and Soviet architectural historian I E Grabar' wrote, 'Not one significant building

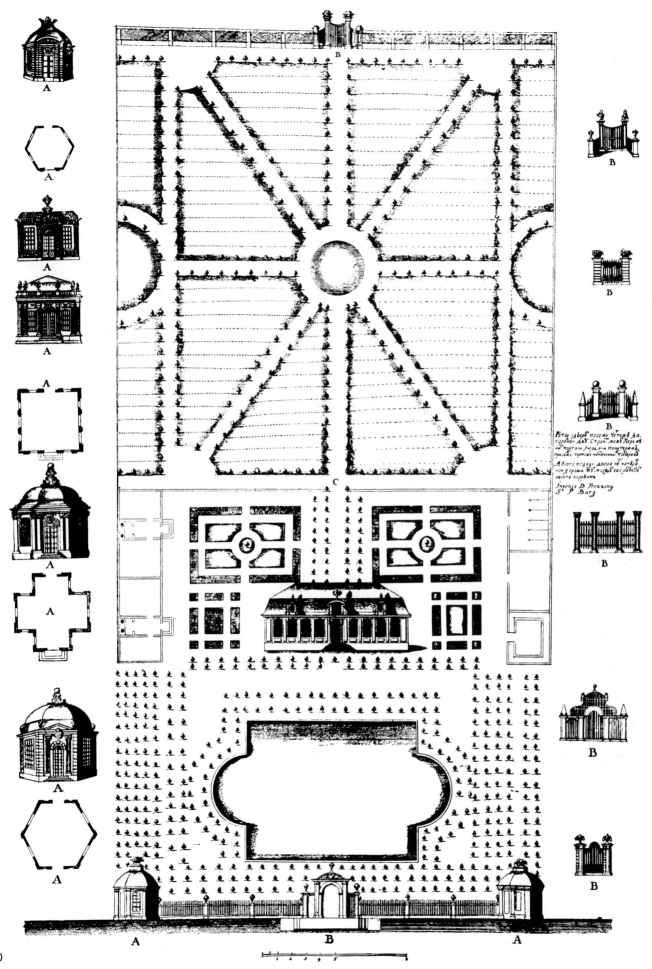

21,22 Manuscript title page of first Russian edition of Vitruvius' *Ten Books*, 1757, translated by Stepan Savitskii, and a page from one of the first Russian-produced architectural manuals of the mid-eighteenth century.

23 Ivan Michurin, Church of the Resurrection, Barashevskii alley, Moscow, 1734.

[in St Petersburg] was constructed without the direct participation of the Tsar at all stages of its creation, from the first designs to individual details.'[15] The first translated manual proved no exception, and the appearance of an architectural manual amongst the very first Russian secular publications itself therefore comes as no surprise.

Vignola was published again in 1712 and 1722, the former (from which most of the present illustrations are taken), was a second edition of the final 1709 variant; the latter was in larger format, with fewer engravings, and based on a Rome edition of 1617.[16] A draft of the 1722 edition was found amongst Peter's personal papers.[17]

Vignola's *Regola* was to be the only strictly architectural book actually to reach publication before Peter died in 1725 – if we discount a mysterious book on 'house-building' (literally 'the architectural structure of the house': *arkhitekturnaia domovogo stroeniia*) apparently on sale in St Petersburg in 1716 but not identified in any later catalogues of published books.[18] There were however a number of translations which remained in manuscript form.

The earliest of these manuscript translations was probably Prince Dolgorukov's *Arkhitektura tsyvilnaia* (*Civil Architecture*, as opposed to military), of 1699, which was extracted from an edition of Palladio on his own initiative whilst the Prince was studying navigation, on the Tsar's orders, in Venice.[19] Several translations were officially commissioned but never printed, among them Mikhail Shafirov's translation of 1708 from a 1694 Dutch edition of Vincenzo Scamozzi;[20] a translation of a work by J-B Lauterbach on 'civic architecture',[21] and another of a building manual published in Dutch by J Dankert.[22]

In 1715 a manuscript translation of Vitruvius's *De architectura libri decem*, carefully amended by its translator, was sent to Russia by an unidentified Russian studying in Amsterdam, and was preserved amongst Peter's private papers.[23] In the 1720s a further series of translations were either commissioned or completed in manuscript, including a book on 'the art of architecture' by Le Clerc, several works on parks and gardens and some books of engravings of buildings in France and Italy.[24] Amongst the latter, two in particular survive, G G Rubens's *Admiranda romanarum antiquitatum . . .* (originally published in 1693) and *Veteris arcus Augustorum triumphis insignes ex reliquiis . . .* (1690), which attest to a growing Russian interest in Antiquity.[25]

Petrine translators, faced with composing a technical vocabulary for topics quite new in the Russian language, had a daunting task. This problem extended over every scientific field, as well as into maritime and ship-building matters. In architecture, some headway had already been made in the previous century, when some elements of the Order system, such as *baza* and *kapitel'* entered the vocabulary, as they did the architecture, via the Ukraine and Byelorussia.[26] Even by the end of Peter's reign, though, in 1725, architectural terms were far from being standardised in Russian. In the 1709 edition of Vignola, for example, captions to engravings appear variously in Russian, French and Italian. When G M Fontana prepared a glossary of Russian terms to help the whole translation effort, he often resorted to a simple transcription or transliteration of the Italian, so that *plinto*, for example, becomes in Russian *plintus*. Elsewhere he gave alternatives, so that either *kolonna* or *pilastr* (in each case given in Cyrillic letters, not the original Italian) are both rendered by the Russian *stolb*, meaning column.[27]

## Libraries and decrees

Works specifically devoted to architecture were only one of the many sources of Western images which penetrated the consciousness of Petrine Russians. Many more works were published on military architecture and fortification, such as translations of E F Borgsdorf's *Unüberwindliche Festung* (originally from Ulm, 1703) and François Blondel's *Nouvelle manière de fortifier les places* (Paris, 1683). At the same time, published works on a variety of topics dear to Russian hearts – triumphal arches, fireworks geography, topography – were embellished with architectural engravings.[28] In 1718 a book of engravings on parks, gardens and their accoutrements *Kunshty sadov* (*The art of gardens*) was published in St Petersburg.[29]

An equal influence upon forms of new building were the numerous published decrees about acceptable modes of building in St Petersburg, and to a lesser extent in Moscow, which reflected both the concern of earlier eras for fire prevention and control, and the new preoccupation of Peter's age with regularity and planning in the whole built environment. A decree of April, 4, 1714, for example, banned construction in timber in certain parts of St Petersburg and advised new settlers to obtain their building plans from the city's chief architect Domenico Tressini, an Italian Swiss hired by Peter in 1703. '*A kakim manerom stroit', brat' chertezhi ot Arkhitektora Trezina*' read the instruction: 'As to the manner in which houses are to be built, drawings should be obtained from Architect Tressini.'[30] Individuals were allowed to use their own designs instead of Tressini's 'model plans' if they first submitted them to the appropriate chancellery for approval, but on September 14 that year, cruel punishments were threatened to those who dared to erect a house in the capital 'without an architectural plan' – '*bez chertezha arkhitektorskogo*'.[31]

Measures such as these reflect fundamental changes in Russian

24,25 Tressini, 1712–33, Cathedral of the Peter and Paul Fortress, St Petersburg's successor to Zarudy's Menshikov Tower in Moscow 10 years earlier: view from the south, L, and early 19th-century view from the north-east, R.

architectural traditions. In the two capital cities at least – in old Moscow and new Petersburg – rule-of-thumb was being replaced by mathematical precision. The slow transfer of vernacular skills from generation to generation was being replaced by reference to Western authorities on the Classical Orders. A supply of technical and theoretical works was now essential.

The Russian edition of Vignola naturally needed to be supplemented by other works in their original languages. One of the richest repositories of architectural books was Peter's own library, the catalogue of which lists over one hundred works in this category, some of them inherited from his seventeenth-century ancestors. Apart from the three Russian-language editions of Vignola, for example,[32] Peter owned several foreign-language editions (from Venice, 1603; Rome, 1617; Amsterdam, 1610), and three works by Scamozzi. Other titles on his shelves ranged from the classical authority, Vitruvius (*De architectura libri decem*, Amsterdam, 1649; *Les dix livres de l'architecture*, Amsterdam, 1681; *ibid*, Paris 1684), through Renaissance theoreticians Alberti and Palladio (he had the former's *L'architettura* from Venice, of 1565, and several Palladios including an English version with 'notes and observations' by Inigo Jones, of 1715), to seventeenth century writers with a marked Baroque bias such as J Furtenbach and J Vredeman de Vries (respectively their

*Architectura universalis, oder die gesammte Baukunst*, Ulm 1635, and *Perspective*, Amsterdam 1629–30). In his library were also a number of much more modern works, such as Colen Campbell's *Vitruvius Britannicus or the British Architect*, which appeared in London in 1715, some of these sent to Peter personally as gifts.

Descriptions of the residences of foreign royalty and aristocracy figured prominently in Peter's collection, amongst them *Nouveau Théâtre de la Grande Bretagne, ou Description exacte des palais de la reine et des maisons les plus considérables des seigneurs et des gentilhommes de la Grande Bretagne*, published in London in 1702.[33] There is a hint here of Peter's desire to emulate his contemporaries, not to lag behind in grandeur and stylishness. Examinations of other private libraries reveal that architectural works, both treatises and descriptions of cities and individual buildings, often acquired during trips abroad, were owned by many educated Russians of Peter's era.[34] Such books had started to become available in Russia in the latter half of the seventeenth century, for example in the libraries of the Chancellery, or *posol'skii prikaz*, and the Armoury, in the Moscow Kremlin, and also in the libraries of such statesmen as A S Matveev and V V Golitsyn.[35] The increased official travel of Peter's era provided these classes with even greater opportunities for their acquisition, just as his building demands increased the need for them.

26 Georg-Iohann Mattarnovy (German), 1717–34, the Kunstkamera, built to house Peter's library and the collection of 'monsters and rarities' assembled on his travels: Russia's first natural history museum and the basis of the future Academy of Sciences library.

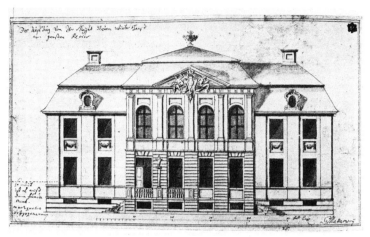

27 G-I Mattarnovy, 1716–19, design for the river elevation of Peter's second Winter Palace.

## Architectural education

How were such books utilized by the Russians? Architectural practice in Peter's reign, especially in prestige projects, was dominated by foreigners who were already well acquainted with architectural manuals. The first Russian architect whose library was catalogued was P M Eropkin, and that was in 1740, fifteen years after Peter's death. Certainly architectural books could be approached on a variety of levels, by literate and illiterate alike. In the case of 'lay' collections, it is possible that such works performed the function of present-day coffee-table volumes, demonstrating the owner's refined and cosmopolitan tastes. As to Peter's own books, however, there is direct evidence that they formed part of an active, working library. As with collections on Peter's other special interests such as fortification and navigation, they were used to provide originals for translation, to give inspiration for royal projects (the grand royal palace complex at Peterhof being a conspicuous example), and as the basis for advice to technicians.

The published architectural manuals, both those translated from foreign texts and increasingly, after the end of Peter's own reign, the home-produced ones, were used first and foremost in the training of a new generation of Russian architects.

The first apprentice builders and draughtsmen to be schooled in new methods came through the Moscow Armoury (Oruzheinaia palata), itself, as we have noted, a respository of architectural books since the end of the seventeenth century. After the foundation of St Petersburg in 1703, the majority of Russian architects were trained in the capital's 'architectural teams' (arkhitekturnye komandy), supervised by foreigners, and as pensionery on study trips abroad, to Holland and Italy.

Until recently, these study trips had been regarded as the main form of training employed under Peter to create the next generation of Russian architects in the new mould. Archival research has shown, however, that pensionery started to become very much the minority soon after the city's foundation, and 'already by the second decade of the eighteenth century the number of student architects being trained in Petersburg was several times greater than the number of pensionery abroad.'[36] The pensionery were encouraged to purchase books on the spot and bring them back to Russia,[37] but the principal textbook of that student body in Petersburg – indeed at first the only textbook – was the Russian Vignola.

Activities of the capital's foreign architects were controlled by the Chancellery for Building, which must therefore take credit for introducing, in Elena Borisova's words, 'a new type of architectural education' whereby, 'for the first time in the history of Russian architecture, training was not the private affair of individual master architects, but was one function of a [central] architectural organisa-

tion of designing and construction teams.'[38] These teams, moreover, were multi-disciplinary: they comprised 'not just the [foreign] architect and his pupils, but also masters and pupils from other building specialisms.' Since the young Russians were simultaneously serving as the main assistants in real building jobs, this team system also produced 'a complete integration of the work of the foreigners and their pupils'.[39]

The first such team was that organised in the later 1700s around Peter's first imported architect, Domenico Tressini. In 1707, Tressini was assigned two young graduates from the Mathematical and Navigational School, and in 1710 they were joined by four more students, including one Mikhail Zemtsov, originally sent up from the Moscow Armoury schools to learn Italian at the Chancellery for City Affairs in Petersburg:[40] outstandingly talented from the first, he was to become the leading Russian architect of Petersburg in the next generation. Of all these multi-disciplinary offices, the fullest archives survive from Tressini's, and they reveal much about the training given in these teams.

'As is evident from the documents of a slightly later stage', writes Borisova, 'theoretical classes in the teams of Tressini and other architects consisted basically of studying and drawing the five Orders of architecture as presented in the treatise of Vignola. Despite the fact that it was already far from the only architectural manual well known in Russia by this period, it is the only one that we encounter in the lists of textbooks which remain from 1720 onwards. The fact that it is not named directly in the earlier documents cannot mean it was unknown to students of the 1710s. There can be no question that the students who joined Tressini at or after the date from which Vignola's treatise existed in a Russian translation must have used that book extensively.'[41]

Borisova notes that students with foreign-language skills 'probably helped their fellows in the study of untranslated architectural books'; but 'the vast majority of these architectural students would have confined themselves to studying the Orders according to "the architectural book" of Vignola, as soon became the tradition.' Although 'hardly a single student exercise has survived from this early period', it seems clear that this theoretical side of their education proceeded through 'copying with the help of drawing instruments, careful repetition of the various figures reproduced in the treatise' till they could be done 'by heart', to freer work on 'the preparation of drawings'.[42]

The records show that 'From 1713, Tressini's original pupils became full members of his professional team, taking active part in the construction of the city. Their success in the field of practice', says Borisova, 'is attested by the fact that already in 1715, Tressini raised the question of augmenting their salaries "till they are in proportion to their jobs", whereupon Zemtsov's salary was doubled.'[43]

A document of 1720 indicates the level to which Tressini's teaching activity had increased. In Borisova's words: 'It shows that he had already had to divide his pupils into several groups. His classes with them took place in special accommodation comprising a small and a larger "palace" (*palaty*) where the students were instructed in "the preparation of drawings" (*risovanie chertezhei*). The heavy load put on the students by academic and practical work is indicated in the fact they often had to continue this drawing work into the night, for which purpose they were specially issued with candles.'[44]

In 1718, Zemtsov moved over to the team of another newly arrived foreigner, N Miketti, presumably to help introduce him to the system. In 1720, that group was joined by four graduates in 'nautical navigational sciences' from the Naval Academy, among them the 20-year old Ivan Michurin, who went to Amsterdam three years later to continue his training as a *pensioner*.[45] Michurin returned in 1725 to Moscow, where during the 1730s he was to become chief architect, a leader of the city's new planning commission, and also founder, in turn, of the first architectural school in Russia's original capital.

Thus were disseminated into Russia, relatively very rapidly and directly, the results of Peter's architectural initiatives. Building upon the haphazard foundations laid in previous decades, his own very organised programme distributed a wide variety of materials to introduce the untrained Russian builders, and their patrons, not only to the basic principles of the Western Classical idiom, but also to the styles and artists of different eras within that tradition. The availability of printed materials, the influx of foreign specialists into Russia, and wider access to foreign travel for Russians themselves, all served to meet the demands of a ruler determined to recast his people's surroundings in the image of the West.

## Notes

1  A particularly rich and detailed source on these aspects of Peter's youth and travels is: Robert K Massie, *Peter the Great, his life and world* (Gollancz, London, 1981); The other most recent books on Peter in English are: M Raeff, *Peter the Great changes Russia* (Lexington, 1972); M S Anderson, *Peter the Great* (London, 1977) and A de Jonge, *Fire and Water: a life of Peter the Great* (London, 1979).

2  N A Evsina, *Arkhitekturnaia teoriia v Rossii XVIII veka* (Architectural theory in Russia in the eighteenth century), Moscow, 1975, p 24.

3  For a richly illustrated and scholarly introduction to the history of Old Russian architecture see: H Faensen & V Ivanov, *Early Russian Architecture* (London, 1975). Also useful as standard sources, if dry and weakly illustrated, are relevant chapters of the following: Tamara Talbot Rice, *A concise history of Russian art* (London, 1963); George Heard Hamilton, *The art and architecture of Russia* (Pelican History of Art, London, 1954, 1975), and R Auty and D Obolensky, eds, *A companion to Russian Studies, vol 3: An introduction to Russian Art and Architecture* (Cambridge, 1980).

4  See: L A J Hughes, 'The seventeenth century Renaissance in Russia', *History Today*, 1980, February, pp 41–45.

5  See: L A J Hughes, 'The Moscow Armoury and innovations in seventeenth century Muscovite art', *Canadian-American Slavic Studies*, XIII, 1979, pp 204–23.

6  See: LAJ Hughes, 'Moscow Baroque architecture: a controversial style', *Transactions of the Association of Russian-American Scholars in the USA*, XV. 1982, pp 69–93.

7  Russian sources on such books are listed in: LAJ Hughes, 'Western European graphic material as a source for Moscow Baroque architecture', *Slavonic and East European Review*, LV, 1977, pp 433–43.

8  TA Bykova & MM Gurevich, *Opisanie izdanii napechatennykh kirillitsei 1689-ianvar' 1725 g.* (Description of publications printed in Cyrillic type between 1689 and January 1725) Moscow-Leningrad, 1958, p 321.

9  Its publication is recorded in: TA Bykova & MM Gurevich, *Opisanie izdanii grazhdanskoi pechati 1708 – ianvar' 1725* (Description of publications printed in civic script 1708 – January 1725) Moscow-Leningrad, 1955, pp 100–102 (abbreviated hereafter to *OIGP*), and P Pekarskii, *Nauka i literatura v Rossii pri Petre Velikom* (Science and literature in Russia under Peter the Great), II, (St Petersburg, 1862, pp 212–14.

10  Documents on the books publishing history were consulted in: *Pis'ma i bumagi Petra Velikogo* (Letters and papers of Peter the Great), IX, Moscow-Leningrad, 1948, p 376, pp 1236–7.

11  Pekarskii, *Nauka i literatura*, II, p 213; *Pis'ma i bumagi*, IX, p 1236.

12  Pekarskii, *Nauka i literatura*, II, p 376.

13  *Pis'ma i bumagi*, IX, pp 1236–7.

14  *Ibid*, p 24.

15  I E Grabar', *Russkaia arkhitektura pervoi poloviny XVIII veka: issledovaniia i materialy* (Russian architecture of the first half of the eighteenth century: research and materials), Moscow 1954, p 112

16  *OIGP*, p 131; pp 399–400; Pekarskii, II, *Nauka i literatura*, p 281.

17  E I Bobrova, comp, *Biblioteka Petra I. Ukazatel' – spravochnik* (Peter the First's Library: an index and handbook) henceforth *BPI*, Leningrad, 1978, p 20, no 14.

18  Pekarskii, *Nauka i literatura*, II, p 685.

19  See A A Tits, 'Neizvestnyi russkii traktat po arkhitekture' (An unknown Russian treatise on architecture), *Russkoe iskusstvo XVIII veka. Materialy i issledovaniia* (Eighteenth century Russian art. Materials and studies), Moscow, 1968, pp 17–31.

20  Evsina, *Arkhitekturnaia teoriia*, p 37. The original may be in Peter's library, see: *De Grondt-Regulen der Bouw-Konst* (*BPI*, p 149, no 1477).

21  Evsina, *Arkhitekturnaia teoriia*, p 41. See *BPI*, p 133, no 1249, for what is seemingly another edition of Lauterbach.

22  Evsina, *Arkhitekturnaia teoriia*, pp 41–2.

23  V Shilkov, 'Russkii perevod Vitruviia nachala XVIII veka' (An early eighteenth-century Russian translation of Vitruvius), *Arkhitekturnoe Nasledstvo*, (Architectural heritage), VII, 1955, pp 89–92.

24  Evsina, *Arkhitekturnaia teoriia*, pp 57–9.

25  Bobrova, comp, *Biblioteka Petra I.*, pp 36; 41; 147.

26  See: L A J Hughes, 'Byelorussian craftsmen in late seventeenth-century Russia and their influence on Muscovite architecture', *Journal of Byelorussian Studies*, III, 1976, p 340.

27  *OIGP*, p 103.

28  These and other titles are listed in *OIGP*. See also Bobrova, comp, *Biblioteka Petra I.*

29  *OIGP*, pp 234; 524–7.

30  *Polnoe sobranie zakonov rossiiskoi imperii* (Complete collection of laws of the Russian Empire), V, St Petersburg, 1830, no 2792.

31  *Ibid*, no 2932. On the architectural history of Petersburg, see: S P Luppov, *Istoriia stroitel'stva Peterburga v pervoi chetverti XVIII veka* (The history of the building of St Petersburg in the first quarter of the eighteenth century), Moscow-Leningrad, 1957. Material in English will be found in the early chapters of: I A Egorov, *The architectural planning of St Petersburg* (Ohio, 1969).

32  See note 25 above, for the complete catalogue.

33  *BPI*, p 156, no 1576. Other examples include G Perelle, *Les places, portes, fontaines, églises et maisons de Paris* (Paris, n d; *BPI*, p 143, no 1396), and several volumes by G-B Falda on the palaces of Rome (*BPI*, p 123, nos 1106–8)

34  On publishing and book collections during the period, see: SP Luppov, *Kniga v Rossii v pervoi chetverti XVIII veka* (The book in Russia in the first quarter of the eighteenth century) Leningrad, 1973.

35  See: L A J Hughes, 'Western European graphic material as a source for Moscow Baroque architecture', *Slavonic and East European Review*, LV (1977), pp 433–43.

36  E A Borisova, '"Arkhitekturnye ucheniki" petrovskogo vremeni i ikh obuchenie v komandakh zodchikh-inostrantsev v Peterburge' (The 'architectural pupils' of the Petrine era and their training in the teams of foreign architects in St Petersburg), in: T V Alekseeva, ed, *Russkoe iskusstvo pervoi chetverti XVIII veka* (Russian art of the first quarter of the eighteenth century), Moscow, 1974, pp 68–80.

37  Grabar', *Russkaia arkhitektura*, p 178.

38  Borisova, 'Arkhitekturnye ucheniki', p 68.

39  *Ibid*, p. 69.

40  *Ibid*, p 69, referring to materials in the State Historical Archives, TsGIA SSSR.

41  *Ibid*, p 70.

42  *Ibid*, p 70.

43  *Ibid*, p 70, quoting materials in TsGIA SSSR and GPB.

44  *Ibid*, p 70, quoting materials in TsGIA SSSR.

45  *Ibid*, p 75–6.

# Christina Lodder
# THE COSTAKIS COLLECTION: NEW INSIGHTS INTO THE RUSSIAN AVANT–GARDE

*AD* has been privileged to have the fullest and most sympathetic support of George Costakis in preparing this extended review of his published collection, and would like to offer its profound thanks.

Copyright in all the visual material remains his own, so that we are greatly indebted for his permission to reproduce so many works here, as we are also for points of elucidation over details. Like all who have found aesthetic and intellectual stimulus in the arts of Russia, we salute his achievement in assembling this rich material, and wish him a happy retirement to Greece with the Western half of his rare collection.

Ed.

Two years ago, in the autumn of 1981, Harry N Abrams and Thames & Hudson launched on the world a large tome containing twelve hundred illustrations of Russian avant-garde art that almost no-one had ever seen before – despite the fact that numerous major names of twentieth-century art were amongst the artists represented. Certain Western specialists had an inkling of what this 'George Costakis collection' would contain: they had been privileged, if briefly, to visit the owner's Moscow apartment during the last decade or so. A few of them had already been invited to New York earlier that year to help Angelica Zander Rudenstine and her staff at the Guggenheim Museum with detailed cataloguing, dating and background notes for the book.

For the rest of us, and indeed for art history in general, this material remains an undigested feast of new images and whole new painterly languages. As curators to George Costakis, the Guggenheim explicitly 'resisted the temptation' – in Rudenstine's words – 'to delay publication of . . . this unique visual material . . . for several years while much more detailed art historical research was carried out', and 'precisely because of the scarcity and inaccessibility of works in this field'. That decision must be warmly applauded.

Though mainly painterly, these works have many implications for design and architecture. In some areas this is material specifically conceived by its authors as preparation, as 'laboratory work', for formal invention in functional problems. A selection of these works which accompanied George Costakis out of Moscow have been shown in the United States during the last year, at the Guggenheim itself, in Chicago and elsewhere. *AD* celebrates the first European showing of this collection at London's Royal Academy by inviting one of those original cataloguing advisors to give a first in-depth assessment of the collection's revelations, as they emerge from the pages of this rich, but most modestly priced, book.

1 George Costakis.

This book is exceptional. New 'finds' of quality material are normally worked over for years, by specialists in learned journals, before they are thought saleable to the mass public. Not that a body of work so large as this makes a debut in the art world very often.

The circumstances surrounding this whole collection are unique, emerging as it does from the straightened circumstances of Revolutionary Russia into the West of the eighties via the surviving relatives and friends of the artists themselves and one single, perceptive collector. Also unique is this bold and careful popular publication of visual material *in extenso*, before it has been located and interrelated by a detailed interpretive narrative. It is a symptom of the material's immediacy and power (for it is certainly not 'popular' material), that it can stand more-or-less alone like this on its visual merits.

For years now, George Costakis' ever-growing collection has been a major source on the Russian avant-garde for Soviet and Western scholars alike, though none have known it more than partially. Twenty years ago, when these same publishers launched Camilla Gray's pioneering re-evaluation as *The Great Experiment*, Costakis' collection was already her central source in several areas.[1] But where Gray illustrated only a tiny number of Costakis' works, the present volume makes available over one thousand of them, in superb reproduction.

The vast majority are items which have come to the West, by Soviet government agreement, with Costakis himself, returning to Greece whence his family came before the Russian Revolution. There are also works that have remained in Moscow in Costakis' gift to the Tretiakov Gallery – which comprised over half his total collection when he left in 1978.

The illustrations reproduced in this article and on the back cover and page 1 are all copyright © George Costakis 1981, and are taken from the following sources: a) photographs provided by George Costakis; b) *Russian Avant-Garde Art: The George Costakis Collection,* Angelica Zander Rudenstine (ed), preface by George Costakis, Thames & Hudson, London/Harry N. Abrams, New York (527pp, 609 illustrations in colour, 592 in black and white, £35.00); c) *Art of the Avant-Garde in Russia: Selections from the George Costakis Collection,* Margit Rowell and Angelica Zander Rudenstine, The Solomon R. Guggenheim Museum, New York, exhibition catalogue; d) photographs supplied courtesy of the Royal Academy of Arts, London.

Whilst eschewing interpretation of the material itself at this early stage, the publishers have provided here some attractive and useful background on the collection as a whole. Frederick Starr, former Secretary of Washington's prestigious Kennan Institute for Advanced Russian Studies, and best known to architects as the biographer of Mel'nikov, contributes a lively and illuminating introduction to the period and the collection. He puts it in the context of other 'great collections' in Russian history, and traces its growth from the beginning, in the later 1940s, through all the vicissitudes attending an obsession with near-forgotten material. There follows a vivid, and sometimes delightfully personal article by George Costakis himself entitled 'Collecting the avant-garde'. Here colour photographs of his Moscow apartment show the collection very much as I recall seeing it: covering every available wall space.

The bulk of the book presents the works of some 65 artists, in alphabetical order. Initial biographical notes are by a Moscow historian of this period, Vassilii Rakitin, sometimes accompanied by a period photograph of the artist. With a few exceptions, works are then illustrated chronologically. Over half are in colour. The quality of reproduction here contributes significantly to the book's enjoyment and scholarly value through the accuracy of colour rendition, and the sensitivity with which it preserves qualities of the diverse media used in this period.

Notes on each work contain the usual descriptive apparatus, plus discursive comments with bibliographical references where appropriate. They indicate the work's present location (Tretiakov or Costakis), and usually also the source from which Costakis acquired it. At times this information on provenance has romantic or even pathetic overtones: this, and a certain myth-making are perhaps inevitable in the circumstances, when families have preserved the works through difficult years. Future historical research would have profited from a more systematic inclusion of detailed provenances, but in other respects the cataloguing is exemplary. Where the much smaller exhibition catalogue is interpretive, with material difficult to locate amongst introductory articles and seven thematic sections, this volume is a model of clarity. It ends with a useful detailed chronology covering events in 'The Visual Arts', 'Literature and the Performing Arts' and 'Politics', during the years 1894–1934. This is by John Bowlt, Director of the Institute for Modern Russian Culture at Blue Lagoon, Texas, and displays his usual broad erudition.

These are the technicalities. The excitement is not so much here, as in the revelations which the visual components provide.

What can we learn immediately from this material?

\* \* \*

Amongst much else, it brings to light for the first time in the West the works of certain Russian avant-garde artists whose names, even, have hitherto remained almost entirely unknown – notable among them are Antonina Sofronova, Aleksei Morgunov, Vera Pestel and Solomon Nikritin.

A few works by Sofronova were exhibited at the Gmurzynska Gallery, Cologne, in 1980, but those few examples are further illuminated by the thirteen abstract compositions reproduced here. These demonstrate her bold use of an abstract vocabulary of colour and line to produce taut and emphatically two-dimensional compositions. Numbers 1070, and 180–2, are particularly fine examples. (*All numbers hereafter refer to figure numbers in the book itself.*)

Some works by Morgunov are already located in Western collections, but this volume makes available a much wider range of his work; it enables us to establish a more accurate perspective on an artist who was a significant member of the Union of Youth group and active participant in avant-garde exhibitions of the pre-Revolutionary decade. In the case of Nikritin, the Costakis collection reveals an artist who epitomises the concerns of the whole generation of young painters who were trained by the avant-garde. He graduated in 1922 from the Higher Artistic and Technical Studios in Moscow – the VKhUTEMAS – to become active in avant-garde organisations and in extending the vocabulary of abstraction, before reverting in the later twenties to an expressive, figurative art.

These new names – and there are others – help establish a fuller picture of the artistic environment in which the great innovators moved, but there are plenty of revelations about them too. Most important in the present context are the material from INKhUK; from the Suprematists and other leading trends, and the theatrical and design-related material by Constructivists and Petr Miturich. I shall examine these in turn.

### The INKhUK portfolio

One of the most interesting groups of material in the Costakis collection is the portfolio of 22 drawings which he acquired from the archive of the Institute of Artistic Culture, INKhUK, held by the wife of the sculptor Aleksei Babichev. It helps to fill the sort of gap that is most

2 A view of the interior of Costakis' flat in Moscow, c 1975, with some of the major items in the collection on display.

3 Rodchenko, *Oval Hanging Construction* No 12, c 1929.

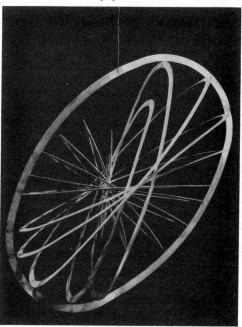

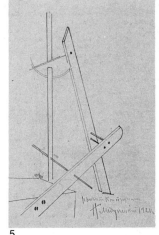
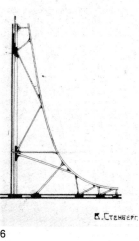

4  5  6

tantalising but characteristic for the specialist in certain areas here. This is the gap produced by the paucity of visual material to correlate with the relatively rich theoretical material which the various Soviet archives contain.

This is particularly true of the Moscow VKhUTEMAS, the Higher Artistic and Technical Workshops, and of the research institute which provided its theoretical underpinnings, INKhUK. This portfolio is of central importance because it illustrates a vital moment in the emergence of Constructivism within INKhUK in the spring of 1921.

After INKhUK was set up in May 1920 on the basis of Vasilii Kandinskii's programme, it concentrated its attention on examining artistic elements in relation to their physiological effects 'from the point of view of the effect of the artistic means employed on a man apprehending it [the work of art]'.[2] In accordance with Kandinskii's ideas this detailed study of the physical effects of the artistic elements was intended to create 'a bridge to the explanation of their influence on man's psychology'.[3] Thus INKhUK conducted experiments to study the physiological influence which colour exerted on the observer, trying to establish colour equivalents for musical chords and a definite relationship between specific forms and particular colours. In the questionnaire which Kandinskii circulated among INKhUK members he also tried to establish whether colour generally prompted any specific emotional response. Among the conclusions reached in the course of such investigations was the observation that blue creates paralysis and a metaphysical sense of the infinite.

Between June and November 1920 a dissatisfaction with the spiritual dimension of this psychological orientation emerged amongst such INKhUK members as Aleksandr Rodchenko, Varvara Stepanova, Babichev and Liubov Popova, who sought to develop a less subjective approach. This culminated in their setting up the Working Group of Objective Analysis, defining their aim as 'the theoretical analysis of the basic elements of a work of Art'.[4] Opposed to the inherent subjectivity of Kandinskii's approach, they believed that 'the process of observation must follow strictly defined logical paths and methods . . . [and] conclusions obtained in this way constitute the material which is the content of the science of art'.[5] One of the crucial components was the series of debates which they conducted concerning the distinction between, and the definition of, the artistic categories of 'construction' and 'composition'. This theoretical investigation which can be followed in the minutes of the Group's meetings that are preserved in the INKhUK archives in Moscow, was developed in visual work which is now for the first time available to us in this portfolio. The direct relationship between theoretical and practical work was fundamental to their method. This is underlined in their report of 1923 which described their programme retrospectively thus:

1 Theoretical: the analysis of the work of art, the conscious definition of the basic problems of art (colour, texture, material, construction etc). The work was conducted with paintings,

4  Installation photograph of the third OBMOKhU exhibition which opened in Moscow in May 1921, showing abstract three-dimensional works by Aleksandr Rodchenko, the Stenberg brothers, Medunetskii and Ioganson.
5  Konstantin Medunetskii, *Design for a Construction* 1920. INKhUK folio, no 27.
6  Vladimir Stenberg, *Construction Drawing*, 1920. INKhUK folio, no 6.
7  Aleksandr Rodchenko, *Untitled*, October 1921.
8  Aleksei Babichev, *Composition*, 1921. INKhUK folio, no 19.

frequently in galleries.

2 Laboratory: group work according to independent initiative or according to a task (for example all members were presented with work on the theme 'composition and construction').

In this folio, we now have the results of precisely that piece of 'laboratory work'. As a scholar privileged to have had access to these archives in Moscow, it was exciting to be presented in New York with visual material which confirmed the deductions I had drawn from those dusty archives. Five of these works are signed and dated April 1921 by the artists. This confirms that they are the visual expression of the theoretical conclusions which the artist had reached in those debates, and that they represent the formal crystallisation of their ideas at this point.

The 'construction versus composition' debates took place at meetings between 1 January and 22 April 1921, and it is plainly no coincidence that the First Working Group of Constructivists was formally set up towards the end of that period, ie in March 1921.[7] This debate was clearly a central catalyst in defining certain trends in an area where we have hitherto been very short of visual material that could be dated with precision. The two main visual landmarks for this period of emergent Constructivism are the Third OBMOKhU Exhibition which took place in Moscow in May 1921 and the Constructivists' Exhibition of January 1922 at the Poets' Café (Kafe Poetov) in Moscow, which comprised work by the Stenberg brothers and Konstantin Medunetskii. The catalogue of the latter expressed an allegiance to a utilitarian dimension in rather vague and incoherent terms, the artists called themselves Constructivists and their works were presented as 'laboratory work', or structures with a utilitarian potential. Apart from the Medunetskii sculpture which now resides in Yale, the only available visual material consists of a few random, undated photographs of individual works, and the two well-known photographs of the Third OBMKhU Exhibition. These indicate only that the Stenberg works were executed before May 1921. The vague catalogue statement of January 1922 had been preceded by the far more precisely formulated declaration of the First Working Group of Constructivists of March 1921 which was not published until August 1922. Whereas the archival texts have made it possible to illuminate the development of the theoretical principles of Constructivism in early 1921, this Costakis material now supplies a visual dimension to that development.

What we have are a set of pairs of drawings, in each case a 'composition' and a 'construction', by Babichev, Karl Ioganson, Boris Korolev, Nikolai Ladovskii, Medunetskii, Popova, Vladimir Stenberg,

16

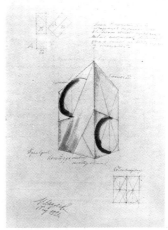

7                8                             9                          10

9  Nikolai Ladovskii, *An Example of a Composed Structure*, 1921. INKhUK folio, with no number. Text reads: 'The entire structure is governed by the rectangle *A*, which generates geometric similarities and displacements for which *A* is the centre'.

10  Nikolai Ladovskii, *Model of a Constructive Structure*, 1921. INKhUK folio, without a number. Text reads: 'Given two planes *A* and *B*, forming a biplanar angle, it is necessary to make a constructive structure that reveals both the angle and the given properties of each of the planes'.

Stepanova and Nikolai Tarabukin; a single 'construction' drawing by Ivan Kliun; a 'composition' by Rodchenko, and certain other related materials by Varvara Bubnova, Ioganson, Popova and Nadezhda Udaltsova.

Two things of great interest emerge from the work of those who formed the First Working Group of Constructivists, namely Rodchenko, Stepanova, the Stenberg brothers, Medunetskii and Ioganson (the seventh member of the Group was Aleksei Gan). Firstly we can now make some correlation between the theoretical statements of individual artists and their visual material. Secondly, we can now see the extent to which their visual allegiance to the technological dimension of their common programme varied. This portfolio therefore provides a more subtle picture than before of this particular and crucial moment in the development of Constructivism.

The purest embodiment of this technological commitment at this stage is to be found here in the work of Medunetskii and Vladimir Stenberg (nos 79–80, 84–5). The latter's drawing of a 'construction' (no 85), displays a direct reliance on the formal vocabulary of engineering structures. Resembling a girder section, this provides an interesting illustration to Medunetskii and the Stenbergs' later, still rather eliptical definition of

| Constructivism as economy | – space |
| utility | – the logic of everyday life |
| expediency | – the use of the present industrial material with uninterrupted action of its content on the formation of the construction |
| rhythm | – the elements of engineering in construction are simultaneously the organising beginnings of its rhythm.[8] |

The explicity technological content of Vladimir Stenberg's construction raises the possibility that he, his brother and Medunetskii played a far more active role in the development of Constructivism at this stage than has hitherto been supposed. Whereas Rodchenko, for example, was later so prominent with his design work, his practical two- and three-dimensional work at this stage seems still far more concerned with Euclidean geometrical themes than with engineering ones (nos 83, 1018, 1019). However, as early as 14 January 1921, Rodchenko's statements are clear declarations of the utilitarian principle and are a far more precise formulation of a potential working method than the statements of Vladimir and Georgii Stenberg. Rodchenko declared

'composition' to be 'an anachronism' because it was related to the outmoded artistic concepts of 'aesthetics' and 'taste'. 'The new approach to art' said Rodchenko 'arises from technology and engineering and moves towards organisation and construction'.[9] A week later, on 21 January, Rodchenko was asserting adamantly that 'the real construction is utilitarian necessity'.[10]

Ioganson's pair of drawings are less related to static building structures than those of Vladimir Stenberg, but amplify his interest in the actual jointing of rectilinear components which was manifest in the works that he exhibited at the Third OBMOKhU exhibition. According to Moholy Nagy, the configuration of at least one of his constructions could be changed by pulling a string.[11] This interest in jointing is evident from his drawing 'Construction' (no 67). His inscription on the back of this drawing states that 'A cold structure in space or any cold combination of hard materials is a cross, either right-angled . . . or obtuse- and acute-angled' (no 68). This indicates some of the complexity of this period. Here we see some of the psychological considerations of Kandinskii's approach being retained within this more rigorous framework of emergent Constructivism. The wording of this inscription was almost exactly repeated in a paper which Ioganson delivered at INKhUK on 9 March 1922 entitled 'From Construction to Technology and Invention'. More importantly, in 1922, Ioganson argued that there were two types of construction, 'aesthetic' and 'technological', and that the only valid construction was one that was made for 'its real translation onto the rails of practical necessity'.[12] He concluded his pronouncements by stating 'From painting to sculpture, from sculpture to construction, from construction to technology and invention – such is my path and such is, and will be the final aim of every revolutionary artist.'[13] Until now Ioganson's work has been known only from the single photograph, reproduced by Moholy-Nagy and the two surviving photographs of the Third OBMOKhU Exhibition. Our knowledge of his work is thus very usefully amplified by these two ink and crayon drawings.

Amongst the pairs of drawings contributed by artists who were not members of the First Working Group of Constructivists, the pair by Popova are interesting as definitions of her interest at this precise moment. Her construction (no 81) is concerned with the interpenetration of planes existing in space. Her composition (no 82) is concerned with interpenetrating forms, but they are securely retained within the one plane. There is a complete absence of any technological dimension or structural coherence in her 'construction'. This absence remains true of her compositions with completely defined and rectilinear elements which appear in the associated drawings of this portfolio (nos 91 and 92) of December 1921 and early 1922. These contain that sense of surface composition which was to serve her in such good stead in her later fabric design work.

Babichev was a sculptor who never embraced the exclusively utilitarian position of the Constructivists, and his drawings (nos 65 & 66) provide a particularly clear formulation of 'construction' as a purely

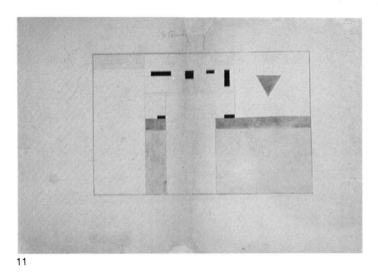

11

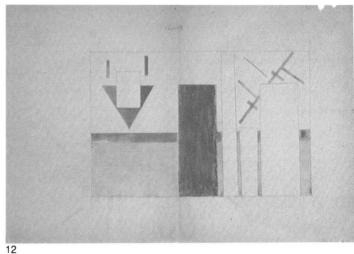

12

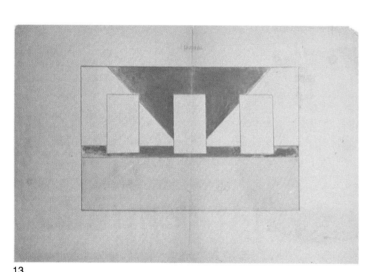

13

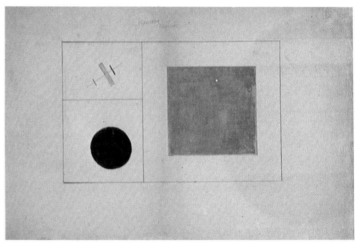

14

11–14 Suprematist wall decorations created by Malevich's students at Vitebsk, c 1920–21.

УСТРОЙТЕ
„НЕДЕЛЮ КРАСНОГО ПОДАРКА"
ВЕЗДЕ и ВСЮДУ.

15 Artist unknown, suprematist wall decoration, created by Malevich's students at Vitebsk, c 1920–21.

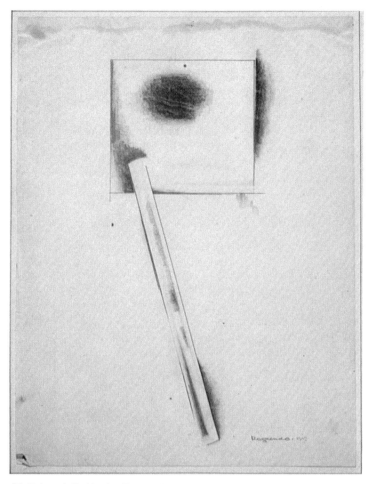

16 Aleksandr Rodchenko, Composition, 1917, INKhUK Folio No 11.

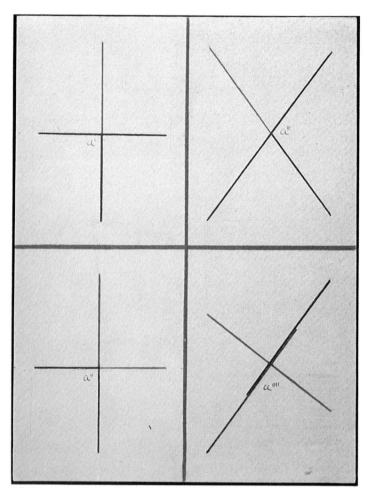

17 Karel loganson, *Construction*, 1921. INKhUK folio, no 17.

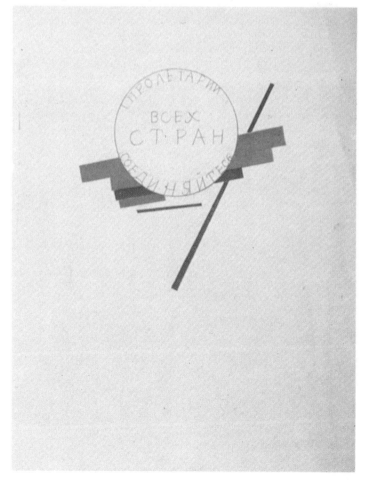

18,19 Kazimir Malevich, front and back cover designs for the programme of the first 'Conference of the Committees for Rural Poverty in the Northern Region', 1918.

20 Kazimir Malevich, *The Violin*, nd.

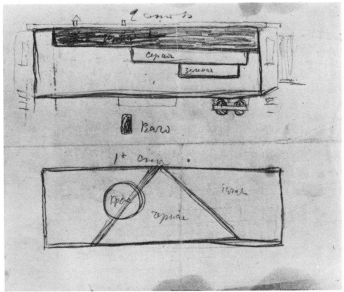

21 Kazimir Malevich, *Sketch for an Agit-Prop Train*, c 1920.

22 Suprematist agitational poster, author unknown c 1920. The text reads: 'Proletarians of the world unite! The organisation of production is the victory over the capitalist structure'.

artistic concept. He defined 'composition' as the continuous interrelationship of forms, and 'construction' as the organic unit of material form obtained through the exposure of their functions within the formal structure.[14] In his 'composition drawing' the forms, although clearly defined, have no specific spatial relationship, and are piled on each other in a way that remains planar. His construction however, resembles an abstract sculpture in which the relationship of each unit to the others and their mutual respective functions are clearly defined. Here we find the crucial move, from the composition which is floatingly two-dimensional to the image which is directly reconstructable in real space, because it provides some concrete reference points for an exact dimensioning in the third dimension. This illustrates the momentum inherent within this move from the two-dimensional art work into three-dimensional, abstract works of art, which then carries it on from the three-dimensional art work to the real, and potentially utilitarian object. This move is fundamental to the development of Constructivism in post-Revolutionary Russia; that is why this portfolio is so important.

A slight anomaly within this portfolio are Ladovskii's two drawings (nos 74–77). These seem to relate far more directly to the exercises he had already devised and used for teaching future architects at the VKhUTEMAS (published in detail in his group's journal of 1926),[15] than they do to the far more fundamental questioning of the nature of structure and construction being conducted by the artist members of INKhUK. The relative superficiality of Ladovskii's drawings indicates perhaps why the later researches of this ASNOVA group never developed any great innovative momentum, and certainly never dispensed with the belief in the role of psychology which had characterised the early period of INKhUK.

**The Suprematist dimension**

The Kazimir Malevich paintings in the Costakis collection cover his entire creative period from 1903 to 1933. They also represent virtually all phases of his development through Impressionism, Post-Impressionism, Symbolism, Fauvism and Cubism, to his own innovation of Suprematism. This range of material is far wider than that within either of the other two major Western holdings in the Stedelijk Museum in Amsterdam and the Museum of Modern Art in New York. It provides examples of aspects of Malevich's work which have hitherto not been accessible to the Western public. This is particularly true of the early period. His earliest Impressionist phase is represented here by *The Church* of 1903 (no 474). This shows his initial debt to Monet's paintings which he would have had an opportunity to know through the Impressionist exhibition in Moscow in 1896, and the collection of Shchukin. Particularly striking among these early works are the Symbolist paintings such as his *Woman in Childbirth* of 1908 (no 478). These illuminate the metaphysical aspects of Malevich's approach to painting and his enthusiastic response to peasant painting as a manifestation of the peasantry's spiritual intuition, which he describes in his autobiography.[16] The spiritual dimension of such works adds credence to the hypothesis that the development of Suprematism owed a debt to Malevich's metaphysical pursuit of the fourth dimension.[17] The obvious interest in oriental art manifest in *The Shroud of Christ* of 1908 (no 479) suggests affinities with Uspenskii's interest in Eastern philosophy and metaphysical striving which were central to his concept of the fourth dimension. There is a more direct Eastern influence in this work than in any paintings which have previously been available from this period of Malevich's development, and the explicitly religious content is, as far as I know, unique in his oeuvre. These paintings amplify the spiritual dimension of Malevich's work and relate it far more closely to the artistic philosophy of his friend Mikhail Matiushin.

The influence of Gauguin and Matisse, evident in the *Self Portrait* of 1910 (no 480), now in the Tretiakov Gallery in Moscow, provides a link with Malevich's interest in peasant scenes and the primitive art of the Russian peasantry that inspired those peasant canvases of 1912 which are among the few important series not represented amongst this Costakis material. Malevich's subsequent understanding and assimilation of Cubism are clarified by the undated painting of *The Violin* (no 494), which appears to be closely related to the drawings of Cubist paintings that he included in his theoretical writings, *The Non-Objective World*, and his artistic charts. One of the most important works formerly in the Costakis collection and now in the Tretiakov gallery is his *Portrait of Matiushin* of 1913 (no 482) which was painted while the two artists were working on the Futurist opera *Victory over the Sun*, Matiushin composing the score and Malevich designing the decor and costumes. Although still firmly linked to Cubism, there are certain elements in the *Portrait of Matiushin*, such as the white line, which presage the radical new developments that Malevich was shortly to pursue in his painting. Malevich himself attached considerable importance to this work and included it in all his major exhibitions.

Although neither Malevich's Cubist period, nor his whole Suprematist œuvre are extensively represented here, the few examples which Costakis has are notable ones. An important aspect of Malevich's work which is included in the collection however, and which is available nowhere else in the West, is the agitational material done by Malevich and his pupils during the First World War and Civil War periods. A preliminary glimpse of this material was provided by the examples in the Beaubourg's *Paris-Moscou* exhibition of 1979, but these of course returned to the Soviet Union thereafter.

Malevich's patriotic posters of the First World War exploited dramatically and colourfully his knowledge of Russian folk art and in particular the traditional peasant woodcuts, or *lubki*. The selection available in this volume (nos 960–963) have a vitality and exuberance which comes across particularly strongly in the company of contemporaneous designs by other artists. This is the first time that any such posters have been reproduced in quantity. In 1918 Malevich was sent by the Moscow Department of Fine Arts, IZO, to help the Red Army in its urgent efforts to consolidate Bolshevik power,[18] and he may again have participated in the design of posters here; certainly the collection includes two Suprematist schemes for the agitational trains of the type which disseminated propaganda along the front line of the Civil War (nos 500–501). In 1919 Malevich moved to Vitebsk at Chagall's invitation, to teach in the art school there and under his artistic influence the Smolensk branch of the Russian Telegraphic Agency, ROSTA, produced posters in a Suprematist idion (nos 972–973). This is where Lissitzky produced his well-known Suprematist poster *Cleave the Whites with the Red Wedge* under the influence of Malevich's presence, and the application of Suprematist compositional principles to such practical tasks inaugurated a new direction in Suprematism itself.

Included in the collection are eight unattributed Suprematist water colours which are explicitly concerned with the decorative organisation of wall surfaces (nos 514–542). It is diverting to speculate as to whether the pair which are composed around a triptych of blank rectangles (nos 516 and 520) were destined to embellish the images of Marx, Engels and Lenin, or merely three windows. Authorship of these eight drawings is unknown, and some are very gauche; only no 521 has a clarity and balance suggestive of that higher order of compositional skill which would be associated with Malevich himself. Certainly the application of Suprematist principles to the decoration of interiors was an activity of which he approved, and for which he had set down principles in writing.[19] In December 1920 he had written to Kudriashev stressing that Suprematism had to adopt a more 'constructive' attitude towards the world and at INKhUK too he had emphasised the need for his UNOVIS group to participate in the reconstruction of the new society.[20] Malevich's typographical designs for the programme of the First Conference of Rural Poverty Committees in 1918 (nos 497–8), and the posters (nos 972–3) attest to the fact that Suprematism had already shifted its attention to a wider context.

23 Ivan Kliun, *Design for a Monument to Olga Rozanova*, 1918–19.
24 Olga Rozanova, *Preliminary sketch for the Construction 'The Cylist'*, 1915.

25 Ksenia Ender, *Untitled*, 1924.

26 Vladimir Tatlin, *Drawing for a Corner Counter-Relief*, 1915.
27 Vladimir Tatlin, *Corner Counter-Relief*, 1915. Contemporary photograph from the brochure *Vladimir Evgrafovich Tatlin*, which was published at the 0.10 exhibition in Petrograd in December 1915.

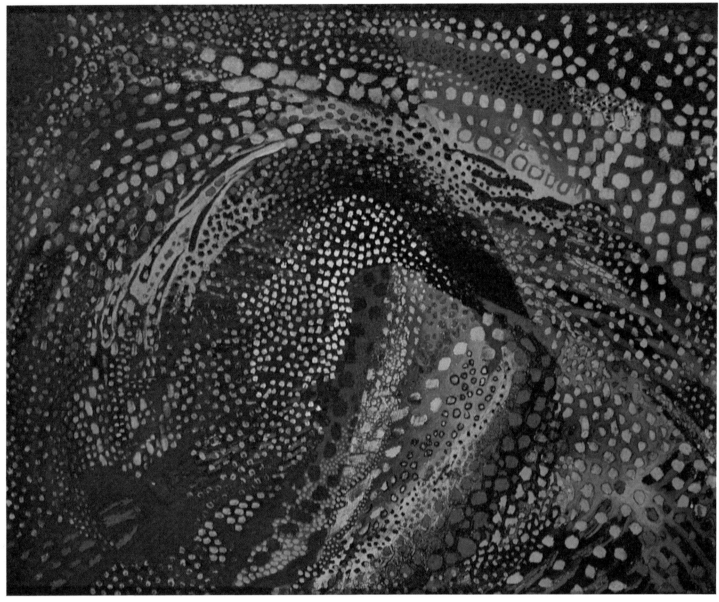

28 Mikhail Matiushin, *Painterly-Musical Construction*, 1918.

29 Kazimir Malevich, Patriotic poster against the Germans, 1914. The text reads: 'The French allies have a wagon full of defeated Germans and our English brothers have a whole tub of them'.

30 Kazimir Malevich, *Patriotic Lubok Against the Austrians*, 1914–15. The text reads: 'An Austrian went to Radziwill and landed straight onto a peasant woman's pitchfork'.

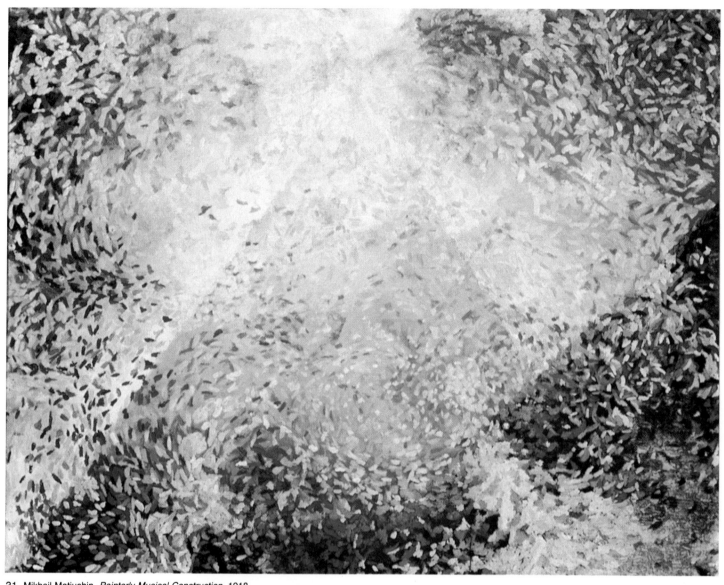

31  Mikhail Matiushin, *Painterly-Musical Construction*, 1918.

32 Kazimir Malevich, *Portrait*, c 1910.

Finally the collection gives us some examples of those very little known works which Malevich produced in the 1930s, when he returned to easel painting and reworked the artistic formulae of Impressionism and peasant art which had preoccupied his early career. The *Portrait of Una* (no 523) has that even, sunny illumination by then associated with Socialist Realism, but in his *Portrait of the Sculptor Pavlov* of 1933 (no 524) he returned to a fine Cézannist brushstroke and situated his spotlit subject against a background of cut-off picture frames such as we are used to seeing in works by Manet and Degas. Previously almost nothing of Malevich's later period, that is dating from after his Bauhaus visit of 1927, has been available in the West.

Malevich's pupil Ivan Kliun is extensively represented in Costakis' collection. These two hundred and more Kliun works enable us to establish for the first time a relatively comprehensive picture of the development of an artist who is little known in the West. His early Symbolist landscape of 1905 (no 125) is clearly influenced by Borisov-Musatov's handling of the Russian countryside. Of the works that follow, one of the most exciting is the Cubo-Futurist relief made from wood, wire, metal, and porcelain entitled *The Landscape Rushing By* which was exhibited at the Last Futurist Exhibition 0.10 in December 1915 in Petrograd (no 135, and dustjacket). Comparison with the more figurative, far less advanced *Cubist at Her Toilet* which was exhibited at the same show would suggest that this work is unlikely to have predated its exhibition by as much as this present catalogue indicates. However George Costakis has informed me that this work is dated 1913 on the back in Kliun's hand. This suggests a far more rapid line of development in Kliun's work than has hitherto been assumed. There is a drawing entitled *The Aviator*, dated 1912 (no 254, top), which does bear affinities with the sketches for *Landscape Rushing By*, and which also argues for the earlier date. The relief itself provides a classic illustration of the principle of *sdvig*, or dislocation, which was central to Russian Futurist poetics and art. Also in the Costakis collection are a fascinating series of sketches in which he uses Suprematist forms three-dimensionally in designs for a monument to be erected to his friend and fellow devotee of Malevich, Olga Rozanova, who died in 1918 (nos 288–9; 293–6).

Amongst Kliun's Suprematist works are a series of canvases, c 1917 (nos 145–51), which while deriving from Malevich's approach, also seem to bear some affinities with Kandinskii's evolving interests in the interrelationships of certain forms and colours, epitomised by Kandinskii's INKhUK questionnaire of 1920. Kliun's series of canvases, elucidated by reference to nos 268–9, of 1931, raise interesting topics for speculation. Having broken with Malevich and Suprematism in 1919, Kliun's works of the 1920s encompassed a vast variety of styles and he managed to rework most of the current artistic trends. Among the most popular with him, especially at the end of the 1920s, was Purism, which with its highly stylised forms but figurative content conformed to the Party's demand for a comprehensible and realist art. George Costakis has established that Kliun used Purism quite consciously, as a kind of official cover for the fact that between 1930 and 1933 he was creating a new style of non-objective painting which was distinct from Suprematism and which consisted of coloured oval, organic forms; unfortunately no examples of this appear in the present book or exhibition.

Some of the most interesting Kliun paintings of the 1920s are canvases like *The Red Light: a Spherical Composition*, of 1923, (no 162), in which the nebulous form of a glowing red sun is set against a dark background. This seems to denote an interest in cosmic phenomena which is illustrated in other works such as *Spherical Composition* of 1923 (no 185). This one resembles nothing so much as a green comet and its vapour trail, that is perhaps prescient of Soviet sputniks.

The non-chronological arrangement of Kliun's work in this book has its logic, but it is confusing in relation to the development of the individual's œuvre. Elsewhere in the book each artists' personal chronology is preserved to great effect. Abandonment of this principle with Kliun is partly due to the desire to maintain the integrity of a collection of thirty-two sheets of sketches which the editor convincingly identifies as an œuvre-catalogue assembled by the artist himself in the 1930s, and which juxtaposes material in a highly unchronological way. Indeed the dating of this whole corpus of work is sometimes highly problematic and the resolution of such questions will take much longer than has been available for the preparation of this volume.

Olga Rozanova is an artist whose reputation will be considerably enhanced by the public availability of this collection. She has a particular role in it, because it was her paintings such as *Untitled (Green Stripe)* of 1917 (no 1067) which apparently first attracted Costakis to the visual character of the Russian avant-garde whilst he was still collecting Old Masters and antiques. Being amongst his first acquisitions in this field, Rozanova's works are the seed of the whole collection. *Untitled (Green stripe)* is among the few examples of Rozanova's abstract painting since she died in 1918. Her pre-Revolutionary career was closely linked to the Futurists, and illustrated here are several of her works in this area including the collages she and Aleksei Kruchenykh devised for the book *The Universal War* which are already well known and have been exhibited in London.[21] A real revelation, on the other hand, are the annotated preparatory sketches for her two constructions of 1915, *The Automobile* and *The Cyclist* which were exhibited at the 0.10 exhibition in Petrograd. These sketches (nos 1036–9) constitute the only surviving information about the genesis of those works, which we know otherwise only from newspaper reports and photographs. Although there are Rozanova paintings in Russian museums, they are rare in private collections both in the USSR and in the West, and this is one of the few examples known to me – paintings being of course unique objects whereas the collage books were produced in editions. The paucity of her works is perhaps attributable to her early death in that chaotic, post-Revolutionary year 1918, and to her concentration in preceding months upon campaigns for IZO, the Department of Fine Arts, to resuscitate craft production in the provinces.[22]

## Other leading trends

Although the Russian avant-garde is characterised by its richness in highly gifted individuals, certain artists stand out particularly, because they pioneered radically different trends in artistic expression. In the estimation of certain Soviet art historians such as Nikolai Khardzhiev and Evgenii Koftun, and of some Western specialists in Russian art, the four leading artists of the pre- and post-Revolutionary avant-garde are Pavel Filonov, Mikhail Matiushin, Kasimir Malevich and Vladimir Tatlin. These men represent the main artistic movements. Of the four, Filonov and Matiushin are still relatively unknown in the West. Apart from one or two articles, nothing of substance has been published here about their work, although a few of their major works appeared at the Beaubourg's *Paris-Moscou* show of 1979, to give Westerners a first taste of the innovations they introduced.[23]

Costakis owns very few Filonov works, but his untitled drawing, his illustrations for Velimir Khlebnikov's *Wooden Idols* and the painting *Head* of 1925–6 (nos 48–51), provide an opportunity to observe Filonov's minute method. These are among the first genuine works by Filonov to be publicly available outside Russia, although examples of his students' work have been circulating for some time. *Untitled (First Symphony of D. Shostakovich)*, of 1925–7 however (no 52), remains in the Soviet Union within Costakis' gift to the Tretiakov Gallery. The *Wooden Idols* drawings illustrate Filonov's attempt to create an exact visual equivalent for the poetic sounds of the text. His self-declared 'analytical method' was a complex intuitive concept of art which used accretions of abstract forms to present a composite vision of the world that would be recognisable and resonant.

His own exposition illuminates the thinking behind his strange images:

Realism is a scholastic abstraction of only two of the object's

33 Vladimir Tatlin, *The Letatlin*, c 1932. The person demonstrating the glider seems to be Tatlin himself.

34 Liubov Popova, *Set design for 'The Magnanimous Cuckold'*, 1922.

predicates: form and colour. . . . [My principle] activates all the object's predicates and its orbit: its own reality; its own pulsation and that of its orbit; its biodynamics; intellect; emanations; interfusions; geneses; its processes in colour and form – in short, life as a whole. My principle presupposes the orbit not as mere space, but as a biodynamic entity . . . in which the reality of the object and its orbit is eternally forming and transforming its colouristic and formal content and its processes. This is absolute analytical vision.[24]

The quality of reproduction in this present volume allows us to grasp the visual implications of these ideas. In this respect it far surpasses the obscure Filonov collection by J Křiž printed in Prague in 1966, which for a long time was our only significant source on this artist.[25] Even better than the *Paris-Moscou* catalogue it conveys the minutely careful application of paint which is characteristic of Filonov's style.

The distinction between Filonov's work and that of his student Sulimo-Samuilo (nos 1097-1100) helps create a framework for reliably assessing Filonov attributions without reference back to the vast collections which the Russian Museum in Leningrad and the Tretiakov in Moscow received from his sister; very few of his works are available anywhere in private collections.

Matiushin's work has also been little known hitherto except for his colour charts, which Malevich exhibited with his own work in the West in 1927, and the striking canvases like *Movement in Space* of 1917–18 which came to Paris-Moscou fifty years later.[26] The Costakis collection now shows us three more paintings that illustrate various aspects of Matiushin's ideas during the period 1918–20 (nos 526–9).

All these works reflect the approach to colour which he was to investigate further within the State Institute of Artistic Culture, GINKhUK, in Petrograd from 1923 onwards. The results of his research were published in his *Reference Book on Colour* of 1932. The group of students who worked with him in Leningrad are all well represented here: the talented Ender family of Boris, Ksenia, Mariia and Iuri, as well as Nikolai Grinberg (nos 534–682). Of immense variety and intensity, their works illustrate interesting ramifications of Matiushin's ideas, and invite a radical restructuring of established perspectives on the Russian avant-garde. Although Zoia Ender has published some work on the group in Italian, a full study of their paintings and ideas in any language is still awaited.

Matiushin himself had a great interest in organic form, and he developed a theory concerning man's ability to observe natural phenomena which involved developing both physical vision and the cognition process beyond their present limits. His system of *zor-ved* ('see-know') was related to his idea that our perception of three-dimensional space was inadequate because it was uni-directional. To appreciate space fully, man had to acquire a 'total vision' encompassing 360°. Such total vision would be directionless, and therefore limitless; it would thus enable man to perceive the fourth dimension. The works displayed here allow us to make some estimation of how this total vision could be conveyed in painting. In the works by Ksenia

Ender for example, (nos 557–9), the horizon curves around the picture plane in a manner akin to the fish-eye lens. This is an instance where a reader's understanding of the deeper issues at stake in these avant-garde paintings would be enhanced here by more extensive background notes to specific works, though the information included in the biographical notes does often provide a general conceptual introduction. In these circumstances, this stunning body of visually most exciting, but far from self-explanatory works, inevitably remains little more than a visual feast for the non-specialist reader.

Unlike Filonov and Matiushin, Tatlin is well known in the West. This happy situation is particularly due to the exhibition organised in Stockholm in 1968 by Troels Andersen, whose exemplary multilingual catalogue was thereafter widely available and provided an excellent chronology and introduction to the artist's works.[27] Costakis owns very little Tatlin material, but this book has the advantage of reproducing it in colour. Although few, the items represent Tatlin's activities in their full diversity. They include his set design of 1912–14, for Glinka's opera *Ivan Susanin* (no 1103) which is interesting for the planar structure of the stage space; for the use of decorative motifs derived from peasant art, and for its vibrant but limited colour range. The partially preserved *Relief* (no 1108) is impossible to date, or even to attribute definitively to Tatlin since it has obviously lost some crucial components. More rewarding are two drawings (nos 1109 and 1111) which seem to be preliminary sketches for his corner counter-reliefs of c 1915. Although undated and unsigned, one of these (no 1111) relates directly to the corner counter-relief which was exhibited at the 0.10 exhibition in Petrograd and illustrated in the brochure entitled *Vladimir Evgrafovich Tatlin* published by the *New Journal for All* (*Novyi Zhurnal dlia Veskh*) in 1915. This similarity has been pointed out in the catalogue where the relief itself is illustrated as no 1110. The importance of the sketches resides in the light which they throw on Tatlin's working method. Valentina Khodasevich's memoirs suggest that in preparing works for this exhibition Tatlin worked upon the materials directly in a spontaneous and intuitive way, letting the materials suggest the structure of the relief, rather than shaping the materials to a specific predetermined image.[28] The existence of such sketches, however, raises questions as to the accuracy of the implied assumption that Tatlin worked only in this spontaneous way when assembling his counter-reliefs. Certainly in his work for his flying apparatus the *Letatlin*, (no 1118), on which he worked from 1929, he was involved both in extensive studies of material, and in assembling a body of technical data prior to developing the forms of the apparatus.[29] Rejecting the 'hard forms' of the engineers as 'evil' and fragile, and evolving forms appropriate to his conception of the world as 'round and soft',[30] Tatlin produced a richly organic, bird-like form for the glider. Costakis' collection contains only one fragment of the total structure, namely a single-wing strut (no 1120–1) but this is enough to show the qualities of his curvilinear forms and his sensitive handling of the natural willow and cork from which it was made. The Letatlin seemed to attract very little attention when it was exhibited in Paris in

35 Ivan Kliun, *Red Light Spherical Composition*, c 1923.

   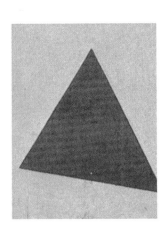

36 Ivan Kliun, a series of small, untitled canvases depicting various geometrical shapes in different colours on a white ground, c 1917.

37  Olga Rozanova, *Untitled (Green Stripe)*, 1917

38 Liubov Popova, documentary photograph of set for *Zemlia Dybom*, 1923.     39 Liubov Popova, political slogans for *Zemlia Dybom*, 1923.

1979, probably due to the fact it was displayed obscurely. The Russians showed greater sensitivity to its achievement when they rehung it in the Pushkin Gallery of Fine Arts in 1981 in the place it had occupied in 1932 – as illustrated in the *AD* report on that show.[31]

As a postscript to Tatlin's Constructivist work, the Costakis collection contains paintings from the 1930s and 1940s. Although essentially figurative, they retain a very strong interest in the painting's surface texture: in works like *Meat* of 1947 (no 1116), Tatlin has scraped the paint away to create particular effects. Equally striking in this painting, and in contemporaneous ones which I have seen in Moscow, is the sense of colour which Tatlin's work displayed even in this period and which provides a strand of artistic continuity in his œuvre. The resonance of the muted three primaries of his monumental *Nude* of 1913 is unforgettable for those who saw it when it was exhibited in Paris in 1979.

For Tatlin, as for many of the other artists, this collection adds a little more to our picture of their work and development.

### The Constructivist dimension: towards design

One of the most exciting items in the Costakis collection is Rodchenko's *Ellipse* hanging construction which was probably made in 1921, just before it was exhibited at the Third OBMOKhU exhibition in May of that year (no 1019). In a collection which consists overwhelmingly of painting, this work is all the more remarkable because it is one of the few three-dimensional objects. The dating here to 'c 1920' is naturally based on the assumption that in this Russian avant-garde period, the conventional time lapse existed between the execution of works and their public display. The conventional relationship does not hold here, however. It was an essential feature of the period – a symptom of its fervent pursuit of innovation and its frenetic creative activity – that an artist's works were commonly last minute executions, produced *ad hoc* for a particular show and often hung with the paint hardly dry. This description from 1915 captures well the flavour that was to continue:

> . . . each tries to put his work on exhibition last to prevent competitors from borrowing his caprices . . . They nail together absolutely anything: soiled gloves, a cheap top hat and call it 'self portrait of Mayakovskii' or similar . . .
>
> On the wall assigned to Larionov there happened to be a fan. Someone started it up. Larionov was called to admire the new effect given to his construction. He approved hugely and set some strings and nails on the fan.[32]

In such an atmosphere, the date of Rodchenko's *Ellipse* is more likely to be early 1921. A similar situation inevitably arises with the dating of numerous other works in this collection. Rodchenko's *Ellipse* is immensely important as the only known surviving example of the series of hanging constructions which he made in 1921 and displayed at the Third OBMOKhU exhibition. In the installation photograph of that show his constructions based on the triangle, the circle and the hexagonal are clearly visible. From illustrations of his work in the magazine *Kino-Fot*, 1922, we know that he also produced a square. Each of these constructions was produced from one flat sheet of plywood whence the forms were cut concentrically. Each set was then rotated to extend the planar figure into three-dimensional space. This exploration of combinations of similar geometric forms was to become a central component of Rodchenko's method in design.[33] Within the Costakis collection this work therefore represents one of the direct take-off points towards solutions for directly utilitarian tasks. Augmenting the Rodchenko material which has recently been made accessible through the Paris-Moscou exhibition and the Rodchenko exhibition at Oxford's Museum of Modern Art, and also through the Karginov monograph from Thames & Hudson, we now have a series of later works by Rodchenko. These highlight his move back towards easel painting, a move made by many of the avant-garde during the later 1920s and the 1930s. But Rodchenko's paintings of the 1940s, unlike Tatlin's, are not always figurative. Some such as *Realistic Abstraction* of 1940 (no 1024), display a concern with the integrity of mechanised form which recalls the solid images of type objects developed by Purism. Other paintings display affinities with Surrealism, and one *Expressive Rhythm* (no 1027) indicates a continued interest in spatial movement though now in two dimensions rather than three. Its parallels with Jackson Pollock serve to emphasise the innovating continuity between the Russian avant-garde and later American developments.

Among the artists very well represented in this collection is Liubov' Popova. Costakis has numerous paintings; several of her sketch-books; linocuts; a series of agitational slogans for the play *The Earth in Turmoil* and other typographical designs, and some important designs for stage sets and fabrics. The book thus gives us material from the whole range of activities upon which Popova was engaged before her death from scarlet fever in 1924.

The earliest work here is a drawing of 1906 entitled *The View of Houses from my Window* (no 724); the earliest painting is a *Still life* of 1907–8 (no 725), which shows her interest in *plein-air* painting and her knowledge of Post-Impressionism. These works help to establish Popova's artistic roots more clearly, and her development is particularly illuminated by the sketchbooks whence the editor has wisely chosen to reproduce extensively.

Here we find fluid figure drawings, such as Popova seems to have

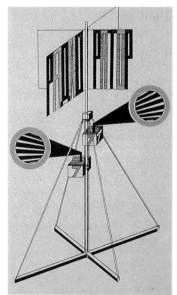

40 Gustav Klutsis, *Construction*, 1922–3.

41,42 Gustav Klutsis, design for agitational stands: *Screen-Radio Orator No 5*, 1922 and *Radio Orator No 7*, 1922.

done throughout her career, but also a series of tree studies which examine the underlying structure of branch formation (eg no 744) and which provide a new sense of the continuity of structural interests which later became manifest in her Constructivist stage designs. This interest in structure is already evident in the numerous Cubist analyses of the human figure dating from Popova's period with Le Fauconnier and Metzinger in Paris during 1913–14, some of which relate directly to figurative paintings in this collection. As a body, this Cubist work contains seeds of the well-known compositions of interpenetrating planes from 1918–19 that she called 'painterly architectonics' (nos 821, 826–7, 848 *et al*), and thus provides another valuable link in Popova's chronology.

The collection helps to clarify the titling and chronology of Popova's paintings in another respect too, since it contains six fascinating postcards – letters sent by Popova herself on cards reproducing her own work. One such, no 815, illustrates a work which has sometimes been attributed to Aleksandra Ekster under the title *2 Lir*. Here Popova herself inscribed the title *Jug on a Table: a Plastic Painting*. This work is therefore securely established as being by Popova, and is accurately titled. It is also established as being the painting Popova exhibited in Petrograd at The Last Futurist Exhibition 0.10 of December 1915, as Number 96 in that show.[34] Sixty-five years later, it was amongst the Popova works displayed in the Moscow showing of Paris-Moscou – see again the *AD* report on that show – and is now in the Tretiakov Gallery. It is so well illustrated in this present book that the variety of painterly textures, and the incorporation of the *objet trouvé* within the painted cardboard relief, are clearly visible. Illustrations of this quality are one of the outstanding features of this book. They compensate most satisfactorily for the geographical inaccessibility of those items from the collection which have remained in Moscow.

Our chronology of Popova's paintings is still far from complete, but her own statement reproduced in the catalogue to her posthumous exhibition provides a framework for the movement in her work towards a constructive approach:

A Cubist period (the problem of form) was followed by a Futurist period (the problem of movement and colour), and the principle of abstracting the parts of an object was followed ... by the abstraction of the object itself ... The problem of depiction was replaced by the problem of the construction of form and line (post-Cubism) and of colour (Suprematism).[35]

For all that clarification, the years 1916–20 incorporate a conglomeration of very different styles, and the wealth of Popova material published for the first time in this book really emphasises the fact that her development was at times so intense and rapid that one style easily gave way to another, without necessarily following a linear and logical progression.

It has always been difficult to explain the change in Popova's approach which occurred between the structurally inarticulate stage sets in a Cubo-Futurist idiom such as *The Locksmith and the Chancellor* of 1921 (no 877), and the first-ever Constructivist stage designs which she did during the following year for *The Magnanimous Cuckold*. For this latter we have both the well-known final elevational drawing and, yet more attractive, a freehand pencil and wash sketch (nos 880, 882). As a scaffold-like structure operating like a 'machine' the *Magnanimous Cuckold* design produced an acting apparatus totally different in conception from the earlier, spatially ambiguous sets. This change of direction may have been prompted by Popova's friendship and collaboration with Aleksandr Vesnin, but Costakis' material reveals a thread of structural interest running right through from her earlier tree and figure studies to paintings like *Spatial Force Construction* (nos 853–6) of 1920–21, and to 'linear construction' drawings akin to contemporaneous work by Klutsis, Rodchenko and Vesnin, that seem related to the stage sets for *Magnanimous Cuckold* as well as to her later work in the theatrical workshops and to 'the varieties of spatial figures' upon which she worked from 1920–22.[36]

Costakis also owns an interesting fragment of Popova's design for the stage set of *The Earth in Turmoil* (no 889), an agitational play based on Martinet's verse drama *La nuit*.

Here Popova's set was essentially a gantry crane to which she affixed various substructures including screens for the projection of newsreels. Here the abstracted mechanical elements of her stripped-down apparatus for *The Magnanimous Cuckold* were replaced by the strongly descriptive, and by real images in photomontage. A vast array of real objects, from field tents and telephones to lorries, were used as props for this play; this was in direct contrast to the complete absence of such props in *The Magnanimous Cuckold*. It was perhaps a response to the play's directly agitational, political purpose, but this use of real industrial objects in *The Earth in Turmoil* heralded a shift within Constructivism away from its initial utopian aspirations towards a more pragmatic compromise with existing reality. The Costakis collection adds to our knowledge of this production yet further with a striking series of agitational slogans which Popova designed for this production (nos 888, 890–906). They are good examples of that free typographical composition with the new simplified post-Revolutionary alphabet which later characterised all Constructivist typography.

Popova's expertise in the manipulation of two-dimensional graphic elements was also evident in her textile designs. These are part of that practical compromise with industry and the environment which

43

44

45

47

43 Liubov Popova, *Textile Design*, c 1924.

44 Liubov Popova, *Design for Embroidered Book Cover*, c 1923–4.

45 Another Popova textile design of 1924.

46 Liubov Popova, *Prozodezhda, Actor No 5*, 1921. Costume design for Meierkhol'd's production of *The Magnanimous Cuckold*. (ph the Arts Council of Great Britain)

47 Replicas of dresses and fabric designs of the early 1920s by Stepanova, Popova, Aleksandra Ekster and Nadezhda Lamanova, displayed in the exhibition *Moscow-Paris 1900–1930* in Moscow, 1981. (ph Catherine Cooke: see *AD* 1981 11–12 pp 72–9)

48 Liubov Popova, *Spatial Force Construction*, 1921.

Popova inaugurated in 1923 with *The Earth in Turmoil*. Costakis has some very interesting examples which represent her attempt to participate directly in industrial production for the creation of the new society.

Among artists hitherto very little studied is Gustav Klutsis, a committed Communist and a soldier in the Latvian Rifles who fought for Bolshevik power before resuming his artistic studies in the Moscow Free Studios under Malevich, until the latter moved to Vitebsk.

In works like the *Dynamic City* painted between 1919 and 1921 (no 339), the influence from Suprematism is strongly evident. Costakis' large collection of Klutsis material reveals with new clarity his move from a Cubist inspiration, through Suprematism, to an interest in three-dimensional structures; it contains a whole series of drawings exploring structure and plane that appear related to contemporaneous explorations by Lissitzky. The spatial ambiguities of some of Klutsis' drawn structures are particularly interesting, however, as each one offers several possible interpretations in three dimensions. The linocut series show this particularly well (nos 378–84, 386–7).

These explorations of spatial structures sometimes refer directly to engineering structures such as pylons and the Eiffel Tower but are sometimes more abstract. They indicate a very intensive aspect of Klutsis' activity. The State Archive of Literature and Art in Moscow contains two enormous bound volumes of Klutsis' sketches and drawings which relate directly to the linocuts and which illustrate the intensity of Klutsis' investigation of such structures. The linocuts therefore provide easily accessible evidence of what formed a very significant aspect of Klutsis' approach to the design process – ie an exhaustive exploration of possible configurations to be generated on the basis of certain components and of certain types of junctions and relationships. The agitational stands represent the practical application of this kind of abstract investigation in two dimensions to a concrete situation in three dimensions, and thus they form a direct link with other Constructivist design methods in furniture and architecture.

The collection contains a large and remarkable selection of these stands, each for a different agitational function, which Klutsis designed in 1922 and which are of particular interest for the development of the early, skeletal style of Constructivist architecture epitomised by the Vesnin brothers' *Leningradskaia Pravda* project of 1924. Some, like no 368, were platforms for political speakers. Others, such as no 366, were news-stands with loudspeakers, a newsreel screen and a bookstall for agitational literature. All were examples of 'laboratory work' being applied to real tasks, and they may have their origin in the Stenberg brothers' first integral 'stands' designed for their constructions in the Third OBMOKhU exhibition in Moscow in 1921. Klutsis was then a student in the VKhUTEMAS and would

undoubtedly have seen their work.

As to Klutsis' influence on furniture and interior design, his teaching position under Rodchenko in Dermetfak is obviously significant. Certain components of the well-known Workers's Club interior which Rodchenko designed for the 1925 Exposition des Arts Decoratifs in Paris – most notably the folding screens and bookshelving – have distinct similarities with Klutsis' agitational stands. In these areas the collection gives a rich sense of the collective character of these explorations and of the successive moves towards evolving the Constructivist approach to design.

Towards the end of the twenties Klutsis, like many other avant-garde artists, concentrated on the immediately agitational fields of graphic and poster design. He wrote extensively about his favourite technique of photomontage, seeing the photomontage as part of a total system of interrelated forms of socially reconstructive activity.[38] Many of his posters from this period have been widely reproduced; most are directly political, and use only red with the grey, black and white of the photographic image. Here in the Costakis collection however there are a wonderful series of richly polychrome postcards, which Klutsis produced for the Moscow Spartakiada in 1928 (nos 400–4). Printed in vibrant green, yellow and blue as well as red these display Klutsis' ability to manipulate colour as a graphic element alongside the photograph, and they link very appositely with his earlier colour teaching.

Among the less-known members of the Russian avant-garde who deserve more extensive research, and who are represented in Costakis' collection, is Petr Miturich. Although almost unknown in the West, Miturich is famous in the Soviet Union as a sensitive and skilled draughtsman who produced small figurative drawings in the twenties and later. However, there are other aspects to his creativity which were more radically innovative and which represented a different way of applying artistic knowledge to the reorganisation of the new environment. This collection unfortunately does not contain some of Miturich's most innovative investigations but it does contain two examples of his purely artistic work, which will now be permanently accessible in the West: one two-dimensional, one three-dimensional. Miturich's pencil sketch of the cover design for Khlebnikov's *Boards of Destiny* (no 683) is directly related to the ten little graphic cubes (no 684) which formed part of a vast series through which Miturich explored the extension of his graphic vocabulary into three dimensions. Costakis' selection of ten cubes represents only a very small number of Miturich's permutations of the three-dimensional potential of graphic form. His spatial posters and paintings had the more ambitious task of projecting entire graphic compositions into a more active spatial dimension.

49 Gustav Klutsis, *Construction*, c 1920–2.
50 Gustav Klutsis, *Photomontage Printed in Colour on Postcard*, 1928. The text reads:

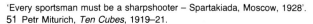
'Every sportsman must be a sharpshooter – Spartakiada, Moscow, 1928'.
51 Petr Miturich, *Ten Cubes*, 1919–21.

Miturich is amongst those artists who have profited from the exposure of his work at the Paris-Moscou exhibition and from his inclusion in this collection, because between them these two bodies of material have brought together examples from almost the whole range of his œuvre. The interest in curvilinear form evident here found a more explicitly utilitarian application in his investigations of the energy potential of organic form, most dramatically in the designs he called *volnoviki*. These were new forms of transport which exploited an undulating motion observed in nature: ships based on the form and motion of fish, for example, and a flying apparatus based on a vast bird.[39] Drawings were displayed at the Paris-Moscou show, in both its Beaubourg and Moscow variants, but not reproduced in either catalogue. Miturich extended these principles of undulating motion to the organisation of a whole energy-efficient urban environment. Works that we have here relate to the genesis of those ideas.

Of Costakis' originally vast collection, only a small portion is now in the West, and among this material there is much of a documentary and manuscript nature which has not been reproduced in this book, yet will also have an important part to play in making our knowledge and understanding of the Russian avant-garde more profound. Meanwhile this volume provides a very stimulating introduction to the collection's most important items. Its cool, unprejudiced presentation will make it a vital reference point for future research.

It expands our knowledge of the well-known names. There is material by lesser-known figures which one hopes will lead to the necessary re-evaluation of their roles. The nature of Costakis' sources – often surviving families – has meant that the works here tend to be ones which artists themselves retained as important to their own development. Russian avant-garde material is represented in public and private collections in the West, but it is hardly widely accessible. The exhibition should not be missed, but as a purchase this book is infinitely better value than the catalogue which accompanies the show. That has a mere thirty coloured reproductions amongst 260 often weak black-and-white ones. If you can find the few extra pounds, the book is sumptuous for its price: indeed, worth saving up for.

## Notes

1 Camilla Gray, *The Great Experiment: Russian Art 1863–1922* Thames & Hudson, London, 1962; republished in paperback as *The Russian Experiment in Art 1863–1922*, 1971.

2 *Institut Khudozhestvennoi Kul'tury v Moskve (INKhUK) pri Otdele IZO NKP. Skhematicheskaia programma rabot Instituta Khudozhestvennoi Kul'tury po planu V V Kandinskogo*, Moscow 1920. This text is reprinted in I Matsa, *Sovetskoe iskusstvo za 15 let. Materialy i dokumentatsiia*, Moscow-Leningrad, 1933.

3 *ibid.*, p 126.

4 N Tarabukin, 'Polozhenie o gruppe ob'ektivnogo analiza', MS, private archive, Moscow.

5 *ibid.*

6 'Institut Khudozhestvennoi Kul'tury', *Russkoe iskusstvo* 1923, No 2–3, p 85.

7 The protocols of these debates are contained in 'Protokoly zasedanii uchenogo soveta INKhUKa' ('Protocols of the meetings of the Scientific Committee of INKhUK') which form part of the INKhUK archive, Moscow. A discussion of these debates is given in S O Khan-Magomedov, 'Diskussiia v INKhUKe o sootnoshenii konstruktsii i kompozitsii (ianvar' – aprel' 1921 goda)', *Tekhnicheskaia estetika*, 1979, No 2, and in C Lodder *Russian Constructivism*, London, 1983. During these debates the First Working Group of Constructivists was set up within INKhUK in March 1921. It consisted of Aleksei Gan, Aleksandr Rodchenko, Varvara Stepanova, Kazimir Medunetskii, Georgii and Vladimir Stenberg and Karl Ioganson. See 'Programma uchebnoi podgruppy konstruktivistov INKhUKa', MS, 1921, private archive, Moscow.

8 G Stenberg, V Stenberg, and K Medunetskii, 'Tezisy po dokladu 'Konstruktivizm'', MS, private archive, Moscow, p 1.

9 'Protokol zasedaniia uchenogo soveta INKhUKa', MS, 14 January 1921.

10 'Protokol zasedaniia uchenogo soveta INKhUKa', MS, 21 January 1921.

11 L Moholy-Nagy, *The New Vision. From Material to Architecture*, New York, 1930, p 109.

12 K Ioganson, 'Ot konstruktsii k tekhnike i izobreteniiu', a paper delivered at INKhUK on 9 March 1922, MS, private archive, Moscow.

13 *ibid.*

14 A Babichev in 'Protokol zasedanii a uchenogo soveta INKhUKa', 14 January 1921.

15 *Izvestiia ASNOVA*, No 1, 1926.

16 K Malevich'Detstvo i iunost Kazimira Malevicha (Glavy iz avtobiografii khudozhnika)' in N Khardzhiev, *K istorii russkogo avangarda*, Stockholm, 1976, p 112.

17 Malevich's development of Suprematism and its relationship to the fourth dimension is discussed in L Dalrymple Henderson, *The Artist, 'the fourth dimension', and non-Euclidean geometry 1900–1930: a romance of many dimensions*, Ann Arbor 1980; C Douglas, *Swans of other worlds: Kazimir Malevich and the origins of Suprematism 1908–1915*, UMI 1980, and S Compton, 'Malevich and the Fourth Dimension', *Studio International*, April 1974, pp 190–5.

18 E A Speranskaia, ed, *Agitatsionno-massovoe iskusstvo*, Moscow, 1971, p 96 and p 126, n 189.

19 Larissa A Zhadova, *Malevich: Suprematism and Revolution in Russian Art 1910–30*, London 1982, Documentary appendices.

20 K Malevich, letter to Koudriashev, dated December 1920, now in the Costakis collection.

21 This book was published in a limited edition. Several copies exist in the West and have been frequently exhibited with other items of Russian art, as for instance, at the *Tatlin's Dream* Exhibition of 1974 at Fischer Fine Art, London.

22 Details of the craft workshops are given in *Gazeta IZO*, No 1, 10 March, 1921.

23 Among the small quantity of literature on these artists in English, is A Povelikhina, 'Matiushin's Spatial System', *The Structurist*, No 15/16, 1975/6, pp 64–71, and various articles by John Bowlt on Filonov, including 'P Filonov: an alternative tradition', *Art Journal*, Spring 1975, pp 208–16.

24 P Filonov, 'Deklaratsiia ''Mirogo iskusstva'' ', *Zhizn' iskusstva* 1923 no 20 pp 13–14. This translation is taken from J Bowlt, 'Pavel Filonov: his painting and his theory', *Russian review*, Vol 34, no 3, 1975 p 285.

25 J Křiž *Pavel Nikolaevich Filonov*, Prague 1966.

26 *Paris-Moscou 1900–1930* Centre Georges Pompidou, Paris 1979, pp 184–5.

27 Troels Andersen *Vladimir Tatlin* Moderna Museet, Stockholm, 1968.

28 V Khodasevich 'Bylo . . .', *Dekorativnoe iskusstvo SSSR* no 3 1980 p 41.

29 K Zelinskii 'Letatlin', *Vecherniaia Moskva*, 6 April 1933, translated in Andersen, *Vladimir Tatlin*, p 78.

30 V Tatlin, quoted by Begicheva, 'Vospominaniia o Tatline', MS, private archive, Moscow.

31 Catherine Cooke 'Moscow notes: from the opening of ''Paris-Moscow 1900–1930'' at the Pushkin Museum, Moscow', *AD* 1981, no 11–12 pp 72–9; the Pushkin Museum exhibition of Tatlin works was described in its catalogue, *Vystavaka rabot zasluzhennogo deiatelia iskusstv V E Tatlina*, Moscow – Leningrad, 1932.

32 E Adamov, 'Pis'mo iz Moskvy', *Kievskaia mysl'*, 6 May 1915, p 2 cited in Andersen, *Vladimir Tatlin*, p 7.

33 Some later implications of this for a design methodology are discussed by V F Koleichuk, 'Programmed form generation in design', *Environment and Planning B*, Vol 7, No 1, 1980 pp 19–30.

34 See G E Gordon, *Modern Art Exhibitions 1900–1916* (Munich 1974) Vol 2, p 884. In Popova's posthumous exhibition this work was titled *Jug on a Tabe (A relief)* and dated 1915 (*Katalog posmertnoi vystavki khudozhnika konstructora L S Popovoi*, Moscow 1924, p 10, no 16).

35 Popova cited by P, 'L S Popova', in *Katalog posmertnoi vystavki* p 6.

36 See here Christina Lodder, 'Constructivist Theatre as a Laboratory for an Architectural Aesthetic', *Architectural Association Quarterly*, Vol 11, No 2, 1979, pp 24–35.

37 TSGALI, fond 1334, op 2, ed khr 238–9.

38 G Klutsis, 'Fotomontazh kak novyi vid agitatsionnogo iskusstva, in *Izofront. Klassovaia bor'ba na fronte prostranstvennykh iskusstv. Sbornik statei ob'edineniia 'Oktiabr'*. Moscow-Leningrad, 1931, p 121.

39 The models and plans for such structures are preserved in a private archive in Moscow. For a discussion of Miturich's work see C Lodder, *Russian Constructivism, op cit*.

## Catherine Cooke

# 'FORM IS A FUNCTION X': THE DEVELOPMENT OF THE CONSTRUCTIVIST ARCHITECT'S DESIGN METHOD

Constructivism in architecture has been subject to very various interpretations. By admirers and denigrators alike, it has been presented as a philosophy predominantly concerned with the function of architecture as a social catalyst, with what Soviet terminology calls literally 'social construction'. It has been presented as an obsession with the space-forming role of structural technologies, with 'building construction'. It has been presented as an obsession with 'constructing possible shapes', that is as an overwhelming concern for formal construction: at worst, as formalism. No wonder the literature, and admirers of the resulting architecture, are confused. How can a small corpus of work have acquired dogmatic labels of such diversity?

The answer is simple. Like any serious professional architect, the Constructivist group were obsessively concerned with all these dimensions of the architectural problem. They were practitioners par excellence, crippled though they were by poverty of resources. Leading members of the group were unquestionably amongst the finest practicing architects of their period anywhere. Not for nothing did every one of them remain, through changing times, at the centre of Soviet architectural practice and education right through till his death or old age. Unlike most others however, they were not prepared to leave questions of the interrelationships between these different dimensions of the architectural problem to chance, or to 'intuition'.

In the words of Lenin quoted in their journal, they believed that 'In order really to know an object, it is necessary to comprehend, to study, all aspects of it: all its internal and external connectivities.'[1] Their's was what today would be called a 'systems' approach, or in the older and more general Russian term, a *kompleksnyi* approach. It addressed the design problem as an integrated complex; it was concerned with

**ПЕРВАЯ КОНФЕРЕНЦИЯ ОБЩЕСТВА СОВРЕМЕННЫХ АРХИТЕКТОРОВ. ERSTE KONFERENZ DER OSA**

ГРУППА УЧАСТНИКОВ КОНФЕРЕНЦИИ ОСА

1 The Constructivist architects at their First Conference, 1927.

solving the problem as a whole. 'Form is a function, x,' said their leader Moisei Ginzburg, 'which has always to be evaluated afresh by the architect in response to the changing preconditions of the form-making.'[2] In modern jargon, which is not so far from their own at times, they aspired to model the entire decision space surrounding that form.

There is a direct generic relationship to much modern thinking here, but also a crucial difference from most of what has passed for systems

thinking about environmental problems thereafter. The Constructivists were not nihilist in the face of architecture's traditional concerns with the delineation and organisation of real space, or with the necessity for expression in architecture through well-understood languages of form. Compared to the aesthetic concerns of the 1930s, or of recent years, their's was distinctly a poetry of the concrete rather than the rhetorical, but men of Ginzburg's sophistication were too deeply rooted in what Russians call 'architectural culture' to deny that their objective must be poetry.

A recent Soviet theorist M R Savchenko has described 'architectural research' as having properly 'a dual orientation, towards both spatial and societal aspects of architecture', that 'dual orientation' being 'repeated in a distinction between a building's *parameters* and its *properties*'.[3]

Systematic Soviet analysis of these two dimensions of the design problem, and their infinite interrelationships, stretches back directly to Constructivist thinking in the 1920s. '*Parameters*' says Savchenko 'are direct measurements of a building and its spaces, of the consumers involved and of the activities it accommodates. *Properties* are measurements of consumers' reactions to that same building . . . They are therefore measurements through an ''intermediary'', measurements of decisions made, of symbolic situations overlaid, as the user ''enters into'' the actual building . . . Properties, like parameters reflect the object as a whole, but they do so through the prism of social attitudes to the architecture in the context of some corpus of architectural values.'[4] In a textbook for students, another recent Soviet commentator has accurately described Moisei Ginzburg as the principal Soviet pioneer of 'systematic attempts to develop a theoretical basis for design as a field of human activity'.[5] Whether wittingly or not, she speaks correctly of Soviet pioneers, not Russian; although before the Revolution, as we shall see, there had already been significant thinking in this field. However these were the areas – the characteristics of the object and the manner of its interaction with people – in which the Constructivists believed there must be principle. They saw it as their professional obligation to their Marxist-materialist society to develop organised bodies of testable knowledge in these fields – what Russian calls *nauki*: literally 'sciences' – out of which solutions could in the broadest sense be 'constructed'.

Some issues of vocabulary have to be elaborated here, in as far as English allows it. Whether we speak of 'designing', 'creating', 'building' or 'constructing', the Russian language has numerous words available, and each has a distinct meaning which only context can attach to their synonyms in English.

If we return to the forms of 'construction' I mentioned earlier, we already encounter the distinction which is crucial to understanding the aims of Constructivism. In 'social construction' and 'building construction' the Russian noun is *stroitel'stvo*. *Stroitel'stvo* takes place in real space and time: the *stroitel'* is the builder on a real site with muddy boots. 'Social construction' in this sense may be a strange concept to us, but this understanding of the phrase illuminates the way Soviet thinking envisages possibilities in this area. In the phrase 'formal construction', by contrast, we are using the word *konstruktsiia*. Its meaning is indicated by the fact that a major Russian dictionary like Smirnitskii will indicate that this word often has linguistic connotations.

A grammatical construction is a *konstruktsiia*. It should not be forgotten here that the Constructivist movement had some roots amongst those precursors of linguistic Structuralism, the Russian Formalists, and also amongst the literary circles around the journal *LEF*. Thus in the final analysis *stroitel'stvo* is a material process where *konstruktsiia* is an intellectual one.

When the early Constructivist artists like Aleksei Gan and Aleksandr Rodchenko formulated the profile of that 'artist-constructor' whom they aspired to produce through their curricula in the VKhUTEMAS, he was not a *khudozhnik-stroitel'* – an artist-*builder*: some legatee of the Arts-and-Crafts tradition. He was a *khudozhnik-konstruktor* – an artist-*designer*. And here are further innuendos. The *konstruktor* is a specialist, highly qualified designer in industry: in engineering, for example, or today in electronics. To him *dizainer* would be a term of insult implying he is a mere stylist. Already nineteenth-century Rationalists in Russia used the adjective *konstruktivnyi* as high praise, for a manifestly 'built' piece of architecture. Smirnitskii represents the active verb *konstruirovat'* very precisely with the alternative translations 'to construct; to design; to form; to organise', and Constructivists were *Konstruktivisty*. They were concerned with how an architect organises or structures his thinking; how he organises the actual work of designing, and how he 'constructs' a set of appropriate forms.

They were also very interested in *stroitel'stvo* in all its dimensions. As loyal Soviets, social construction, and particularly 'the building of socialism' were the unquestioned raison d'être of their work. Material construction is the physical means whereby architecture exists at all: the materialist, in particular, must have the constraints and possibilities of all its media at his finger tips. In problems of *konstruktsiia* however, the choices are rooted in philosophic or aesthetic principle rather than physics. Aesthetic principle defines choices amongst possible systems of formal construction. The overall approach to the task of designing; the ordering of data and prioritising of objectives; the methods of synthesis and the criteria of evaluation: these are the philosophic problems of *konstruktsiia*.

Moisei Ginzburg, leader of the Constructivist architects, insisted 'There can be no question of any sort of artist losing creativity just because he knows clearly what he wants, what he is aiming for, and in what consists the meaning of his work. But subconscious, impulsive creativity must be replaced by a clear and distinctly organised method, which is economical of the architect's energy and transfers the freed surplus of it into inventiveness and the force of the creative impulse.'[6] In the words of another, younger, founder-member of the group Nikolai Krassil'nikov: 'Intuition is not eliminated thereby; it merely comes to occupy its proper place.'[7] Constructivism was distinguished by its refusal to leave these *methodological* problems to the mercy of 'intuition'.

In the light of this, what follows is perhaps less unexpected.

Constructivists believed that the Soviet architect's mode of working must exhibit the same holism as the material and cognitive worlds in which he was 'constructing'. Precisely in order to 'guarantee' that a monistic integration of the material and the cognitive aspects of the world was preserved in design work, they formalised their 'method of functional creativity', or in later shorthand, their 'functional method'.[8] This was a set of procedures whereby the totality of factors they saw impinging upon a design would be taken into account objectively, 'moving from the first priority to the second', in generating a 'basic spatial organism' and in its technical and formal refinement. Bodies of background knowledge were the subject of 'laboratory work'. As Ginzburg explained in 1927: 'Methodologically, in order to subject the whole productive process of the architect to evaluation, Constructivism has recourse to many other scientific disciplines, and uses the laboratory method, of separating out one reaction, that is of taking one integral process' – in today's jargon, one subsystem – 'into temporary isolation from the others, in order to get the most favourable conditions for analysing it.'[9] Considerable work was done by these Constructivist

architects in generating new 'classes of spatial organism', or building types and in exact analysis of what Savchenko would call their 'parameters' (as well as some of their 'properties', though this field generally belonged to Ladovskii's Rationalists and others). Given the very short period – hardly four years – over which they were working as an organised group, their œuvre was impressive as a demonstration of the standards they believed necessary. Some examples are illustrated here.

How does all this relate to the familiar roots of Constructivism: to Tatlin's Tower of 1919–20; to the geometrical 'structures' of Rodchenko and the First Working Group of Constructivists around 1921; to the ideas of Aleksei Gan, revered as a founder theorist of Constructivism but known to us professionally only as a graphic- and exhibition-designer?

If we examine what these artists said, in the texts with which they illuminated their intentions, we find a development of ideas that is

2 An advertisement in *SA* 1927 no 1, urging readers to 'Demand' from the State Publishers their 'catalogue of scientific journals'.

directly continued into the thinking of Ginzburg and the other Constructivist architects through the middle and later twenties. There is also a distinct continuity within architecture itself, between nineteenth and early twentieth-century-theorists and Constructivist architectural theory. These roots are undoubtedly real: amongst leading members of the profession there is a continuity of personal biographies across the divide of the Revolution – as there is of building technologies and much else – which conventional readings of this period wholly ignore. But given the political obligations to 'forget the old ways', these continuities were not part of the logical argument which the 'new men' were trying to construct. I shall therefore examine some of them retrospectively, after tracing the thinking of the 'new' generation in its own terms.

### Tektonika, Faktura and Konstruktsiia

The fullest exposition of the Constructivist architects' working method was published at the peak of their activity, in late 1927, as a paper by Ginzburg in their journal *Contemporary Architecture* (*SA*). The same issue contained much of the foreign work, by Gropius and others, sent to their First Exhibition.

Entitled 'Constructivism as a method of laboratory and teaching work', the article was 'a schematic plan of the course in the theory of architecture being given by the author in the architectural departments of VKhUTEMAS and MVTU [Moscow Higher Technical School]'.[10]

This was how Constructivists taught design. It was how they themselves operated in designing, and it was the framework whereby different 'laboratory investigations' by themselves and others – in building science, in social aspects of their briefs, in visual psychology, in development of formal languages and the rest – were organised into the process of designing new buildings to catalyse the process of 'building the new way of life'.

That five-part 'schematic plan' has been further edited into Diagram 2. Diagram 1 traces the development of the ideas in that schema through Ginzburg's earlier writings. These stretch back over the two preceding years of *SA*'s publication, 1927 and 1926, beyond the formation of the Constructivist architectural group OSA in late 1925, to Ginzburg's seminal 'manifesto' of a constructive architecture, the book *Style and Epoch* of 1924, and earlier articles.

This consecutive enrichment and increasing detail of his thinking is a feature of Ginzburg's work in this period: through the writings one grows in understanding of the group's aspirations as they are further articulated. As a man of broad, largely European education, of wide reading and already significant professional experience, the sources of his thinking are complex. In respect of the three main ideas concerning us here, namely: the catalytic role of architecture and the built environment in effecting social change; the need for an organised method of working whereby the designer can respond logically, and the proper range of factors to be embraced by that 'method', there are also direct sources within the thinking of Constructivist artists in the three years following the Revolution, when Ginzburg himself was far away from the Moscow-Petrograd avant-garde axis, working and writing down in the Crimea.

*   *   *

Much later, in 1928, Ginzburg was to dismiss Tatlin's Tower to his colleagues as 'idealistic symbolism'; as manifesting only 'the acute wish of a talented man to communicate emotionally.'[11] In its time, however, that grand and original scheme had been seminal to their own thinking.

Many putative 'sources' and 'meanings' have been attributed to this monument to the Third International. The latest rich array can be found in John Milner's new book, reviewed elsewhere in this issue.[12] Art historians may find satisfaction in such vague speculation; for architects it is more fruitful to examine the designers' own explanatory statements. Russians of this period do not use words pointlessly: even paper, as Lubetkin has reminded us, was an extraordinarily precious commodity. In his nice phrase, this 'was a wonderful time for poetry':[13] texts were concise and closely wrought. They deserve equally careful reading.

When Tatlin took his dismantled model Tower from Petrograd to Moscow in December 1920 to re-erect it for the Eighth Congress of Soviets, he and his three assistants published a brief newspaper statement entitled 'The work that faces us', often translated, more passively, as 'The work ahead of us.' An English translation is available in several sources.[14]

Here they explained the role which Tatlin's 'reliefs and contre-reliefs' had played, since 1914, as 'laboratory scale' preparation for the Tower project, and indicated how such explorations of 'materials, volume and the way these come together (*konstruktsiia*)' could be the starting point for new disciplines. These would be 'comparable in their severity' to those of Classicism, but where the Classical language had been constrained by the structural limitations of marble, these new languages would be liberated by the potential of 'modern' materials 'like iron and glass'. 'In this way' they declared, 'an opportunity emerges of uniting purely artistic forms with utilitarian intentions. . . . The results are models which stimulate us to inventions in our work of creating a new world' and which 'call upon [us] to exercise control over the forms encountered in our new everyday life.' Ridiculing Fedor Shekhtel's *moderne*-style Iaroslavl Station in Moscow with its 'applied art' from Abramtsevo (Map Guide no 130), they postulated this new path to a 'synthesis of painting, sculpture and architecture'. Non-functional 'art', be it two- or three-dimensional, in modern technological materials, must now serve as 'lab work' for the formal aspects of functional tasks. They saw this as the proper parallel in 'art' to 'what happened from the social point of view in 1917'.

During that same year of 1920 another group of artists, based permanently in Moscow, had started talking in very similar terms. The debates of early 1921 in which they juxtaposed the old artistic principle of *kompozitsiia* to their new concern with *konstruktsiia* have been outlined elsewhere in this issue in the context of George Costakis' collection. So too has the formal emergence of a 'First Working Group of Constructivists' in the spring of 1921.

In this group's declaration the vocabulary is already more explicitly politicised. 'The group's sole premise' they declared, 'is scientific communism, based on the theory of historical materialism.'[15] These phrases were the common currency of the period: what matters is their interpretation of the underlying philosophical concepts. Important for its continuity with Tatlin's statement was their affirmation of 'the necessity of synthesising the ideological and formal parts [of their task] so as to direct the laboratory work onto the tracks of practical activity'. Yet more important, they started to frame some concepts which could help effect this synthesis operationally. Those 'elements of the group's work' which would make an 'organic link' here were three synthetic concepts which they termed '*tektonika, konstruktsiia* and *faktura*'. The definitions are brief but already they demand mastery of enormous and diverse fields. Through principles of 'organisation' embraced by a 'science' of *konstruktsiia*, Constructivists will effect 'an organic link' between political values, industrial techniques and the specific possibilities of manipulated materials. *Tektonika* is a synthesis of the first two; *faktura* is the latter. '*Konstruktsiia* is formulating activity taken to the extreme.' The First Working Group which was formed around these ideas comprised the seven artists Aleksandr Rodchenko, Varvara Stepanova, Georgii and Vladimir Stenberg, Kazimir Medunetskii, Karl Iogansen and Aleksei Gan.

Aleksei Gan was soon to develop these themes more fully in his book *Constructivism* of 1922, and with them the First Working Group's radical views on the past and future of 'art'.[16] He opened the book with punchy restatements of the Group's view that the traditional concept of 'art' must die naturally with the old culture, but here as throughout he builds a yet more explicitly Marxist-materialist rationale around their thoughts.

'The present publication' he declared, 'is an agitational book with which the Constructivists begin the fight against supporters of traditional art.' The enemy are those unable to grasp the 'fact', which their own Marxist rationale makes logically inevitable, that there cannot be a peaceful evolutionary transition in Russia's concept of art if there has been a violent Revolution in her politics.

Portions of this book have been translated into English, but editing has distorted the emphasis.[17] Much of its explicit politicality has been drained by omitting long quotations from the Communist Manifesto. More significant here is omission of the climactic sections that direct Constructivist energies towards architecture and the whole urban environment, and of the full definitions of their three new 'disciplines'.

Artists who work 'on this side of October 1917' says Gan, 'should not be reflecting, depicting and interpreting reality. They should build practically and express the planned objectives of the new and actively working class . . . which is building the foundation of the future society . . . as an organised force in possession of a plan.' 'The master of colour and line, the combiner of spatio-volumetric solids . . . must all become Constructivists.'[18] But that too means organisation. 'In order to produce practitioners and theoreticians of Constructivism who are qualified, in a Marxist sense' he warned, 'It is essential to channel [our] work into a definite system; to create disciplines through which all the Constructivists' experimental work would be directed.'[19] They all had teaching jobs, in the new VKhUTEMAS particularly, and 'the production of qualified Constructivists' – of 'artist-constructors' – became the objective of their curricula.

Here in Gan's 'definite system' is our first hint of a 'method'. Its components would be those new synthetic 'disciplines' of *tektonika, faktura* and *konstruktsiia*, but now, from Gan, we get fuller definitions.

'With *tektonika* as their first discipline, Constructivists are trying to chop away the ignorance and tyranny exercised by architects and

Тектоника ▬▬▬▬▬

Фактура ▬▬▬▬▬▬

и Конструкция ▬▬▬▬▬

3 'Tektonika, Faktura and Konstruktsiia', from Gan, p 56.

4 Rodchenko's 'spatial constructions'.

builders under capitalism. *Tektonika*, or tectonic style organically emerges and is formed on the one hand out of the characteristics of Communism itself, and on the other from the appropriate utilisation of industrial material. The word tectonic is taken from geology, where it signifies violent restructurings coming out of the Earth's core.

'*Tektonika* is a synonym of organicness, of an eruption from the inner essence.

'*Tektonika* as a discipline must lead the Constructivist in practice towards a synthesis of the new content with new forms. He must be a person educated in a Marxist way, who has eliminated from his life all vestiges of "art" and has started advancing his knowledge of industrial material. *Tektonika* is his guiding star, the very cerebrum of his experimental and practical activity.

'Constructivism without *tektonika* is like painting without colour.'[20] Of the three concepts, this is perhaps the most obscure; the final sentence, which seems to compound the obscurity, in fact offers a key. Every professional act of the Constructivist must be coloured, or informed, by the understanding that a violent restructuring of underlying relationships has profoundly changed the way industry should shape and distribute material in space.

*Factura* is simpler. This word emphatically 'must not be understood from the painter's point of view', 'as just the handling of a surface'. On the example of cast iron, it implies 'the character of the whole processing', the melting, casting and turning, say, 'whereby it becomes an object'. As 'the appropriate use of material' *faktura* 'means the selection and processing from the raw material'. Also, 'more specifically, *faktura* is the organic condition of processed material or the new condition of its organism.' 'It is material consciously chosen and appropriately used in a manner that does not limit the *tektonika* or obstruct the *konstruktsiia*.'[21]

In the light of much that has been said earlier, the meaning of *konstruktsiia* should be clear. In Gan's words:

'*Konstruktsiia* must be understood as the assembling and ordering function within Constructivism.

'While *tektonika* comprises an interconnection of the ideological and the formal and as a result gives a unity of conception, and *faktura* takes account of the state of the material, *konstruktsiia* reveals the actual process of putting together.

'Thus the third discipline involves giving form to the concept through the use of processed materal.'[22] *Konstruktsiia*, in short, was design, but these expansive new synthetic disciplines still omitted the sciences of real space.

In challenging 'the combiner of spatio-volumetric solids' and 'the master of colour and line' to become Constructivists, Gan was not suggesting that they leave those skills behind them. On the contrary. 'A system must also be worked out in the field of producing forms', and he explained how that system would be developed by quoting his colleague 'the Constructivist Rodchenko', 'elucidating one of his experiments in spatial constructivism.' The works concerned would be items from his 'spatial inventory' or studies of similar geometrical forms from the period around 1920–21, which are well known.

Rodchenko had written: 'I have devised these latest spatial constructions as experiments, specifically to make the designer (*konstruktor*) bound by the law of appropriateness of applied forms, to constrain him to assemble the forms according to laws, and also to show their universalism, how from identical forms he may assemble (*konstruirovat'*) all possible constructions, of diverse systems, kinds and applications.'[23] Here was 'art' already consciously executed as lab work for design. Contemporaneous photographs indicate that such exercises were already central to Rodchenko and Stepanova's teaching[24]

Rodchenko and his immediate colleagues did not pursue these ideas into architecture. Others were to carry the baton forward in that direction, and Gan thrust it at them unequivocally.

'The planned working out of the whole area of the urban territory, of its individual districts and also its proper solution in the vertical dimension, in the *tektonika* of its masses and volumes, in the *faktura* of its materials and the *konstruktsiia* of its structures – these' he declared 'are the basic tasks of our Constructivism, which arose in the fresh cornfields of the proletarian revolution and is actively and consciously fighting for communism.'[25] In developing their 'definite system', their 'primary objective' must be 'to establish a scientific foundation for the approach to constructing buildings and services that would fulfill the demands of Communist culture in its transient state, through all stages of its future development out of this period of ruin'.[26]

Already here, if vaguely, is the idea later central to architectural Constructivism, that form must accommodate or respond to social evolution. Yet more importantly, however, Gan introduces the notion that architecture, by its spatial organisation, itself actively influences that evolution.

5 Moscow street scene, by Georgii Golts, 1925: the small buildings and spaces against which Gan inveighed.

He raises the question negatively: 'As the material, technological "organs" of society, the capitalist towns that we inherited are staunch allies of counter-revolution. Soviet communism has already discovered that the capitalist town not only cannot accommodate even the most timid measures of Revolutionary reorganisation, but more than that! *It stubbornly obstructs the path of that reorganisation*. Its small and awkward buildings have been totally unable to accommodate the operational requirements of the various new Soviet organisations. They are too cramped, just as the streets and squares which we inherited have not afforded the spatial conditions that we need for mass parades and vast assemblies.'[27]

'We must get human consciousness organised' he declares. 'We must force the active revolutionary groups and the working masses to see this disformity, this misfit, to see it just as clearly as they see a misfit when some reorganisation brings disorder into their own home.'[28] The logical implication is present here, though Gan does not develop it: if a 'misfitting' environment can obstruct social change, a 'fitting' one can foster it. If spatial organisation can be a negative catalyst, it can also be a positive one. Over the next few years, that view of architecture was to become the central motivation of the Constructivist architects, as they also pursued in greater detail the implications of Gan's other injunction, 'to develop a system of forming objects in general'.[29]

## Moisei Ginzburg

Gan's book *Constructivism* came off the presses in 1922. During the previous year there had returned to Moscow a young architect who previously spent three wartime years there, from 1914–17, at the Polytechnical Institute. Son of an architect in Minsk, this twenty-nine year old Moisei Ginzburg had had a head-start to early professional maturity. He had been amongst the last young Russians to complete a university education abroad before the First World War. Three years at the Milan Academy had left him experienced in both the beneficial disciplines and the inhibiting limitations of the classical architectural education.[30] His stay had coincided with Marinetti's most active and noisy years, but behind the verity and appeal of that vision he plainly perceived all too clearly the lack of any practical signposts for the professional. Returning to Russia in 1914, he balanced his education with the engineering-oriented courses at the Moscow Polytechnical School. After four years down in the Crimea during the Revolution and Civil War, in practice and studying the regional vernacular, he was an exceptionally travelled young architect amongst the generation to which he returned in the decimated and isolated Moscow of 1921.

6 L to R: Georgii Golts, unknown, Andrei Burov, Le Corbusier and Ginzburg while Corb was in Moscow, late 20s; Moisei Ginzburg.

Ginzburg's student years in Moscow, during the War, had been the period of Tatlin's first experiments into three-dimensional 'constructions' and the 'culture of materials'. His four years absence had seen those beginnings evolve into politically committed programmes and educational curricula. Architect friends of Tatlin like the Vesnin brothers, all a decade older than Ginzburg, were already engrossed in exploring the consequences of this committment for architecture; but at a time when words attracted more attention than designs for which

there were no materials, they were more at home at the drawing board than the typewriter. Ginzburg, like Aleksandr Vesnin, was attracted by ideas being expressed by Maiakovskii, Osip Brik and others in the journal *LEF*, and during 1922 the two became the nucleus of a small architectural group amongst these literary Constructivists. Already having several articles to his name in the journal *Amongst the Collectors*,[31] Ginzburg also moved quickly to the centre of reviving professional circles in the old-established Moscow Architectural Society, MAO, and a year later became chief editor of its new journal *Architecture*.[32] During the next few years, talking, writing and teaching were the active architect's most rewarding media, and Ginzburg used them all.

MAO was the main forum for progressives of the pre-Revolutionary generation. Ginzburg's two editorial colleagues on *Architecture* were Leonid Vesnin, eldest brother of the successful pre-War trio, and Edgar Norvert, an established expert on building rationalisation. Amongst their larger editorial committee were two leading pioneers of new building techniques Ivan Rerberg and Aleksandr Kuzntesov, and two leading architects-turned-planners Aleksei Shchusev and Vladimir Semionov. The new position in which the whole profession found itself was expressed by the latter in the first issue of *Architecture*, under the title 'Priority tasks', in terms which show the young avant-garde was far from alone in its concerns. 'It will soon be ten years since any of us built anything' began Semionov. 'Our very approach to work has to change. Where previously we converted reliably proven technical knowledge into concrete facts, we now have to blaze entirely new trails not just in architecture, in the narrow sense of that word, but also in the broadest sense of architecture, as creative construction (*stroitel'stvo*), where logic, the way of life, community attitudes and every side of civil life all make their demands equally. Before the Revolution we knew neither this complexity, nor this responsibility.' Professionally, it will be 'the task of the future public architecture to understand these new conditions, these new requirements of the present time, and to find forms answering the real situation'. But 'The battle requires organisation, and the changed circumstances call for new methods.'[33]

As editorial writer for this issue, Ginzburg took the opportunity to offer some pointers from other circles. 'Contemporary researches in the field of artistic form' he wrote, 'are speaking of a new phase of creative activity' which must take account of 'that new element of our lives . . . psychology and . . . aesthetics: the machine.' 'Architecture today must find sources of inspiration in the best achievements of engineers and of industrial architecture' he declared, and in a four-page article, all six illustrations were 'Grain elevators in Buffalo, New York.' With 'the descent of artists from Olympia' to become 'master-craftsmen . . . in the real world' said Ginzburg, they have brought a 'healthy . . . coarsening of our concept of the creative process'.[34]

The other Moscow forum where Ginzburg was active was one fully sensitive to the traditional refinements he invoked in that remark. RAKhN, the Russian Academy of Artistic Sciences, was formed in 1921 as a talking shop on a modernised model of eighteenth-century European academies. It was dedicated 'to discovering the inner, positive laws on whose basis aesthetic works are produced in each branch of art, and to deriving from that the principles of synthetic artistic expression'.[35] Ginzburg read numerous papers in the architectural section lead by Ivan Zholtovskii. In February 1924 he presented the argument of a book he had already completed entitled *Style and Epoch*. It was typical of the approach observed by one recent Soviet writer to be characteristic of RAKhN, that 'theory and history are bound together as a single topic of investigation'.[36]

## Style and Epoch

*Style and Epoch* was seminal to the whole development of Constructivist thinking about architecture. It also provides an important point of comparison with Western thinking, in particular that of Le Corbusier, who to Soviets always occupied the foreground of it.

With its further illustrations of Buffalo grain silos, and now also of aeroplanes, the book looks sufficiently like *Vers une architecture* for Corbusier to have felt no doubt immensely flattered when his inscribed copy arrived in the mail.[37] (It is still held in the Fondation Corbusier.) One can only speculate as to how it might have influenced his approach if he had been able to read the text. Precisely how and when the message of *L'Esprit Nouveau* arrived in the Soviet Union remains to be discovered, but as far as Irina Kokkinaki has ascertained, the first copies to arrive were those which 'Le Corbusier sent to the Commissar of Enlightenment A V Lunacharskii . . . in 1922, long before the establishment of diplomatic relations between the Soviet State and France.'[38] In early 1923 MAO's *Architecture* referred in its 'Survey of journals' to there being 'a few copies in Moscow in private hands' with more expected by the 'university and neo-philological libraries soon'.[39] The strength and authority of Ginzburg's ideas already derived, however, from the very wide range of stimuli on which he drew. The architectural philosophy expounded here can be seen as a natural, indeed logical synthesis of the various influences in his training, his early professional life, and the Moscow circles around him.

While *L'Esprit Nouveau* was not the only influence behind Ginzburg's book, the end product was plainly modelled closely upon it. *Style and Epoch* shows us that this material which the West has always found to be an indigestible lump had already been critically digested in the Soviet Union. Yet more significantly, it had already been used as the first stepping stone to an operational method that would bring to architecture the qualities so lauded in engineering, rather than just the forms.

Happily we now have an English translation of this work, which is reviewed elsewhere in this issue.[40]

Out of those initial observations about the honesty of form in grain silos, cars and aeroplanes, Ginzburg had built a consistent little Marxist-theoretical work (though he did not call it that), which makes *Vers une architecture* look more than ever like a loose piece of journalism. Although then, and later, Corbusier made many comments upon historical architecture, he never attempted to pull them together into any theory of the general development of architectures. Gan had insisted that 'The theory of historical materialism through which the Constructivists are assimilating history in general and the basic laws . . . of society must serve them equally as a method of studying the history of art' to develop 'a science of the history of its formal development.'[41] Here Ginzburg produced a first such analysis of architecture.

For all Corbusier's eulogies on the logical and precise methods whereby engineers create forms, nowhere did he attempt to build a bridge into the practice of architecture. All too clearly he had no aptitude for the sort of calculations involved. Ginzburg by contrast, with the engineering emphasis of his polytechnic degree, was a prototype of his own vision of the architect. His mentor Aleksandr Kuznetsov had addressed the last pre-War Congress of Russian Architects a decade before on the theme that 'The architect, according to the definition of the London congress, "*is an artist with a scientific education*".'[42] Insisting as Ginzburg did that architectural creation is a monistic process and a distinct activity (though elements from many others are synthesised into it), he saw however that only those whose central concern was architecture could build a bridge from engineering that was useful to it. While circumstances made Corbusier's fundamentally romantic book a major inspiration to architectural thinking world-wide, there is no doubt that Ginzburg's is the more useful and thoughtful work, which would have served the practice of architecture better in that role. To those exploring Constructivism's implications for architecture, it provided both historical legitimacy, and an operational starting point for their approach to building design.

To Corbusier, 'style' was never much more than an attribute of

artefacts. To Ginzburg it was 'some kind of regularity, a similarity through conformity to the same laws (*zakonomernoe edinstvo*)'[43] which relentlessly characterises every branch and product of the life of a human, historical period. It can only be identified through as intimate an understanding of the period's 'social, economic, climatic and national particularities' as of its 'artistic environment'.[44] Wolflin's *Renaissance and Baroque* had influenced him here, and he quotes it widely. Crudely summarised, it was Ginzburg's observation from extensive historical study that what one might call the 'health' of architecture follows that of cultures and their respective Weltanschauungs, as they pass through phases of fresh, creative 'flowering', 'organic' maturity and decline into 'decorative' rhetoric.[45] It was to illustrate this theory of a cyclical process that he used the historical examples which Corbusier would have found familiar. With his concern for historical objectivity, as well as dynamic processes, Ginzburg also paid considerable attention to the Gothic, which had never fitted Corbusier's formal predilections.

Ginzburg called the first phase of a typical architectural cycle *konstruktivnyi*: 'constructive'. Neatly he spans the gap here between the limited nineteenth-century architect's understanding of that term, and the broader meaning already established amongst Soviet artists. In a constructive phase, says Ginzburg, unprejudiced responses are being made to the mass of what are, axiomatically, new social and technical problems. In these periods, the chief task in every field of design is that of 'devising the characteristic plastic types for the epoch', and the present coincidence of social and technical revolutions made their own period unquestionably one of them.[46] In these periods, 'the new style will always be aesthetically strong and organically logical'.[47] In Viollet-le-Duc's terms, the '*principes*' will be pure, for 'the architect is facing the very basic problem of the delimiting of space with material forms, and this requires the creation of elements working constructively'.[48]

In the present, early-Soviet period however, Ginzburg perceived factors making it 'doubly constructive'. Exceptional economic stringency required the maximum possible economy of material in that 'delimiting', and therefore a maximising of the constructive work done by the building elements. But it also happened that the principles on which every branch of their contemporary life was organised, or more accurately aspired to be organised, were precisely those embodied par excellence in the machine: the principles of honesty, structural simplicity, objectivity, precise organisation and thus economy of all the

7 Tatlin's Tower and Buffalo grain elevators brought together in *Style and Epoch*, chapter 5.

means. Returning to themes we have already observed in his writings he declared: 'The essence of this machine, which is beginning to play such an exceptional psychological role in our lives, consists in the naked constructiveness of its component organisms.'[49] 'The machine is creativity at its most organised, the greatest clarity and power in the formulation of the creative idea.'[50] 'In the machine there can be nothing superfluous, accidental, "decorative"', and never forgetting architectural history: 'In essence we find in the machine, before all, the clearest expression of that ideal of harmonious creativity long ago formulated by the first Italian theoretician, Alberti.'[51] It was in this sense that the machine was the symbol of their present epoch, and these characteristics of the style of every 'constructive' period thus happened, in this one, to be also the characteristics of its own particular Weltanschauung. How then could the correct architectural style of the young Soviet Union be anything but 'constructive'?

This argument was to be the primary source of the Constructivist architects' strong self-confidence. It gave them a conviction that their stance was historically 'correct': a conviction quite as strong as that which motivated their political leaders. The particular characteristics and prototypes of modern 'organisedness' gave them the starting point for their method of design.

As forms said Ginzburg in Style and Epoch, 'neither the engineering structure nor the machine gives us an expressive spatial solution, which is what constitutes the distinguishing mark of architecture'.[52] 'How' he asked, 'are we to build a bridge between these contemporary ensembles and the architectural monuments, once we realise that this is possible only through the principles of creativity and not through the actual forms? We will try to continue our analysis.'[53] His 'continued analysis' showed the machine to be potentially an appropriate model for the organisation of any functionally interconnected agglomeration of specialised and diverse activities, dynamic and static. Here was already a quite sophisticated methodological concept that left Corbusier's mere image of the house as a 'machine à habiter' in the realm of aphorisms.

From this general idea of the machine as an organisational prototype, Ginzburg developed a two-stage analogy. The first stage was an analogy between the machine and the factory, which

is a collective of machines; . . . all linked together by desirable necessity just as the parts of an individual machine are, . . . and at the same time it is also a 'dwelling', not for people primarily but for machines, but [in a way that makes it] an architectural object none the less, with all the spatial connotations of that.[54]

'Industrial architecture' therefore 'serves as the connecting link, . . . but factories and silos cannot be the sole contents of modern architecture.'[55] So, secondly,

Precisely as we established the analogy between the machine and the industrial building, an analogy may be established between the industrial building and the architecture of the dwelling or the community building. Just precisely as the industrial building is not the conscious imitation of a machine, but comprises forms that have been generated organically and quite independently, while reflecting the same contemporaneity through whatever are their own unique characteristics, so here in precisely the same way is it a question of building an analogy,[56]

Style and Epoch did not pass unappreciated by the architectural profession. 'In the excellent book of M Ia Ginzburg' said the established Leningrad architect and planner Professor Karpovich, reviewing it for the city's main environment journal Questions of the Communal Economy, 'the reader will find not only theoretical discussions on style in architecture, but also absolutely practical approaches to the creative problems of contemporary architecture.' The book demonstrates, said Karpovich, that 'the study of the machine can give a new stimulus to the creation of new architectural forms', though 'it shows us how far today's Constructivists are from the creation of such new forms'.[57] Karpovich was a relevant commentator on the book's originality, when nothing else emerging in Moscow, from such fora as RAKhN or INKhUK, was comparable. Its main competitor in sophistication at this date, in the pursuit of an approach to the whole architectural problem, was the work of his younger Leningrad colleague A E Rozenburg, a hospital design specialist before the Revolution, whose book of the previous year, A Philosophy of Architecture, was more synoptic, but less pregnant.[58]

## OSA's 'method of functional creativity'

From the basic analogy established in Style and Epoch, Ginzburg and his colleagues developed the central concepts and procedures of their design 'method'. First however they formed themselves into a group, and started a journal.

MAO had proved itself inadequate as a platform for advancing genuinely new aesthetic ideas. Anathema to the young and engagés was the passive 'professionalism' of Edgar Norvert's view that 'the posing of general social questions and questions about the new way of life is outside the domain of the architect'. Too dominant was his opinion, expressed in Architecture in 1923, that architecture could not serve society until distinct social forms had crystallised out of the present transitional period.[59] The psycho-formal work of Nikolai Ladovskii and his colleagues in ASNOVA, said the Constructivists, 'could only acquire a genuinely scientific materialistic basis if it was always made clear what real problems the theoretical work was directed at', and 'if the methods being applied in solution of these tasks were fundamentally those of the architect, so that they could be put to real and practical use in the present-day architect's work as an organiser of building.'[60] In late 1925, Ginzburg and the Vesnin brothers formed a Constructivist architectural group to fill the gap, and called it OSA: the Union of Contemporary Architects.[61]

Ginzburg and the three Vesnins, Leonid, Viktor and Aleksandr, represented a bridge between progressives of the older generation and the younger avant-garde. Aleksei Gan was a central participant from the first, in launching their journal during the next year; in staging their exhibition, and in developing theory. He and Aleksandr Vesnin brought a direct link to the aesthetic debates of the First Working Group and the attitude to materials of Tatlin, whom Vesnin knew well. Ginzburg and Leonid Vesnin brought the experience of pre-Revolutionary Russian pioneers of a technologically and aesthetically 'modern' architecture, particularly through their connections with Norvert, Artur Loleit and Aleksandr Kuznetsov, who had founded the architectural department where they taught at MVTU. Much of the group's authority derived from the fact it was a synthesis of this broad thinking and experience. Their method sought to formalise 'correct' relationships between these very diverse components.

After the demise of others, OSA's journal SA (Contemporary Architecture) was Russia's only purely architectural journal during the four pre-Five-Year-Plan years 1926–30. On page 1 of number 1, it was launched with an article by Ginzburg entitled 'New Methods of Architectural Thinking'.[62] Here as in his next two major articles on this theme (see Diagram 1),[63] as already in Style and Epoch, he adressed both theoretical and operational questions. These now became two distinct categories of 'variables': the 'general unknowns' and the 'particular' ones.

'General unknowns' were those identifying 'characteristics of the epoch as a whole' whose influence must permeate the entire design and construction process. In Style and Epoch he had discussed these 'social, economic and national peculiarities' of a culture as inevitably influencing building form.[64] From further analysis of their own emerging culture Ginzburg now identified four such 'peculiarities' of the Soviet situation. These were the fact of a collective, rather than an individual, client, which was trying to build 'a new way of life'; the concommitant shift in architecture's position, to become one part of a larger social and economic plan; the conjunction of these factors to produce a new, ideological and technical status for norms and standard types, and the overriding, methodological obligation under the new ideology, to 'solve the architectural task, like any other, only through precise evaluation of its "unknowns" and the pursuit of a correct method of solution'.[65] The deductions were not all novel, but the codified statement was new.

In Style and Epoch Ginzburg illustrated Tatlin's Tower as an example of the new approach. So complex and unrealisable in the decimated state of Russia, it had been reduced to a piece of technological symbolism in the public mind. Here therefore he

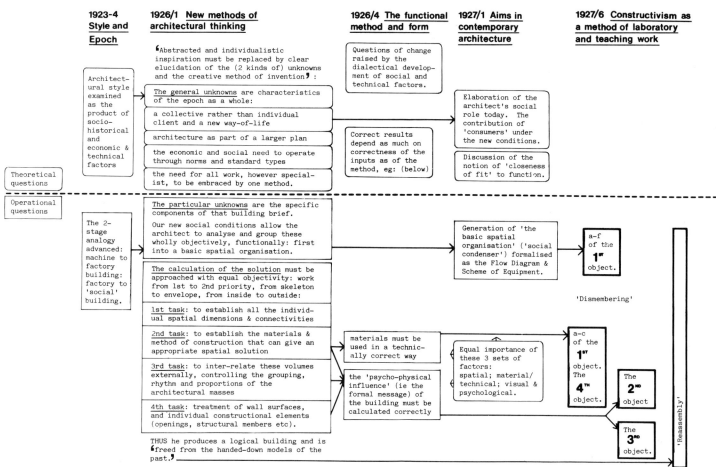

| 1923-4 Style and Epoch | 1926/1 New methods of architectural thinking | 1926/4 The functional method and form | 1927/1 Aims in contemporary architecture | 1927/6 Constructivism as a method of laboratory and teaching work |
|---|---|---|---|---|

**1923-4 Style and Epoch**

Architectural style examined as the product of socio-historical and economic & technical factors.

**Theoretical questions**

**1926/1 New methods of architectural thinking**

'Abstracted and individualistic inspiration must be replaced by clear elucidation of the (2 kinds of) unknowns and the creative method of invention':

The general unknowns are characteristics of the epoch as a whole:

a collective rather than individual client and a new way-of-life

architecture as part of a larger plan

the economic and social need to operate through norms and standard types

the need for all work, however specialist, to be embraced by one method.

**1926/4 The functional method and form**

Questions of change raised by the dialectical development of social and technical factors.

Correct results depend as much on correctness of the inputs as of the method, eg: (below)

**1927/1 Aims in contemporary architecture**

Elaboration of the architect's social role today. The contribution of 'consumers' under the new conditions.

Discussion of the notion of 'closeness of fit' to function.

---

**Operational questions**

The 2-stage analogy advanced: machine to factory building: factory to 'social' building.

The particular unknowns are the specific components of that building brief. Our new social conditions allow the architect to analyse and group these wholly objectively, functionally: first into a basic spatial organisation.

The calculation of the solution must be approached with equal objectivity: work from 1st to 2nd priority, from skeleton to envelope, from inside to outside:

1st task: to establish all the individual spatial dimensions & connectivities

2nd task: to establish the materials & method of construction that can give an appropriate spatial solution

3rd task: to inter-relate these volumes externally, controlling the grouping, rhythm and proportions of the architectural masses

4th task: treatment of wall surfaces, and individual constructional elements (openings, structural members etc).

THUS he produces a logical building and is 'freed from the handed-down models of the past.'

materials must be used in a technically correct way

the 'psycho-physical influence' (ie the formal message) of the building must be calculated correctly

Generation of 'the basic spatial organisation' ('social condenser') formalised as the Flow Diagram & Scheme of Equipment.

Equal importance of these 3 sets of factors: spatial; material/technical; visual & psychological.

a-f of the 1ST object.

'Dismembering'

a-c of the 1ST object. The 4TH object.

The 2ND object

The 3RD object.

'Reassembly'

Diagram 1: development of ideas in the Functional Method through Ginzburg's writings from 1924.

condemned as 'merely naive ... any attempt to replace the complexities of the art of architecture by forms, however sparkling' derived as 'symbolism ... from other aspects of technology'. Architecture was 'invention like another other', a task of 'organising and giving form to (*skonstruirovat'*) a concrete practical problem not only for the dictates of today, but to fit the needs of tomorrow'. '*From the inventor the contemporary architect must take only his creative method.*'[66] A future issue of *SA* drove home the difference from Corbusier here, with a feature on calculations underlying the design of those seductive biplanes.[67]

The conditions that had produced the architect's 'new social consumer' had also 'freed him' from being a 'peacemaker in irreconcilable conflicts of interest', operating (if only in self-defence) behind closed doors. By the 'method of functional creativity' they

8 'The form of the aeroplane and the methods of designing it' from *SA* 1926 no 3. On p 63 the slogan reads: 'Architects do not imitate the forms of technology, but learn the method of the engineering designer (*konstruktor*)'. On p 65, amidst the mathematics: 'Architects! This is how to understand the materialistic bases of the aesthetic of constructivism.'

aspired to make design 'a unified organic process'. Having a 'single clear aim', the task could be 'hammered out logically ... from first priorities to second ... from skeleton to envelope, from inside to out, as a conscious process from beginning to end'.[68] Such a process would be open to scrutiny of its data and decisionmaking, and thus publicly accountable. It would be a collective act of 'construction' as the public and specialists contributed their components, and much of *SA*'s campaigning was directed at stimulating that participation. The architect's specialism however, was the synthesis: the *konstruktsiia*.

The main rules for that process of *konstruktsiia* had already been worked out. They are only outlined at this stage, but the Constructivists' view of what should be primary in design, and what secondary, is clearly indicated by the ordering of stages within their 'logical process'. 'Spatial parameters, their dimensions and interconnections are the first function of the brief'; 'the spatial organisation is the starting point of the design and the place to which the main thrust must be directed'. Then secondly, the architect must establish the appropriate building materials and method of construction 'as functions of the basic spatial solution'. Thirdly, he must order the 'external interrelationships of spatial elements'. 'The grouping of the architectural masses, their rhythms and proportions will derive naturally from the first half of his activity: they are a function of the material envelopes and inner volumes he has "constructed".' Finally, he will give form to individual components and elements: to apertures, overhangs etc 'all on the basis of calculations or other types of consideration within the brief'. In this linear process, 'one task leads logically from another'. The architect 'is freed from the handed-down models of the past' and is 'forced to seek artistic expressiveness in that which is most important and necessary'. If the resulting architecture is currently 'ascetic', that is not the result of the process, merely of 'youth' in both the builders, and the new life they are building. New systems of compositional principles will develop from the typical spatial patterns of the new problems themselves.[69]

Ginzburg's categories of 'general' and 'particular unknowns' correspond to today's 'state' and 'decision variables'. Gan and the First Working Group had established a role for the former category within the design process, but the mapping of Ginzburg's classification onto their concepts of *tektonika, faktura* and *konstruktsiia* is not exact. The notion of *konstruktsiia* had been absorbed as the premise of their whole approach; that is clear. The concept of *faktura* lay beneath all references to materials and 'appropriate' building methods in Ginzburg's 'second stage', and in his fourth, but more as an assumed rigour of analysis than as an explicit operation. Notions of an 'expressive' relationship between materials and their spatial possibilities stretched back to Tatlin. The complex 'geological' concept of *tektonika* as a synthesis of deep political and technological 'restructurings', is largely subsumed within Ginzburg's category of 'general unknowns', but technological elements of the concept, in particular, also permeate the rest. Gan's 'three new disciplines' had constituted a first redefinition of the 'whole' design problem in their expanded, Marxist-materialist context, but it was crude. In moving from Gan's 'general system' towards a 'method', the architects had articulated the intuitive categories into something approaching real tools.

In his next two papers Ginzburg elaborated certain ideas and introduced others. In 'The functional method and form', published later in 1926, he established a role within his four-stage process for those issues of visual psychology and of 'economy of perceptual energy' being explored by ASNOVA under Ladovskii.[70] From within earlier Constructivist thinking he took up the question of how form should relate to an evolving content. Gan had spoken in general terms; Ginzburg was now explicit. The Constructivist must 'calculate correctly' the complex overlapping relations between old and new within 'the dialectical development of life' at any given time. Then 'the functional method of thinking must always take as the precondition of its material forms not the areas of backwardness, but the landmarks of the new way of life and advanced technology'.[71] How he should take the new way-of-life as his starting point, and why, were the most important topics of his next paper, 'Aims in contemporary architecture', published early the following year.

Here two of the most powerful ideas in earlier Constructivist writing come together. Developing his own 'two-stage analogy' with the machine, and harnessing it to Gan's vision of spatial organisation as a catalytic force in social change, Ginzburg formulated the concept which henceforth became central to all his colleagues' propagandising and design work, the concept of 'the social condenser'.

Out of the basic analogy he identified in *Style and Epoch*, Ginzburg develops the two concepts of the 'scheme of equipment' and the 'flow diagram', which will be the tools for establishing the 'first spatial diagram of the building' in the first stage of the method. The 'scheme of equipment' is a description of the hardware involved in each of the myriad specialised and identifiable events within a building. In machine terms, these are the components of its specialised sub-assemblies. The 'flow diagram' describes the multiple human movements between them, which correspond to the conveyor belts of the factory or the drives of a complex machine. Henry Ford in his autobiography had described achieving great spatial economies in his production lines through rationalisations of this kind: plainly, he reasons, such economies must be equally accessible to the architects of a building. 'For Palladio in the Villa Rotunda' or the pre-Revolutionary palace 'accommodating only the mazurka or the polonaise', functions were not distinguishable said Ginzburg, always enjoying the historical example. 'With building in a socialist country' however, 'the difference is basic, and one of principle'.[72]

The influence of Russia's Taylorist movement for the 'Scientific Organisation of Work' (NOT.) is certainly also strong here. It is not clear when the Constructivists first learnt of the Germans' use of such ideas in building design; probably not by 1925–6 when they started formalising their method, but in 1927 they used material from Bruno

Taut and others as illustrations to their articles.[73] They also noted that Frank Lloyd Wright's houses were models of economic movement.[74] Eclectic or not in its origins, the status and role which OSA accorded to the resulting 'basic spatial diagram' was uniquely defined by Ginzburg's conception of their period as 'doubly constructive'. It constituted an empirical solution of a socially and technically new brief, in the fresh, creative 'flowering' stage of a new era. Within Ginzburg's historical schema it was thus one of the 'characteristic plastic types for the epoch'. With the materialist's view of the power of organised matter, these embodiments of advanced 'landmarks' in social evolution were the architect's most important contribution to Soviet revolutionary objectives. Low-voltage activity and a weak consciousness would be focused through the circuits of these 'social condensers' into high-voltage catalysts of change, in the habits and attitudes of the mass population. This contribution to the act of 'social construction' was OSA's mission as architects; it was their methodological objective that identified them as Constructivists.

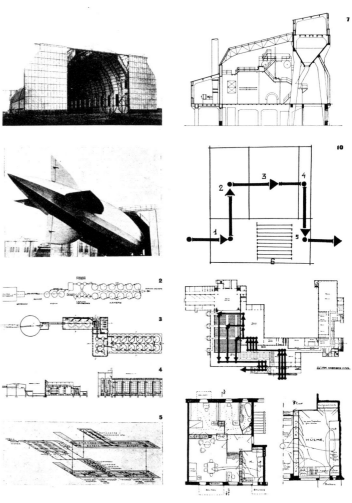

9 The flow diagram and scheme of equipment derived from Ginzburg's analogy between the 'building for machines' and the 'building for people', from 'Aims in Contemporary Architecture', *SA* 1927 no 1.

### The method of laboratory and teaching work

The last column of Diagram 1 shows how directly these arguments developed into the fuller procedures of Ginzburg's 'method of laboratory and teaching work', which is detailed in Diagram 2.

In its logic the process is unchanged; under new numbering, a '4th object' reasserts the *faktura* concept in a concern with industrial production processes.

Most importantly, though, it has finally re-embraced that first category of 'laboratory work' pioneered and developed in teaching by Rodchenko to be, in Gan's words, 'a system for producing forms'. Rodchenko believed that the designer must be 'constrained to

**Dismembering**  The **1**ST object is to <u>establish the FORM of the SOCIAL CONDENSER</u> as the product of:

1:   The social and productive preconditions <u>of the brief:</u>

Consideration
of all the
PRECONDITIONS –
both REQUIREMENTS
and POSSIBILITIES

a.   <u>Study of how these may change through social and technological changes</u> – stressing not the <u>dimensions</u>, but the <u>dynamic,</u>
the changing use of the spaces over time.

b.   <u>Build up the FLOW DIAGRAMS</u> – from individual ones to the overall one, which is THE FIRST SPATIAL DIAGRAM OF THE BUILDING.

c.   <u>Study the SCHEMES OF EQUIPMENT these require.</u>   d.   <u>Establish the DIMENSIONS of that equipment</u>, also the correct FUNCTIONAL
SPACING of it.

e.   <u>Study the ENVIRONMENTAL REQUIREMENTS of the activities and processes taking place</u> – temperature, light, accoustics.

f.   <u>Build up the scheme of the SOCIAL CONDENSER on the basis of this material</u> – establishing an integrated organism
as a SPATIAL PROTOTYPE.

2:   The technical and constructional preconditions <u>of the realisation:</u>

a.   <u>Study of the BUILDING MATERIALS at the architect's disposal</u> – stressing the maximum possible revolutionary reassesment of them,
using as far as possible the most advanced (ie the minimum mass).

b.   <u>Study of the STRUCTURAL METHODS AND SOLUTIONS that are appropriate in the light of the</u> – stressing the most RATIONAL
<u>preconditions of the brief;   study their character and the technical possibilities</u> methods of construction in the
<u>that they afford.</u> light of the spatial possibilities.

c.   <u>Study of the conditions and methods of PRACTICAL REALISATION involved,</u> – the actual METHODS OF BUILDING, seeking the maximum
<u>in relation to each detail and to the architectural whole.</u> INDUSTRIALISATION, 'assembly' rather than 'building'
with all the architectural consequences of this.

Consideration
of PERCEPTION and
VISUAL CLARITY

The **2**ND object is to <u>look at the MATERIAL FORMS crystalised as the social condenser, in terms of the PROBLEM OF PERCEPTION,</u>
so that the useful activity of the condenser is enhanced by the user's clear perception of it.

<u>Constructivism sees FORM as ACTIVE,</u> rather than passive.
It sees the <u>ORGANISATION of PERCEPTION</u> as much as part of its task as the organisation of the material factors.

There are two stages to this:

A:   The following must be studied IN ORDER, from PARTICULAR properties of the particular object, to GENERAL questions:

1. The FUNCTIONAL CHARACTER of the object, its purpose_____ (a)   Perception in respect of the fundamental
2. Its STATE – static or moving?___ characteristics of the object
3. MATERIAL – its properties and faktura, colour etc_____
4. The RELATIVE SCALES of parts and whole._____ (d)   How to ORGANISE PERCEPTION to make
5. The TEKTONIC STRUCTURE of the object. CLEAR the relationships of the elements
   How it is constructed. The links of parts and whole.___ (c)   Perception of   comprising the object, their absolute
   The principles upon which its parts are related. UNITY AND WHOLENESS.   and relative SIZES, clarity of the
6. FORM AS A BOUNDARY, a 3-D volume, a defined space____ OVERALL SPATIAL FORM of it.
7. The main distinguishing marks of the object as a SPATIAL ORGANISATION___ (b)   Perception in respect of SPATIAL INTER-RELATIONS
   and of SPACE in general.

B:   In relation to the perception of these characteristics,
the second stage of the studies ARE THEN GROUPED AS ABOVE, (a)–(d)

Consideration
of the RATIONAL
USE of the FORMAL
ELEMENTS of the
architecture

The **3**RD object is to <u>study THOSE ELEMENTS OF ARCHITECTURE ITSELF</u> which are the OBJECTS OF PERCEPTION, namely, in order of COMPLEXITY

A:   SURFACE   B:   VOLUME, as a system of surfaces
C:   The volumetric coexistence OF MANY BODIES (intersecting, or contiguous, or related but separate)
D:   SPACE   TIME and MOVEMENTS as METHODS OF ORGANISING SPACE;   space as the inter-relation of individual volumes TO EACHOTHER and
the whole;   the LOCATION of an object in space;   space as an ISOLATING factor;   space as the ORGANISATION of NON-RELATED or
PARTIALLY RELATED dimensions (space – street – town etc).

TWO IMPORTANT PRINCIPLES are to be observed THROUGHOUT THIS PROCESS:

1:   None of this laboratory dismemberment must concern itself with ARTISTIC EXPRESSIVENESS IN GENERAL, for Constructivism only
understands expressiveness <u>CONCRETELY</u>, in relation to DEFINITE AIMS AND INTENTIONS, as something specific to its context.

2:   All such studies carry the basic danger of CANONISATION of certain forms, of their becoming fixed elements of the architect's
vocabulary.   Constructivism is LEADING THE BATTLE against this phenomenon, and studies these basic elements of architecture
as something <u>CONTINUOUSLY CHANGING in connection with the changing preconditions of the form-making situation.</u>   It NEVER ADMITS
therefore the FIXING OF FORMS.   <u>Form is an unknown, 'x', which is always evaluated anew by the architect.</u>

Therefore we have ALSO TO STUDY not just the ELEMENTS OF ARCHITECTURE, but the METHODS OF THEIR TRANSFORMATION; we have to
study HOW THAT FUNCTION, X, CHANGES, how a change in the brief effects the form.

Amongst such <u>TYPES OF TRANSFORMATION</u> we may include:

1. change in the object's external relationships;
2. vertical or horizontal dismemberment of it;
3. the cutting of the surface or volume from the
   inside (doors, windows etc);
4. the cutting of the surface or volume from the
   outside (change of silhouette);
5. differences in the object's material, colour or faktura;
6. change in the spatial relationships of its parts;
7. the introduction of mobility into the parts or the whole;
8. the introduction of new (working) elements, and so on.

<u>In all this, 3 things are vital:</u>

1: This method of transformations is PART OF THE ARCHITECT'S
REAL, PRACTICAL TOOLS;

2: That TRANSFORMATION involves not just AESTHETICS, but
reorganisation of the WORKING, CONSTRUCTIVE ELEMENTS;

3: That what we are changing is the MATERIAL OBJECT, but
this is done IN THE CONTEXT OF ITS ESSENTIAL PURPOSE
and of its PERCEPTION BY THE USER.

Consideration of
the POSSIBILITIES
of INDUSTRIALISED
BUILDING.

The **4**TH object is the <u>study of INDUSTRIAL PROCESSES</u>, not as FETISHISM, not to IMITATE industrial forms, but to identify THOSE
CHARACTERISTICS that will be the HALLMARKS of <u>INDUSTRIALISATION in ARCHITECTURE.</u>   Thus we study:

1:   How industrial technology CREATES a functional form.   2:   The particular processes characteristic of industrial production
which LEAVE A STAMP on the character of its products.

This must be done in relation to the INDIVIDUAL COMPONENTS of the building and in relation to WHOLE ORGANISMS (kitchens etc).

**Reassembly**   The **5**TH object is THE RESTORATION OF ORGANIC WHOLENESS.   This applies whether the functional method was being used for ANALYSIS OF
an <u>EXISTING PRODUCT</u>, or for the <u>CREATION OF A NEW PROJECT.</u>   (Either of these processes involves all four sections above.)

Diagram 2: Procedures of the Functional Method summarised from Ginzburg, 'Constructivism as a Method of Laboratory and Teaching Work', *SA* 1927 no 6.

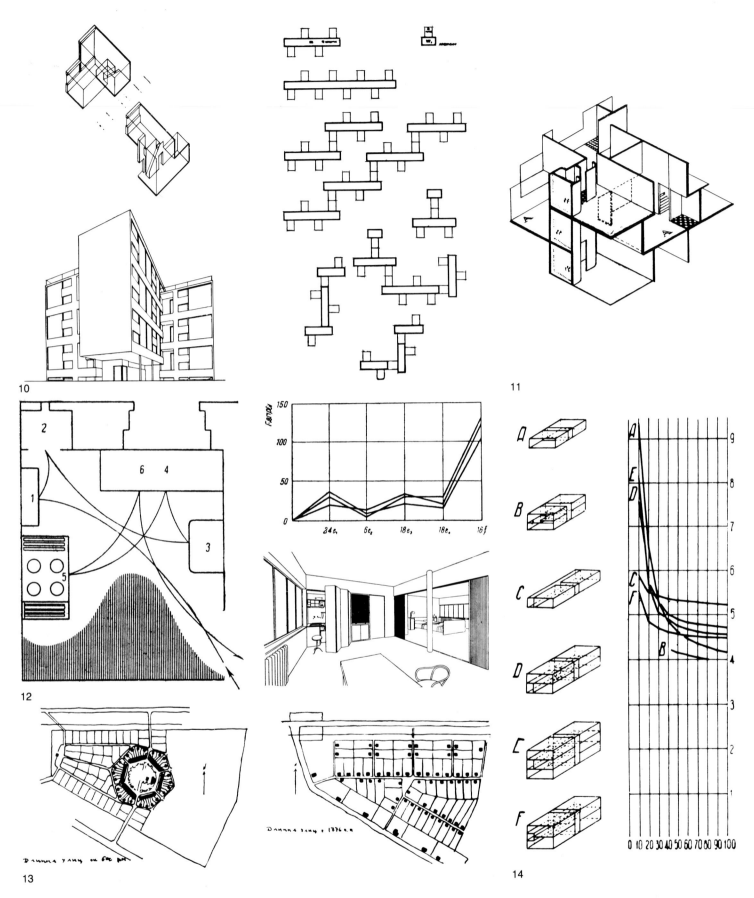

10 Interlocking volumes and multiple plan variants from Vladimirov's scheme for OSA's 'comradely competition' for new housing types.

11 Interlocking spaces in Vegman's scheme.

12 OSA work in the Russian Building Committee (STROIKOM RSFSR): 3 stages from analysing flow diagrams in the 'irrational' kitchens of Mossoviet's new housing, through calculation of the 'dynamic minimum', to the proposed 'kitchen element', L, in their 'rational' apartment designs.

13 Barshch, in *SA* 1927 no 3, pits his mathematics against the Garden City man Markovnikov, to prove 'intensive' residential development more economic of roads, service runs and travel times than cottage housing.

14 Ginzburg, Barshch et al in STROIKOM: useful space plotted against circulation in their six new apartment types, relative to apartment size; the analysis which made them favour Type F.

assemble forms according to laws'; must be able to make 'all possible combinations, of diverse systems, kinds and applications' through understanding the fundamentals of formal 'construction'.[75] In Ginzburg's new '3rd object' Rodchenko's 'rules' have been aggregated into 'types of transformations', whose logic will ensure that the clarity, consistency and flexibility of response to be achieved through the rest of the method, are matched in the logic of an architects formal vocabulary.

In his preceding paper, Ginzburg had recognised that 'the whole Soviet community must be drawn into solving the task' outlined by the functional method. The task thus defined was 'not within the powers of the single architect or even a collective of architects'.[76] The exhaustive precision to which they aspired also demanded bodies of data and research that were decades beyond the Soviet Union's horizon at that time. All the same, some remarkable work was done in broaching these topics.

Working with leading structural engineers, for example, they themselves explored the relative economics of various new structural systems. Using the latest foreign data and research they advanced building science aspects. On lighting issues, they made pioneering studies of the relationships between colour and working efficiency; between fenestration and illumination patterns. This work is published in their journal and elsewhere. Most advanced for its time however was their work on optimising the parameters of their 'spatial prototypes' by quantitative methods.

All their design work involved minimising the lengths of flow diagrams. Underlying the well-known apartment types 'A–F', which Ginzburg and others developed for the Russian Building Committee, STROIKOM, lay very interesting work on the static parameters of spatial organisations produced when the apartment units are linked by circulation systems to form whole buildings. More complex interactions of 'flow' factors were the focus of their mathematical arguments with Garden City adherents, on the relative economic and human merits of 'extensive or intensive' residential development. However, as one young founder-member of OSA pointed out in his VKhUTEMAS final diploma thesis, whilst these limited and essentially technical studies gave 'undeniably useful results', they were still 'considering requirements too much in isolation'.[77] They did not tackle the problem of synthesis. Ginzburg's conspicuous silence on the nature of the 'reassembly' process in the '5th object' of the functional method made it all too clear that this Nikolai Krasil'nikov was right. Here in the very heart of the architect's province, any question of 'a scientific . . . replacement for the habitual intuitive-graphic method of designing [had] hardly been broached'.[78] In his diploma and a joint paper with fellow-student Lidiia Komarova, Krasil'nikov 'tried to open up this question . . . to creep towards . . . a mathematical-graphic method' of solving it.[79]

## 'The application of mathematical methods'

Krasil'nikov believed that 'A scientific theory of the design of form is possible through the dialectical method of thinking by the application of mathematical methods of analysis; that is, by analysis which uses the infinitesimal concepts underlying analytical geometry and the differential and integral calculus, and the theories of probability and mathematical statistics.[80] His thesis was devoted to demonstrating how these techniques could be used to optimise 'the actual form of the building' in terms of 'the material resources for constructing and running it'; 'amortisation and repairs'; 'the time spent by people in all kinds of movement'; 'amortisation of the health of the individual', which was a function of 'sanitary-technical and psychological factors'; the extent to which 'conditions in particular parts of it favour the maximum "productivity" of mental or physical work, and of leisure'. His particular objective was 'the building form which diverges least from the maxima or minima of each of these factors' whilst also achieving 'the maximum cubic volume of building on a given site area'. At the planning scale, he then optimised 'conditions of daylighting, exposure to wind, and ventilation of the whole administrative complex, and links between this building and other parts of the town'.[81] The detailed mathematics are inappropriate here: I have translated the whole paper elsewhere.[82] Some illustrations indicate the flavour. It is clear that the group as a whole were using their mathematics to the limit, as SA published one graph whose strange change of gradient immediately attracts the mathematical eye – and in fact results from a mistake when Krasil'nikov evaluated his quite complex formulae.

As architecture, his circular town of skyscraper office-blocks was somewhat traditionally conceived, but his concern was with method. His attempt to include factors which Savchenko would call 'properties', as well as 'parameters', was important. His procedure for optimising, however, remained linear. He established the best spatial configurations 'in relation to each of these factors individually'. He still started from the optimal flow diagram – albeit one now defined in greater detail, and probabilistically – and compared that to other optima by inspection, in a pre-established order of priorities. Thus far he had not moved beyond the linear *konstruktsiia* of the functional method under which he had been taught.

Krasil'nikov recognised that, as he did the primitiveness of his techniques by the standards of 'higher mathematics', even then. In the subsequent paper with Komarova he recognised that this was still essentially the age-old process whereby the architect examines a series of discreet, alternative forms 'and divines empirically . . . the most successful combinations of those variants he has put to the test'. Under the title 'A method of investigating the generation of building form' they declared 'Our aim must be to advance this process in order to make possible an objective scientific assessment of *all* the possible variants available to the designer.'[83]

15 Further developments of their new 'spatial types' at STROIKOM.

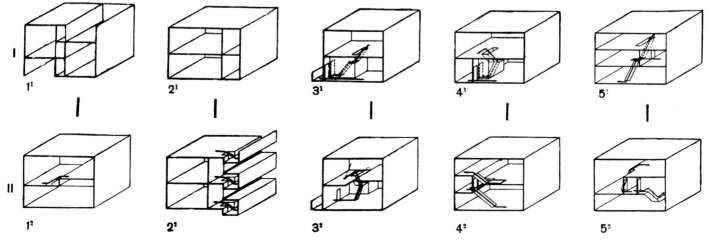

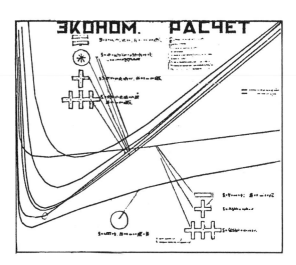

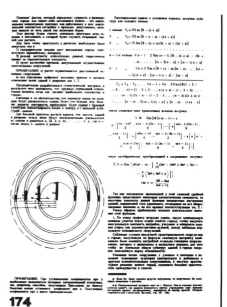

**174**

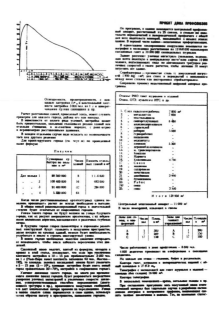

16 Krasil'nikov analyses evacuation time and building surface for his various plan forms.

17 His calculations to maximise built volume on a given city area. The curve's dip, top R, results from his miscalculating one value of his formula.

It was the conceptual step embodied in that '*all*' which was historically important. Since Rodchenko first spoke of 'showing the designer how he may assemble all possible constructions', the idea had remained a chimera to them.

18 Krasil'nikov and Komarova, third and fourth from L, with Leonidov, below Komarova, and other students.

From the premise that 'the form of any body is a function of many variables', Krasil'nikov and Komarova argued that a dialectical process takes place in which even purely quantitative changes in the brief lead to a qualitatively different form, and the 'correct' form emerges from a resolution of competing or conflicting demands. 'A continuous sequence of variants therefore exists.' This concept is quite different from the series of discreet, alternative forms. With two examples, they outlined a mathematical procedure 'for finding the most advantageous possible dimensions' of a given spatial organisation in terms of 'cost, for a given form of construction'. It involved 'drawing up equations' describing 'costs of a specific form of any one part of the building in relation to all different forms of each other part. These equations would produce 'a series of cost curves. These we

can build up into a surface, or system of curves in space, which will give us the position of minimum cost.'[84] In their list of 'all the requirements' for which they would establish were included all the organisational, material, environmental and social factors contained in Krasil'nikov's earlier list of a building's five measures of 'cost-effectiveness, in the very broadest sense'. These in turn embraced the whole 'first object' of the functional method, from structural questions through to 'the flow diagrams and schemes of equipment, always remembering sanitary and hygiene factors such as daylighting'. This clear mathematical formulation of the concept of a multi-dimensional solution 'surface' seems to be unique in the architectural context for its time. It was to be about four decades before automated data-processing techniques emerged, and any architects started handling the enormous computational operations involved in an integrated, multi-variate optimisation of this kind.

With his realistic understanding of engineering, Ginzburg's 'functional method' was an almost literal response to the observation injunction in Bukharin and Preobrazhenskii's *ABC of communism*, of 1919, that 'Marx's chief instruction to his followers was that they should study life as it actually is, . . . precisely after the manner in which we might study a machine.'[85] In its *konstruktsiia*, his whole, essentially linear process was also rooted in a mechanical analogy. With their grasp of mathematics, Krasil'nikov and Komarova sought to indicate the ultimate implications for architecture of a remark from Engels' *Dialectics and Natural Science*, and the almost identical one from Lenin which headed their papers, that 'In order to really know an object, it is necessary to comprehend, to study, all aspects of it: all its internal and external connectivities.' With this concept they brought the functional method several stages closer to later concepts of systems theory, and to later techniques for solving such multi-variate problems. The same two, canonical, ideas had lain behind the early Constructivists' redefinition of design as a function of '*tektonika, faktura* and *konstruktsiia*', but whilst the content and interrelationships of these three 'disciplines' remained ill-defined, their's was a very general model.

As a group, the Constructivist architects refuted charges of trying 'to eliminate the aesthetic emotion'. They were merely seeking to recognise that 'the character of it has changed under the influence of changed conditions of life, new economic priorities and new technology'.[86] Nor, Ginzburg insisted, did 'the functional method of thinking in any way eliminate the extremely complex tasks of architectural form-making'; 'it merely establishes a framework of procedures for that process'.[87]

46

**Precursors**

This is no place to examine the validity of OSA's approach in either its linear or 'simultaneous' stages. In other contexts, such issues have been discussed elsewhere.[88] But nothing, of course, emerges *ex machina*.

These architects, like most of their contemporaries, had little background in the Marxist philosophy on which they premised their design approach. Cut off in general from foreign stimuli, had they other, congruent, models at home? The answer, as I have already indicated, was yes: in the thinking of the Rationalist movement which developed during the later nineteenth century in Russia alongside advancing technology, political pluralism, and the aesthetic codes of realism.

The canonical work of that tradition was Apollinari Krasovskii's *Civil architecture* of 1851, where he was already urging a synthesis between 'emerging camps' of 'aesthetic-rationalists' and 'technological-rationalists'. The former he said, 'see architecture as an art of abstract form, to be composed according to rules established *a priori*'; the latter 'believe that everything in the parts and the whole must emerge purely in response to utility and construction'. 'In our opinion' he declared, 'The true path of architecture lies between these two. Our slogan is the transformation of one into the other: the transformation of what is functional into something beautiful.' Here was the ordering of priorities, and hence tasks, typical of nineteenth-century rationalism everywhere, that was to emerge without fundamental change into the Constructivists' method. More specifically, 'The characteristics of materials and the best possible way of combining different materials together determine the method of building, or the construction, and the form of construction determines the external form of the parts and of whole buildings.' 'Observation of this principle' produces 'architectural truth.' The task of art is then 'to communicate an aesthetic finality to the crude forms of technology'.[89]

These concepts were carried through the next generation by pioneers of cast iron and concrete construction like Ieronim Kitner.[90] As the new century began, theorists of the *moderne* still quoted Krasovskii widely. Some still found his ordering of the design process appropriate; others were blowing the problem open for redefinition.

To V Apyshkov, for example, discussing *The rational in the latest architect* worldwide, declared to students and academicians in 1905 that 'The basic component cell of a rational architecture is a form – maybe still crude and unrefined – but satisfying its functional purpose.' The end-product of the functional method's '1st object' could well be thus defined. 'Architecture's job' Apyshkov continues, describing well the aims of its next two stages, 'is then the further perfection of that cell from an aesthetic point of view, not destroying the level of functional suitability which it already possesses, but merely giving it a more refined delineation or stressing its function'. In familiar language he concludes 'The observation of this rule leads to so-called constructiveness of form, . . . which characterises Hellenic building, as the very highest manifestation of rational architecture.'[91] Tatlin, we recall, had the same model; Ginzburg had gone back only to Alberti.

Others however were already abandoning this linear, essentially mechanical analogy for appeals to another logic which they perceived in natural science. B N Nikolaev, much influenced by new work in geometry and mechanics, by crystallographers' studies of the relationship between morphology and material, had first declared in 1902 that 'It is time to throw out the dead idea that form can have a canon. Form must be as varied as the endless diversity of conditions that generate it, and the only "style" that the creative artist must pursue in his products is the style of nature, where nothing is

19 Krasovskii's *Civil Architecture*, 1851: cover of the accompanying volume on construction and detailing.

ГРАЖДАНСКАЯ АРХИТЕКТУРА.

ЧАСТИ ЗДАНІЙ.

Сочиненіе Аполлинарія Красовскаго.

ЧЕРТЕЖИ.

С. ПЕТЕРБУРГЪ.
1851.

ОБЛОМЫ.

# ФИЛОСОФІЯ

ZΩON TEXNIKON

# ТЕХНИКИ

## ВЫПУСКЪ 3-й                    НАША ЖИЗНЬ.

20  Peter Engelmeier, and cover of *The Philosophy of Technology*, part 3.

superfluous; where everything has meaning and serves the underlying idea . . . Only these principles can create a new architecture that will be a step forward not a mere marking time.'[92] But what were 'these principles'? How were 'meanings' and 'the underlying idea' to be described? Indeed, what aspect of 'nature' could offer a useful new model?

Most interesting here, and most prescient, was the concept advanced by Peter Engelmeier, the engineer and scholar who addressed European Philosophical Congresses and Moscow public lecture halls alike, during the years 1910–12, on the urgency of formulating a modern 'philosophy of technology'. Within a history traced back to Aristotle and forward to nineteenth-century figures like Mach and Rouleau, he sought to describe the nature of design as a creative activity in a technological context, and was to remain equally vocal on similar themes in Moscow professional and teaching circles right through the twenties.

Engelmeier built an analogy between the four 'classes of impulse' underlying any human 'intention', and 'that single formula, $C_m H_n O_p N_q$ . . . by which the chemist describes any one of the infinite number and diversity of natural bodies.'[93] Any 'intention', 'I', was a function of 'Truth, Beauty, Good and Utility', which 'unlike chemistry, can have negative values' (Falsehood, Ugliness etc). Between the 'Divine act' when all coefficients m,n,p,q have the value '+ infinity', and the converse 'Diabolical act', other special cases occur when any three

coefficients are zero. Thus the relations $I=T_m$, $I=B_n$, $I=G_p$ and $I=U_q$ represent respectively 'pure science, pure art, pure ethics with religion, and pure technology in the utilitarian sense.' When one coefficient is large but the rest are not zero, 'we have *applied* science' etc. Any specific 'technological act', or design, may be described in these terms. 'Since we have four dimensions' Engelmeier observes however, 'we cannot represent it by planar graphs'. Thus we are back with the multi- (here four-) dimensional 'solution surface' of Krasil'nikov and Komarova, and far closer to set-theoretic models of the late twentieth-century than to the linear, mechanical ones of the nineteenth.

The stylistic pluralism of Russian architecture in these pre-War years, which the Map-Guide here demonstrates, was clearly echoed by its theorists. What P O Sokolov described in 1912, in his pursuit of 'underlying principles', is a *tabula rasa*. 'The ideal of architectural beauty is just as fluid as all ideals of the human spirit,' he wrote. It cannot be determined once and for all time. The only eternals are the connections between Man and Nature, and the eternal laws governing the world. It is only knowledge of these connections and these laws that can lead to the supreme results and to the fullest success.'[94] In the Constructivists' favourite passage from *Dialectics and Natural Science*, Engels had said much the same. In trying to respond to that new ideology, their generation had this strong tradition of debate within the architectural profession behind them.

21  Engelmeier expounds his chemical analogy.

Волю        черезъ В
± Истину        »        И
± Красоту        »        К
± Добро        »        Д
± Пользу        »        П

получаемъ общую формулу воли:

$$В = И_m \ К_n \ Д_p \ П_q$$

которая имѣетъ два безконечныхъ предѣла: это божественная воля

$$В_{max} = И_\infty \ К_\infty \ Д_\infty \ П_\infty$$

и діавольская воля

$$В_{min} = И_{-\infty} \ К_{-\infty} \ Д_{-\infty} \ П_{-\infty}$$

Между этими предѣлами осуществляется воля человѣка. Но коэффиціенты имѣютъ величины, весьма различныя. Самые типичные случаи имѣютъ мѣсто, когда нѣкоторые изъ нихъ равны нулю. Такъ: когда n = p = q = 0, то воля направляется только на Истину, и мы имѣетъ формулу чистой науки (вмѣстѣ съ философіей по Аристотелевски):

$$В = И$$

Когда m = p = q = 0, то мы имѣемъ чистое искусство:

$$В = К$$

Когда m = n = q = 0, имѣемъ чистую этику (вмѣстѣ съ религіей):

$$В = Д$$

Когда m = n = p = 0, имѣетъ чистую технику (въ утилитарномъ смыслѣ):

$$В = П$$

# Notes

1 *Sovremennaia arkhitektura* (*SA*) 1928 no 6 p 170
2 M Ginzburg, 'Konstruktivizm kak metod laboratornoi i pedagogicheskoi raboty', *SA*, 1927 no 6 pp 160–6
3 M R Savchenko, 'The Nature and Methods of Applied Research in Architecture', *Environment and Planning B*, 1980, vol 7 no 1 pp 31–46
4 ibid p 39
5 V S Naginskaia, *Avtomatizatsiia arkhitekturno-stroitel'nogo proektirovaniia*, Moscow, 1979, p 63
6 M Ginzburg, 'Tselevaia ustanovka v sovremennoi arkhitekture', *SA*, 1927 no 1 pp 4–10
7 N Krasil'nikov, 'Problemy sovremennoi arkhitektury', *SA*, 1928 no 6 pp 170–6
8 In *SA* 1926 no 1 he speaks of a 'metod funktsional'nogo tvorchestva'; in no 4 he speaks of 'metod funktsional'nogo myshleniia' though the article is entitled 'Funktsional'nyi metod', and through 1927 onwards that phrase appears generally.
9 Ginzburg, 'Konstruktivizm kak metod', p 160
10 ibid, p 160
11 M Ginzburg, 'Konstruktivizm v arkhitekture', *SA* 1928 no 5 pp 143–5
12 John Milner, *Vladimir Tatlin and the Russian Avant-Garde*, Yale, 1983, pp 151–80
13 Lecture, 1 May 1969, Cambridge; a version published in: P Coe & M Reading, *Lubetkin and Tecton*, London & Bristol, 1981, pp 191–9
14 T Andersen, *Vladimir Tatlin*, Stockholm, 1968; S Bann, ed., *The Tradition of Constructivism*, London, 1974, pp 11–14; J Bowlt, ed., *Russian Art of the Avant-Garde: Theory and Criticism 1902–1932*, New York, 1976, pp 205–6
15 There is confusion relative to archival sources here, but the essential text is that which appears as 'The programme of the Productivist Group' in Bann, *The Tradition*, pp 18–20, also in N Gabo, *Gabo*, London 1957
16 Aleksei Gan, *Konstruktivizm* Tver, 1922
17 Bann, *The Tradition*, pp 32–42; Bowlt, *Russian Art*, pp 214–225
18 Gan, *Konstruktivizm*, pp 20; 53
19 ibid, p 55
20 ibid, p 61
21 ibid, p 61–2
22 ibid, p 62
23 ibid, p 65
24 cf D Elliott, ed., *Alexander Rodchenko*, Oxford 1979, p. 46
25 Gan, *Konstruktivizm*, p 64
26 ibid, p 53
27 ibid, p 63
28 ibid. p 63
29 ibid, p 64
30 He discusses this in M Ginzburg, *Stil' i epokha*, Moscow 1924, pp 9, 10
31 *Sredi kollektsionerov*, articles in 1921, nos 11–12; 1922, nos 1, 3, 7–8
32 *Arkhitektura*, monthly of MAO; only 2 issues published: 1923, nos 1–2; 3–4
33 VI Semionov, 'Ocherednye zadachi', *Arkhitektura*, 1923 no 1–2 pp 28–30
34 Ot redaktsii, 'Estetika sovremennosti', *Arkhitektura*, 1923, no 1–2, pp 3–6
35 N T Savel'eva, 'Organizatsiia nauki ob arkhitekture v gosudarstvennoi akademii khudozhestvennykh nauk', in A A Strigalev, ed, *Problemy istorii sovetskoi arkhitektury: sbornik*, Moscow 1983, pp 48–56; also Bowlt, *Russian Art*, pp 196–8
36 Savel'eva, 'Organizatsiia', p 53
37 Ginzburg, *Stil' i epokha*
38 I V Kokkinaki, 'K voprosu o vzaimosviazakh sovetskikh i zarubezhnykh arkhitektorov v 1920–1930-e gody', in *Voprosy sovetskogo izobrazitel'nogo iskusstva i arkhitektury*, Moscow 1976 pp 350–82. She also mentions that Lunacharskii published a translation of 'Les yeux qui ne voient pas' in the journal he edited, *Khudozhestvennyi trud*, 1923, no 2 pp 25–8
39 Edgar Norvert, 'Obzor zhurnalov', *Arkhitektura*, 1923 no 1–2 pp 42–4
40 Moisei Ginzburg *Style and Epoch*, introduced and translated by Anatole Senkevitch, Jr, MIT, Cambridge, 1982
41 Gan, *Konstruktivizm*, p 54
42 A V Kuznetsov, 'Arkhitektura i zhelezobeton', *Zodchii*, 1915, no 19–20; version of a speech to the 5th Congress of Russian Architects, Moscow, 1913
43 Ginzburg, *Stil' i epokha* p 13
44 ibid, pp 13–20
45 ibid, pp 119–20; on the cultural dimension he refers to Russian editions of N Danilevsky's *Russia and Europe*, 1888, and O Spengler's *Der Untergang des Abendlandes*, 1923.
46 Ginzburg, *Stil' i epokha*, pp 78, 73–89, 121
47 ibid, p 121
48 ibid, p 111
49 ibid, p 121
50 ibid, p 94
51 ibid, p 93
52 ibid, p 131
53 ibid, pp 128–9
54 ibid, p 132
55 ibid, p 133
56 ibid, p 134
57 Prof V K Karpovich, review of Ginzburg's *Stil' i epokha*, in *Kommunal'noe khoziaistvo*, 1925 no 2 pp 167–8
58 Edgar Norvert, 'Priemy planirovki', in V N Semionov, ed, *Udeshevlenie stroitel'stva*, Moscow, 1925, pp 15–26
60 '*SA* privetstvuet vykhod "ASNOVA"', *SA*, 1926, no 2 p 59
61 On the founding of OSA see: V E Khazanova, comp, *Iz istorii sovetskoi arkhitektury 1926–32; dokumenty i materialy*, Moscow 1970, pp 65–8
62 M Ginzburg, 'Novye metody arkhitekturnogo myshleniia', *SA* 1926 no 1 pp 1–4
63 M Ginzburg, 'Funktsional'nyi metod i forma', *SA* 1926 no 4 p 89, and Ginzburg, 'Tselevaia ustanovka'
64 Ginzburg, *Stil' i epokha*, later parts of Chapter 1
65 Ginzburg, 'Novye metody', p 1
66 ibid, p 2
67 K Akashev, 'Forma samoleta i metody ego proektirovaniia', *SA*, 1926 no 3 pp 65–6
68 Ginzburg, 'Novye metody', pp 1, 3
69 ibid, pp 3–4
70 Ginzburg, 'Funktsional'nyi metod', p 89
71 ibid, p 89
72 Ginzburg, 'Tselevaia ustanovka', p 6
73 ibid, p 6
74 ibid, p 7
75 Gan, *Konstruktivizm*, p 65
76 Ginzburg, 'Tselevaia ustanovka', p 10
77 Krasil'nikov, 'Problemy'
78 ibid, p 170
79 ibid, and N Krail'nikov and L Komarova, 'Metod issledovaniia formobrazo-vaniia sooruzheniia', *SA* 1929 no 5 pp 183–4
80 Krasil'nikov, 'Problemy', p 170
81 ibid, pp 174–5
82 Catherine Cooke, 'Nikolai Krasil'nikov's Quantitative Approach to Architectural Design: An Early Example', *Environment and Planning B*, 1975, vol 2 no 1 pp 3–20
83 Krasil'nikov and Komarova, 'Metod', p 183
84 ibid, pp 183–4
85 N Bukharin and E Preobrazhenskii, *Azbuka kommunisma*, 1919; Penguin 1969, pp 66–7
86 Ginzburg, *Stil' i epokha*, p 122
87 Ginzburg, 'Funktsional'nyi metod', p 89
88 L J March, 'The Logic of Design and the Question of Value' in March, ed, *The Architecture of Form*, Cambridge 1976; Philip Steadman, *The Evolution of Designs*, Cambridge 1979, Chapter 15
89 A K Krasovskii, *Grazhdanskaia arkhitektura*, St Petersburg, 1851 pp 4–5
90 On Kitner etc see: Catherine Cooke, 'Russian Perspectives', in I Latham, ed, *E E Viollet-le-Duc 1814–1879*, London, 1980, pp 60–3
91 V Apyshkov, *Ratsional'noe v noveishchei arkhitekture*, St Petersburg 1905 p 59
92 B N Nikolaev, *Fizicheskie nachala arkhitekturnykh form*, 1905; originally the paper 'Rol' fizicheskikh nachal v arkhitekture', read to the St Petersburg Society of Architects, 15 October 1902
93 P K Engelmeier, *Filosofiia tekhniki*, vyp 3, Moscow 1912 pp 92–4 (a lecture of 1911). C,H,O and N are the elements Carbon, Hydrogen, Oxygen and Nitrogen, in the format of a standard molecular formula.
94 P P Sokolov, *Krasota arkhitekturnykh form: osnovnye printsipy*, St Petersburg, 1912, pp 25–6

Irina Kokkinaki

# THE FIRST EXHIBITION OF MODERN ARCHITECTURE IN MOSCOW*

*Exhibitions of modern architecture were in vogue worldwide in 1927. In their journal SA the Constructivist architects of OSA recorded them. In a review of their own activities that year they recorded invitations which they themselves had received to participate – 'from New York, from Brussels and from Prague'. They were gratified at the positive press response 'amongst Americans' to the fifty works they sent to the New York show. 'But the other invitations unfortunately had to be declined' as they record, 'because they arrived almost simultaneously whilst OSA was in the thick of organising the First Exhibition of Modern Architecture in Moscow.'†*

*That first exhibition was to be the last, but its two months run at the peak of building activity in the 1920s made it a major landmark in the history of modernism in Soviet architecture. Without access to archival materials, however, background aspects of its organisation and important details of its content have remained obscure. Irina Kokkinaki fills many of those gaps for the first time.*

Catherine Cooke

On the eighteenth of June 1927, in the VKhUTEMAS building at number 11, Rozhdestvenskaia Street, Moscow, was opened the Soviet Union's 'First Exhibition of Modern Architecture'. It had been organised by the Chief Administration for the Sciences under the Commissariat for Enlightenment (Glavnauka) and by the Union of Contemporary Architects, OSA, on the basis of an initiative taken by the latter in the preceding autumn of 1926.[1]

The exhibition was an important event in the country's architectural life, and it was intended to be so. The organisers had a triple aspiration for the exhibition: that it should bring the ideas of contemporary architecture to the attention of the 'broad masses of the population in the USSR'; that it should oppose 'unprincipled eclecticism with the united front of contemporary architecture', and that it should draw conclusions from completed works, expose mistakes and indicate a path towards 'actively overcoming present building conditions'.[2] In his introductory essay to the catalogue P I Novitskii, the head of Glavnauka's artistic department and the Rector of VKhUTEMAS, wrote that 'The exhibition committee has tried to attract the cooperation of all architects working in the area of modern architecture who are bound together through the requirements imposed by our real conditions and the epoch of socialist construction.'[3]

As we shall see, far from 'all' the modernist architectural groups participated. Invitations were sent very selectively by the organisers, and some who were invited refused. That selectivity certainly did not pass unnoticed even in the general building press,[4] far less in the profession as a whole. In that respect, the exhibition helped exacerbate the factionalism already strong amongst the less-than-unified 'front' of modernist architects. At the same time, it represented a historically unique juxtaposition of Soviet work to its nearest European parallels. Commentaries by OSA as organisers, and in the wider building press, indicate strong awareness of that dimension and interpret it variously.

In its first task of acquainting broad sections of the population with the ideas of contemporary architecture the exhibition was fairly successful. It received numerous, and on the whole, positive reviews in the press.[5] It was visited by 5,000 people from 30 towns in the Soviet Union and from Germany, France, Austria, Italy, Czechoslovakia, Japan and other countries too. About forty excursions were organised from institutes of higher education in Moscow, Leningrad, Tomsk, Kiev, Odessa, Baku and Saratov, and from industrial enterprises, administrative organisations and individual factories.[6] In this article I shall try to reconstruct the picture of modern architecture which an exhibition visitor would have taken away with him, and to examine something of how that corresponded to the reality. We shall also consider how far the organisers did manage to consolidate the efforts of innovative architects in the interests of a 'united front of modern architecture' opposed to eclecticism.

\*    \*    \*

At the initial stages of discussion it had been planned to house the exhibition in the Tsentrosoiuz pavilion down in the park created for the All Union Agricultural Exhibition of 1923 – the present Gorkii Park in central Moscow. A somewhat earlier opening date had also been projected.[7] (In the event the show ran until 15 August.) The initial planning committee had comprised A A Feodorov-Davydov from Glavnauka; Moisei Ginzburg and Aleksandr Vesnin, who were Chief Editors of the Constructivists' journal SA, and the young Constructivist architect Georgii Orlov as secretary. At the detailed planning stage in April 1927, these four were joined by Viktor Vesnin and another younger member, G G Vegman. Aleksei Gan, the pioneer theorist of Constructivism and designer of OSA's SA was appointed Chairman of the exhibition committee, and he directed the design and lay-out of the show.[8] He also designed the catalogue.

With that heavily Constructivist committee, it could be no surprise that the exhibition would lay great emphasis upon the achievements of that group.

* This article was first published, without illustrations, in: A A Strigalev, ed, Problemy istorii sovetskoi arkhitektury (Problems of the history of Soviet architecture), TsNIIP-gradostroitel'stva, Moscow, 1980, pp 39–54, whence it is translated by kind permission of the author and editor. The author is a Senior Research Fellow of the Central Research Institute for the History and Theory of Architecture in Moscow. Illustrations have been assembled by Catherine Cooke.

† 'Zhizn OSA' (The life of OSA), SA 1927 no 4/5 p 158.

# ПЕРВАЯ ВЫСТАВКА СОВРЕМЕН-НОЙ АРХИТЕКТУРЫ

ERSTE AUSSTELLUNG DER ARCHITEKTUR DER GEGENWART

The Constructivists' great successes in overcoming academicism and traditional stereotyped modes of thinking, and in the formulation of architectural principles responding to the tasks of the new society, were all well and fully represented in the selection of materials. The wide typological range of projects represented – from industrial complexes to one-off community buildings – was enriched by showing examples of new building types which had arisen in response to new demands formulated by a new social class. In the development of social and functional programmes and in the quest for forms for those socially new architectural organisms, it was precisely the Union of Contemporary Architects that had made the most decisive contribution. In that context, it was natural that little interest should have been accorded to Palace of Labour schemes, to workers' club and designs and new types of apartment housing by such established figures as Ivan Zholtovskii and Aleksei Shchusev. In the rare cases where they tackled an identical brief, as was the case with Zholtovskii's House of Soviets for the Dagestan Republic, these architects quite manifestly failed to overcome their traditionally ingrained understanding of such 'public' buildings as exercises in a palace 'in a chosen style'. Even in their housing design there was little that was truly innovative. Not for nothing on the other hand was a particularly large amount of the Constructivists' section devoted to their work in the development of new housing types. Even more perhaps than any other Constructivist designs in the show, their housing research demonstrated their very significant successes in resolving social, functional and constructional questions alongside those of economical organisation of the internal space and communications patterns in buildings.

**The Constructivists' room**
Works by the leaders of OSA naturally occupied a central position in the whole exhibition. Here were those projects by the Vesnin brothers which had laid the foundations of architectural Constructivism: the Palace of Labour of 1923; the *Leningradskaia Pravda* building from 1924; the ARCOS headquarters of that same year, and the Central Telegraph project from 1925. All were characterised by their emphatic exposure of the reinforced concrete frame, by a structural clarity, by simplicity and compactness of composition, by the transparency of their glazed facades. All were consciously and manifestly pieces of 'design' in architecture. There were works by the same architects from the next two years, 1925 and 1926, which represented Constructivism in a more mature phase, of which several had been built or were then under construction: the Central Institute of Raw Materials complex in Moscow; the headquarters for Sverdlovsk Oblast Executive Committee; the Agricultural Bank building in Ivanovo-Voznesensk (Ivsel'bank), and the hotels complex in the mountains at Matsesta.

The other leader of Constructivism in architecture, Moisei Ginzburg, was equally generously represented. From 1925 there was his Moscow covered market scheme; from the fervidly active year 1926, his projects for the House of Textiles and Rusgertorg Headquarters in Moscow; the University of Minsk complex, and the House of Soviets for the Dagestan Republic, all of them compact but highly specific and articulate plans. Prominently featured in the main OSA room were photos of his newly completed Gosstrakh housing block in central Moscow, conspicuously 'modern' amidst the two-storied nineteenth-century classicism of its environment. In the housing research section his own contributions to the OSA group's 'comradely competition' were also amongst the most substantial. All these schemes reflected Ginzburg's consistent development of the principles of a functional design method, and his search for structural and formal solutions to new building types, together with a gradually increasing complexity in his volumetric and spatial compositions.

Another senior member of OSA who was prominently featured was Ilia Golosov. He was represented in the show by his designs for Rusgertorg, the Electrobank, the Smolensk market, the Municipal Employees Club on Lesnaia street, Moscow – the so-called Zuiev Club – and a scheme for the Matsesta hotels complex. All were examples of his particular synthesis between Constructivism and the romantic and symbolic experiments of his earlier years. All his works were characterised by their compositional dynamism, and by his extension of the range of forms used and their contrasting juxtapositions. The glazed corner cylinders of his club designs and his Electrobank building were a typical motif. His brother Pantelemon exhibited his designs for the State Trading Company, Gostorg, for hospitals in Rostov-on-Don and Samarkand, for the Central Railwaymen's Club and Post Office building in Kharkov. Even more perhaps than Ilia Golosov's work, these were examples of lucid planning and composition.

Surrounding these works in the OSA room were numerous projects by younger Constructivists, graduates of the architecture departments in the VKhUTEMAS; the Moscow Higher Technical School, MVTU, and in the Moscow Institute of Civil Engineering, MIGI, who had received their professional education under Ginzburg, Ilia Golosov and the Vesnin brothers. These works showed vividly the active participation of the younger generation of OSA in real issues of construction. Amongst the housing schemes were reworkings of Moscow City Soviet's elevations for their building programme of 1927 by G G Vegman and A S Fufaev, designs for a cooperative housing block for employees of the newspaper *Izvestiia* by I N Sobolev, and several others. There were investigations of new types of community buildings, such as the workers' clubs by Andrei Burov and Ivan

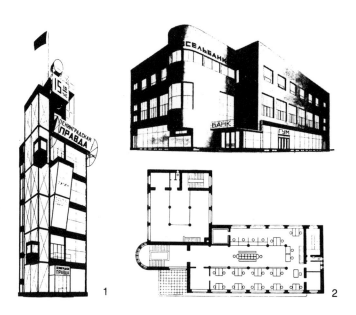

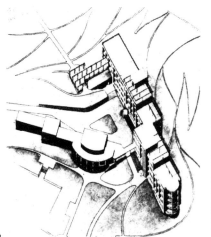

3

Vesnin brothers: 1 *Leningradskaia Pravda* building, 1924. 2 Agricultural Bank building, Ivanovo-Voznesensk, built 1926, perspective and first floor plan. 3 Hotels complex, Matsesta, built from 1926, axonometric and site plan.

Leonidov, and the House of the People in Rostov-on-Don by Vegman, Nina Vorotyntseva and V A Krasil'nikov. There were industrial establishments like the Sugar Industry Research Centre in Moscow by Ivan Nikolaev and A S Fisenko, and the electric power stations at Orekhovo-Zueva and Kupavna by Ia A Kornfel'd. Amongst schemes entered in architectural competitions were projects for Minsk University by V N Vladimirov and V A Krasilnikov, and by Vegman; designs for workers' housing at Ivanovo-Voznesensk by Burov and N P Parusnikov; and for the House of Textiles in Moscow by Kapustina, Kornfel'd and Fufaev.

Some of the projects in this group display an inordinate enthusiasm for glazed surfaces – a thing for which Constructivists were more than once criticised very publicly; others displayed a hypertrophy of scale and a repetitive use of certain formal devices. Nonetheless, some very serious achievements were to be found amongst these new graduates' work. Leonidov's graduation project for the Lenin Bibliographical Institute was a distinctive highlight of the show, presented in its expansive and handsomely made model by the window of the OSA room, and at the same time was an outstanding landmark in the development of a new architecture. The combination of plan drawings and model gave a rich picture of this design by a talented student of Aleksandr Vesnin, which displayed a continuity with the best traditions of early Constructivism as well as a qualitative advance in the extension and renewal of its vocabulary.

V A Pashkov's much less well-known project for that same Lenin Institute displayed a comparable sharpness of conception and boldness of invention, as did Mikhail Barshch and Mikhail Siniavskii's draft project for a Moscow planetarium. Stills from Eisenstein's film *The General Line* showed models constructed to full size as sets for an agricultural laboratory, cowsheds and the pigsties of a 'model farm', all built in 1926 to designs by Andrei Burov. These buildings, created under the strong influence of Le Corbusier's work and in accordance with the ideas of the film's scriptwriter, were intended to act as propaganda for the extensive use – as archival materials explicitly state – 'of new architectural forms for all our ever-expanding range of building requirements'.[9]

Architecture Schools' room: 4 Corner with work from LIGI, Leningrad, and door into OSA room. 5 VKhUTEMAS corner, including S Kozhin's Palace of Labour project, 1926, left of door. 6 Work from MVTU, Moscow, including, centre right, diploma project in factory design by active OSA student, later Union of Architects President, G Orlov. 7 B Movchan, MVTU, mechanised electrified bread factory. 8 Grechina, Kiev School, Artist's House. 9 L Khidekel, LIGI, workers' club. 10 Lavronovich, LIGI, covered market.

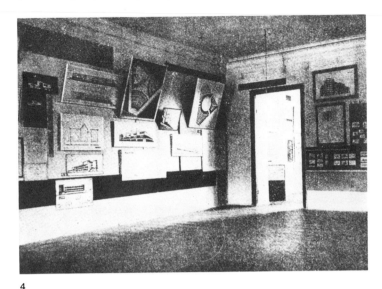

4

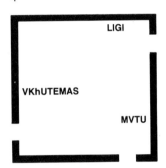

**ARCHITECTURE SCHOOLS' ROOM**

LIGI
VKhUTEMAS
MVTU

5

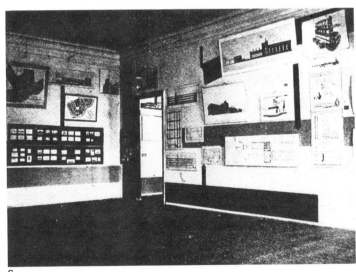

6

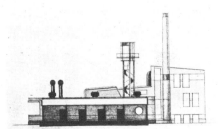

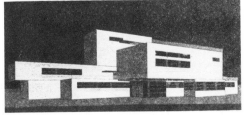

8                9                10

11

12

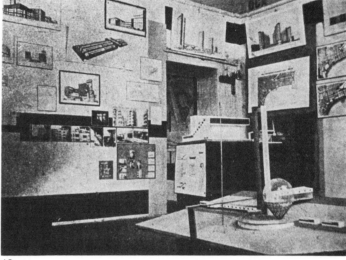

13

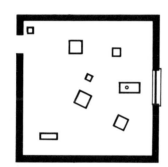

**CONSTRUCTIVISTS' ROOM**

Constructivists' room: 11 Towards door from Schools' room: upper L, I Sobolev, Palace of Labour, 1926; L of door, Ginzburg's Gostrakha housing; foreground, model of Nikolskii et al, workers' club. 12 Towards adjoining end wall, Leonidov's Lenin Institute model near window, R. 13 Towards same corner, from window: Leonidov model; Ginzburg's Gostrakha, centre, with his Orgametal project above, and his covered market, 1925, top; Barshch & Siniavskii central market, over door; R, T Chizhikova, MVTU diploma, replanning Baku. 14 Opposite corner with Nikolskii Club model, L; centre top, A Pasternak & I Viliam, 1926, spinning mill; R of that, 3 I Golosov schemes: Smolensk covered market, top, Zuev Club, centre, and Elektrobank, below. R, top: Kornfel'd, power station. 15 Nikolskii, Gal'perin & A Krestin, workers' club model. 16 I Golosov, Elektrobank, 1926. 17 Ginzburg, Gostrakha housing, built Moscow, 1926–7.

14

15

16

17

Certain of the OSA projects displayed here were thus executed during the final years of younger members' training, but in general works by the country's architectural students were displayed in a special room, devoted to the Institutes of Higher Education, the VUZi.

## The architecture schools' room

With many students' work located in the OSA room, the VKhUTEMAS display here was predominantly devoted to Nikolai Ladovskii's students, members of his Association of New Architects, ASNOVA. There were projects by I V Lamtsov and M A Turkus, including the layout of a communal residential district for a town; a tribune design and a layout for the International Red Stadium, Moscow, by M A Korzhev and S B Glagolev; layouts for a VKhUTEMAS housing area and a new VKhUTEMAS building by G I Glushchenko, T N Varentsov and G T Krutikov, and schemes by I I Volod'ko, N P Travin and several others. Due to ASNOVA's prevarication about participating at any level – even the student level – it is particularly difficult to establish exactly what material was displayed. The exhibition catalogue lists the names of ASNOVA-related participants in a separate supplementary section without any indication of the material they showed. Even this scanty list of specific projects has had to be assembled from information in such secondary sources as journal reviews and other contemporary publications, with certain hints from material in the official VKhUTEMAS archives.[10] It is certainly not complete therefore.

The students of MVTU, who were pupils of Viktor Vesnin and the distinguished pre-Revolutionary pioneer of concrete structures Aleksandr Kuznetsov, presented almost exclusively industrial projects. The most distinguished students here were Ivan Nikolaev, A S Fisenko, Grigorii Orlov who had contributed to the exhibition's organisation so much as Secretary, and G Ia Movchan. All were people who would later become very prominent members of the architectural profession.

Outstanding amongst works sent by the Leningrad Institute of Civil Engineers, LIGI, were the designs of K A Ivanov for a sanatorium and a House of Physical Culture. L M Khidekel's design for a workers' club, executed under the direction of Malevich, received wide publicity amongst the exhibition commentaries, as did projects by the two Krestins: a Department Store by M V Krestin, and a Monument to the Revolution by A V Krestin, a regular member of the studio of OSA's leader in Leningrad, Aleksandr Nikolskii.

Amongst projects from the Kiev Art Institute shown at the exhibition were works by students of A F Aleshin who comprised the newly formed nucleus of Ukrainian Constructivists. There was a cinema for 1,000 by G I Voloshinov, a House of Textiles project by I I Malozemov, a House for an Artist by Grechina, and a tramstop and a Museum of the Revolution by Ignatii Milinis, who was shortly to become a regular associate and collaborator of Moisei Ginzburg in Moscow. The Polytechnic of Fine Arts in Odessa sent certain schemes, and others came from the Siberian Technical Institute in Tomsk, including a cinema project, for example, by the student Ageev.

*   *   *

At this date, Leningrad was the only city outside Moscow to contain a formally constituted branch of the Constructivists' group OSA. Its leader, Aleksandr Nikolskii, headed an active studio where his main assistants were I K Beldovskii, V M Gal'perin, and the young A V Krestin. The largest project which they presented in the show was a first-prize winning scheme for a mechanised bread factory for the organisation LSPO in Leningrad – a complex capable of producing 62 tons of rye bread and 85 of wheat bread every day. There were also designs – and in some cases models – for a meeting hall for 5–10,000 people; an automatic telephone substation for Leningrad; a boulevard cinema and canteen; a tram stop, a workers' club, and certain other schemes. All their work was distinguished by an intense attention to purity of architectural form, to rhythm and proportions. The compositional principles on which certain of the schemes were based, using complex combinations of rectangles shifted, in parallel or perpendicularly in three dimensions, and the nature of the rhythmic structures employed, demonstrated the influence of Malevich's architectural experiments. The spare and economical use of architectural elements was augmented in certain of their schemes by the introduction of intense applied colour on the elevations.

## The housing room

That very important body of material on OSA's housing work, already mentioned, was divided between the OSA room and a special Housing Room. Numerous plans, models and photographs of completed buildings were on display, of which Ginzburg's Gosstrakh building on Malaia Bronnaia in Moscow, perhaps the most visually dramatic, was centrally displayed amongst the group's other work. The housing room proper was principally devoted to the later, group researches resulting from their announcement of a 'comradely competition' amongst themselves to generate ideas about a 'new house form appropriate to the new pattern of living and working of our population'. 'Everything done about housing in the USSR so far' they declared, 'whether theoretical or practical, has been only a set of palliatives. It is now time to develop a new form.' They announced their 'competition' at the very end of 1926, with the date of presentation to be 10 April 1927, specifically in time for assessment to precede display in the exhibition.[11] The result therefore represented only about three or four months work, but the range of new spatial organisations and ideas about the nature of the dwelling unit itself was considerable.

Eight sets of ideas were produced, by Ginzburg, Aleksandr Pasternak, Vegman, Vladimirov, Sobolev, by Vorotyntseva and R

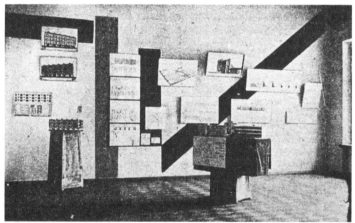

18

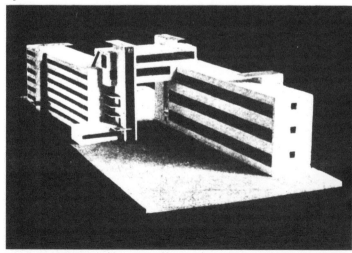

18 Corner of Housing Room, with schemes from OSA's 'comradely competition' of early 1927: L, Nikolskii's scheme, from Leningrad; central pedestal, Ginzburg's scheme, with model.
19 Ginzburg's model.

Poliak together, and by Aleksander Nikolskii and Andrei Ol' from Leningrad OSA. In pursuit of housing adapted to the new way of life, all had focussed upon a type of residential complex that would combine individual dwelling units of various sizes with a varied selection of communal facilities. A great deal of attention had been paid to detailed development of the numerous different dwelling types in both their spatial structure and the lay-out of their internal equipment; to the manner in which they were arranged in relation to each other and the circulation system, and to their access to those communal facilities and social amenities. Most schemes embraced a sizeable complex of buildings; that by Sobolev expanded to the scale of a whole district plan.[12] The presentation of this material at the exhibition was to lead to an invitation for certain of the Moscow group to continue the work as an official research team within the Construction Committee of the Russian Republic's Economic Soviet – the Stroikom EKOSO RSFSR. It was thus the starting point for that well-known range of housing types 'A–F' which would form the basis of their later extensive building commissions, such as the Narkomfin housing complex in central Moscow.

20

## Other modernists

Amongst the exhibitors, 'those people working on the same plane as OSA' formed a special group within the show who were, in the ironical words of one reviewer, 'acceptable, but not orthodox from OSA's point of view'.[13] Here Moscow architects of the older generation presented works which used external attributes of the 'Constructivist style': the exposure of the frame system of verticals and horizontals, lavishly glazed elevations, the use of integral applied lettering and so on. The main schemes in this section were two variants, from 1925 and 1926/7, of Grigorii Barkhin's *Izvestiia* building for central Moscow, and Barkhin's spinning mill for Ivanovo-Voznesensk; buildings for Gostorg and Gosstrakh by B M Velikovskii; the Anatomical Institute for Moscow University, the competition projects for Moscow Central Telegraph and the Matsesta hotels by Aleksei Shchusev, and the expansion and refacing of the Grain Export Department headquarters, Eksportkhleb, a much-watched recent project executed in central Moscow by Sergei Chernyshev. To a certain extent the execution of these first large projects like the *Izvestiia*, Gostorg and Eksportkhleb buildings in central Moscow, which were stylistically close to Constructivism and created by experienced master architects, assisted the process of breaking down stereotyped conceptions amongst the wider population, and a gradual adaptation of the public consciousness to the new forms. At the same time, the compositional devices did not correspond in any organic way to the kind of spatial organisation being developed by the Constructivists, and indeed often did not coexist very satisfactorily with highly traditional organisational concepts in the client establishments themselves, and hence in the internal structure of the so-modern looking buildings.

The principal area of direct overlap between Constructivists and these 'older modernists' was through their joint participation in certain town planning schemes. A wide range of projects was included in the exhibition, and virtually all the genuine bits of professional town planning activity, as opposed to student and other exercises, related to distant parts of the Soviet Union. The most substantial were proposals for the planning of Baku and nearby oil settlements of the Azneft organisation, in which Aleksandr and Viktor Vesnin and others had worked with the pioneer former Garden Cities planner Aleksandr Ivanitskii; for nearby Armenikend and Bailov areas, in which Pasternak, Poliak, M A Kniaz'kov, V V Kratiuk and B N Matnev had worked with Ivanitskii; and a planning study of Tuapse executed by Shchusev with Leonid Vesnin and A S Mukhin. The time when planning could become a major and central concern of the Constructivists as a group was still several years away. With minor exceptions, the work which came from foreign architects was also focussed overwhelmingly upon the problems of the single building complex.

20 Barkhin, spinning mill in Ivanovo-Voznesensk, 1926.
21 Shchusev, competition scheme for Moscow Central Telegraph, 1925.

## The foreign section

Towards the end of 1926, the exhibition committee had sent advance information on the exhibition to selected destinations abroad. They were helped in organising the foreign section of the show by the All-Union Society for Cultural Relations with Foreign Countries, VOKS. In the Moscow archive of VOKS is still preserved an issue of the Belgian journal *7 Arts* for April 1927, published by Victor Bourgeois, containing a report about the forthcoming exhibition with information about the sections planned, the kind of work that would be welcomed and membership of the organising committee.[14] To France, Holland, Belgium, Switzerland, Czechoslovakia, Poland, and Germany went lists of architects invited by name. The invitation sent to Germany, for example, contained the names of Mies van der Rohe, Max and Bruno Taut, Erich Mendelsohn, K Ludek, B Joseph, Walter Gropius and his Bauhaus colleagues, and of two building firms.[15]

The resulting foreign section of the show displayed examples of various branches of European rationalism, in the forms of both design drawings and photographs of completed buildings. Methodologically and formally closest to Soviet Constructivist work was the substantial body of material from Walter Gropius, Director of the Bauhaus. The complex of the Bauhaus' own buildings was prominently featured. Particularly noticeable was the inherent similarity between the general planning solution adopted for that school, created as it was under the marked influence of experimental and speculative designs by Malevich and Lissitzky, and the Dagestan Republic House of Soviets by Moisei Ginzburg, which was one of the first Constructivist designs to demonstrate a clear dismemberment of the unified form and to group the volumetric elements in strict accordance with their functions. The whole construction of the Terten-Dessau housing area by Gropius was illustrated in detail by photographs showing details of the standardised houses under erection, the actual techniques for assembling the pre-fabricated components, and the interior equipment of the living spaces.

In OSA's own work, problems of the industrialisation and standardisation of housing construction, of efficiency in building techniques and of reviving the building materials industry were all given a very prominent place. It was thoroughly consistent, therefore, that they should particularly focus the attention of exhibition visitors upon Bauhaus designs for steel housing, by Marcel Breuer and G Muche in partnership with R Paulik on which they have received rich material. The Bauhaus also sent numerous photographs of furniture, ceramics, lighting fixtures, fabric and typographical work executed by students to their own designs. A page of Gan's exhibition catalogue reproduced in *SA* indicates – in German – some of the contents of this section.[16]

The diverse range of material sent from Germany included Taut and Hoffman's pavilion for the German Trades Unions at the Dusseldorf exhibition and their Printers' House in Berlin. From Ludek there were both mass housing projects, and his demonstration 'House for a Brain Worker' built at the Dresden exhibition of German Culture and Technology in 1925.

From Switzerland came one of the best and most lucid examples of European functionalism to be produced during the whole 1920s; Hannes Meyer and Hans Wittwer's competition project for the League of Nations headquarters in Geneva. This work revealed many parallels in approach with the Constructivists' own design methods. The project was published in *SA* more fully than any other single foreign exhibit, with prominence given to such tools of the Constructivists' own approach as the flow diagram for vehicles and pedestrians, and the acoustic patterns determining auditorium shape. The editorial commentary embraced the scheme with an explicit sympathy that is almost unique in the whole of *SA*. 'In publishing the League of Nations project by Basel architects Hannes Meyer and G Wittwer' they wrote,

we want to make this point clear: we present it not as an example of a bourgeois and, to Soviets, alien conception, but as a **BUILDING**. In its internal contents and its whole treatment, in the handling of the organisational problems, it could readily be 'A Palace of Labour': a place for the assembly of peoples who have taken their fates into their own hands. The spirit of this project absolutely contradicts the bombastic enthusiasms of the League of Nations. It was for just this reason that the competition judges set it aside in favour of designs that proclaimed falsely classical stereotypes.

If we take this project apart, we find here an object perfectly thought out, in the details of its volumetric construction, of its planning, in the treatment and manipulation of its various component materials: the perfect home for congresses of another 'league of nations', which we may call the International of Liberated Peoples from the Whole World.[17]

They went on to quote at some length passages from the architects' notes to the Jury, which focussed upon their specific refusal to engage in any form of symbolism, abstract or rhetorical, and certainly its language was close to much of the Constructivists' own writing in that same vein.

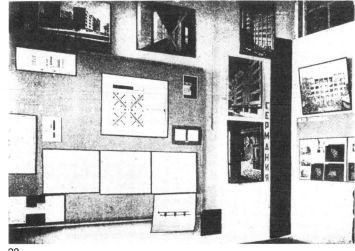

22

23

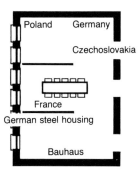

FOREIGN SECTION

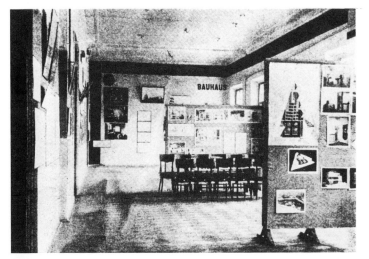

24

25

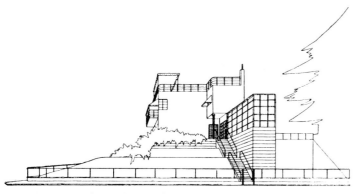

26  Iaromir Kreitsar, Czechoslovakia, villa in Prague.

Foreign section: 22 End of room with Polish display, L, some German work, and Czech section starting R, with housing by J Kroha.
23 General view towards Polish end; screen, front L, with German pre-fabricated steel housing above, and Roneo office furniture below.
24 Opposite end: reverse of screen in 23, with French housing, mainly Mallet-Stevens and Lurçat; Gropius' Bauhaus Building on end wall behind.
25 General view towards Bauhaus end, from Polish end.

A certain analogy with the principles of Soviet Constructivism could also be discerned amongst the Dutch architects' work at the exhibition, for example in Van der Flugt's Van Nelle complex and in Oud's social programme for the Hook of Holland housing development. The plastic treatment of the buildings which developed out of Oud's intentions, however, and to an even greater extent the composition of Rietveld's schemes, showed a completely different design method. Deriving as this did from the theoretical precepts of De Stijl, their approach exploited modern materials and constructional systems, but the point of departure for design was not a functional analysis in the manner understood by the Constructivists. The shop and Shroeder house in Utrecht and the Amsterdam flats which represented Reitveld in Moscow were all good examples of design which proceeded from an interest in the composition of complex, space-defining volumes in their own right.

The French work at the exhibition was equally dominated by an attention to architecture's aesthetic problems. Lurçat was represented by apartment blocks at Serrat and Versailles, and a villa at Obonne. From Rob Mallet-Stevens came apartment houses at Orsay and Boulogne-sur-Seine, a garage, the Alpha Romeo building and a bookshop in Paris. Whereas the majority of Soviet Constructivist designs of the mid-twenties were using the concrete frame as an artistically expressive device, these French architects' attention had been far more concentrated upon the delineation of smooth elevational surfaces and in the punching of asymmetrical window apertures in various configurations, and in enlivening these with small balconies and other three-dimensional details which allied them at times very closely to Art Deco.

From Belgium Victor Bourgeois had contributed material, and there were schemes by Maurice Gaspard. Poland was represented by the Syrkuses, M Shchuka, T Zarnoveruvna, Karchevskii, Kozinskii and some others. Czechoslovakia had sent villa and office building schemes by Ia Kreitser, and a house at Mlado-Boleslav from Irui Kroga with his block of flats in Brno.

\* \* \*

This was the range of architectural materials which the exhibition brought together. Where it had a stylistic unity, this was rooted, as organisers and reviewers indicated, in the common use of certain formal and artistic devices that fulfilled the requirements of a broadly functionalist aesthetic. Virtually every one of the exhibited projects, Soviet or European, used a post-and-beam reinforced concrete frame; there was universal adherence to the approach whereby the building form grew, like an organism, from inside to outside, 'from the bones to the skin'. Equally characteristic of all the work was an expression of inner functional and constructional organisation on the exterior, and a strong formal asceticism: what Ginzburg had called in the first-ever issue of SA, in 1926, 'the cheerful asceticism of those who are building and organising the new life'.[18] These factors in turn determined a certain uniformity in the appearance of the works exhibited, characterised by facades with exposed systems of horizontals and verticals and a glass infill.

Very clear amongst the OSA work was the considerable evolution which architectural Constructivism had undergone during its short life, from the Vesnins' Palace of Labour in 1923 to this 1927 exhibition. Terse framed volumes in the very earliest schemes like the Palace had given way to projects where a single integral body was broken down into cubic or rectangular volumes which were shifted and composed into dynamic and dramatic relationships: intersecting each other in bold right-angled movements, advancing and retreating from the basic mass, heightened by the contrasts of transparent glazed surfaces against solid, blank walls. Golosov's Zuiev Club on Lesnaia Street, and Ginzburg's unbuilt Orgametal building were classic examples of this phase.

Amongst the latest works, designed not long before the show, a further stage of articulation of parts was taking place. The building organisms were broken down very clearly into separate volumetric entities in accordance with their function. Buildings with different purposes were then unified by covered walkways, characteristically forming complex asymmetrical compositions. Typical examples here were Ginzburg's Dagestan Republic House of Soviets, Barshch and Siniavskii's Planetarium, and Leonidov's Lenin Institute. This pavilion principle of building up architectural organisms owed much to the example of the German functionalists, and was subsequently developed further in later Constructivist work. At the same time there were examples of other borrowings from Western colleagues. The horizontal strip window was one element reflecting an influence from Le Corbusier: one of the most distinctive applications of that device was Ginzburg's housing block for the OSA 'friendly competition'. The free-flowing space around ground-level pilotis were another Corbusian device, that one widely used in Burov's filmic farm complex for Eisenstein. These later designs give reason to suggest that the particular originality which developed progressively in Constructivist work from the Vesnin Palace of Labour and Leningrad Pravda schemes right through to Leonidov's designs of the later-middle twenties, was somewhat weakened as a result of the group's embracing their Functional Method during 1926–7.[19]

Certainly the exhibition demonstrated the extent to which Constructivism had established itself in the Soviet architectural profession as a whole. The powerful group at its heart comprised several extraordinarily distinguished architects with great practical experience, great authority in professional circles, and extensive roles in teaching. This was supported in turn by an enormous following of young architects, by recent graduates from the schools, and by current students in Moscow, Leningrad, the Ukraine and Siberia. Into the movement were also attracted certain traditionalist architects of the older generation. The roots of this remarkable professional phenomenon lay in the consonance of the Constructivists' general principles with the ethos of the time; in their declamatory social programme, and also in the simplicity and accessibility of the external devices of the Constructivist aesthetic and the ease with which the 'Constructivist style' could thus be applied. The emergence and adoption of new stylistic stereotypes did owe a considerable amount to the Constructivists' conscious rejection of any profound investigation of formal problems as such, to their simplified formulations of the relationship between functional and constructional structures and their artistic embodiments, and to their dread of the 'danger of abstract and aesthetic interpretations of form'.[20]

27 Tekhbeton section, in the display of modern building materials. Tekhbeton showed samples of their hollow concrete blocks, front, and behind, photos of buildings using them, with tables of building cost and energy savings.

In this connection, it was particularly noticeable that there were no works in the exhibition by those leading architects whose conception of architecture accorded an important place to the aesthetic or 'artistic' problems of design in their own right. The participation of unconverted traditionalists was excluded by the very programme of the show. The old-established Moscow Architectural Society, MAO; the Circle of Architect-Artists; the two Leningrad architectural societies; the Union of Art Workers, Vserabis, and other groups and organisations were not there because they did not receive an invitation to participate.[21]

The curator of the exhibition, P I Novitskii, wrote in the catalogue: 'the present exhibition does not represent any one trend in contemporary architecture. It does not and cannot pursue the aims of any particular group or faction.'[22] However, the agreement to entrust the exhibition's organisation to OSA had already long ago created the preconditions for an exhibition that was far from impartial. It cannot therefore be regarded as surprising that the First Exhibition of Modern Architecture in Moscow was in essence an exhibition of architectural Constructivism. Its incompleteness and one-sidedness with 'an overt bias in favour of the organisers, OSA',[23] was unanimously noted by the reviewers.

In refuting the charges of sectarianism, the OSA leadership cited the official refusal to participate which they had received from ASNOVA. This group had given as their reasons the late date at which they received the invitation 'to take part in organising the exhibition', and the preparation of their own exhibition; according to the Association's work plan, this was timed to coincide with the Tenth Anniversary of the Revolution.[24] Even at the end of 1926, however, ASNOVA were absent from the list of exhibition participants published in SA: 'The participants in the exhibition will be OSA, people working within OSA's general plan, the architecture schools, and foreign architects.'[25] Thus, despite OSA's declaration that there was no factional purpose behind the show, and their propagation of it under the slogan of 'consolidation', it became one more manifestation of divisions between the groups. Tension between them was increased by OSA's sharply critical thrusts at ASNOVA, and by the way they shifted the accusations from the professional to the social and political. The ASNOVA leadership seems to have been totally justified in accusing OSA of appropriating to itself the right to be 'sole judge of the qualities and merits of architectural work by other groups and other individual architects'.[26] They explained their refusal to take part in the exhibition precisely as a disagreement with OSA's intolerable mode of operating.

A number of factors contributed to the generally weak publicity accorded to ASNOVA's design and research activity in its time. A lack of support from the official leadership of artistic activity – in this case from Glavnauka – was a significant one by this date. David Shterenberg, who had been head of the Art Department in Glavnauka's parent body, the Commissariat of Enlightenment, during the first half of the twenties had valued very highly the theoretical and

design activity of Ladovskii and his fellow Rationalists. It was at his suggestion that work of theirs had been included amongst the Soviet exhibits in the Berlin exhibition of 1922 and the Paris Exposition des Arts Decoratifs in 1925. Shterenberg had also played an important role in the ratification of Ladovskii's group as an independent department within the Architectural Faculty of VKhUTEMAS. This patronage had evaporated however during the period after 1925 when Novitskii, who to all intents and purposes now occupied the same position, was a firm supporter of OSA.

At the same time, a great deal of blame for the public and professional ignorance of their own work must lie with ASNOVA themselves, and their own inertia in relation to publicity. As early as 1924 Ladovskii had informed El Lissitzky of the group's intention to mount an exhibition,[27] but it never took place, and only one very slender issue of their journal, ASNOVA News (Izvestiia ASNOVA) ever appeared, in 1926. Even today, it remains Ladovskii's pedagogical system and the diploma work of his students which is best known of all the Rationalists' activities. Meanwhile those few works by ASNOVA members which appeared at the First Exhibition of Modern Architecture through the participation of VKhUTEMAS students showed a variety and freedom of spatial solutions, an expressiveness of composition, innovative proportional systems and rhythmic relationships, that were only typical of the achievements of Ladovskii's group in their explorations of aesthetic problems.

The absence of Konstantin Mel'nikov from the exhibition also significantly impoverished the picture it gave: more perhaps than any of his contemporaries he had attracted the attention of architectural circles abroad, both as the designer of highly innovative projects, and as the relatively very prolific builder of them.

It was significant in this connection that the Soviet display assembled in that same year, 1927, by VOKS, for showing abroad, comprised works by OSA and ASNOVA members and by Mel'nikov, who officially belonged to neither group, on equal terms. The VOKS selection which went to the New York show The Machine Age that year, and which formed the architectural section of the Revolutionary anniversary exhibition A Window on the USSR, to display the achievements of the Soviet state in all areas of the country's economic and cultural life – this selection comprised thirty works by OSA members, eight by ASNOVA members, and seven by Mel'nokov.[28] Unbiased selection in this situation would seem to have produced an exhibition which reflected a truer picture of modern architecture in the Soviet Union to the rest of the world than the Moscow exhibition did to the Soviet public.

The First Exhibition of Modern Architecture in Moscow remained the only such exhibition. As we have seen, it did not promote a unified front of contemporary architecture in the USSR – indeed it was a contributer to the weakening of progressive movements in Soviet architecture. Constructivist criticisms of ASNOVA work, with their appeals to public opinion and their accusations of ideological errors, intensified during the forthcoming year 1928. During that year Constructivism's ideologists Gan, Ginzburg, Aleksandr and Viktor Vesnin, with the future leaders of the All-Union Organisation of Proletarian Architects, VOPRA, namely Ivan Matsa and A M Mikhailov, and sociologists of art including Novitskii, were to form a new artistic organisation called October, on a programme characterised by utilitarian and vulgarly sociological tendencies. In VOPRA's own declaration of 1929, Constructivism would be denounced as a 'reflection in architecture of the psychology and ideology of large-scale capitalist elements within the bourgeoisie', and it was criticised mercilessly along with ASNOVA.[29] Their own systematic fostering of sectarianism at the earlier stage, though, was one of the main reasons for the progressive weakening and increasing defencelessness of the innovative modernists, and the First Exhibition of Modern Architecture, as we have seen, was eventually to serve as a contributor to that process. In the history of Constructivism, however, it remains a historical datum and landmark.

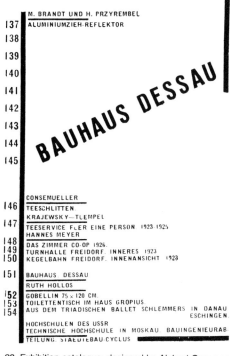

СТАЛЬНАЯ МЕБЕЛЬ ДЛЯ КОНТОР И БИБЛИОТЕК ФАБРИКИ RONEO

СТАЛЬНАЯ МЕБЕЛЬ ДЛЯ КОНТОР И БИБЛИОТЕК ФАБРИКИ RONEO

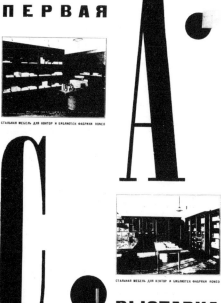

ПЕРВАЯ

А.
С.

ВЫСТАВКА

### Выставка „Современная Архитектура".

18 июня сего года Художественным Отделом Главнауки при участии ОСА в помещении Вхутемас'а открыта архитектурная выставка. Выставка заключает в себе два отдела. Один из них представляет образцы некоторых современных строительных материалов, выставленных „Асбостромом", Конструкторским Бюро Кооп-го Т-ва „Тэкбетон" и фирмой „Церезит". ...

Рис. 1. Жилой дом. Постройка 1910—1913 года.

Рис. 2. Андрэ Лурсэ (Франция). Жилой дом. Выставка „Современная архитектура".

28 Exhibition catalogue, designed by Aleksei Gan: page from the Bauhaus section.
29 Advertisement for the exhibtion from *SA* 1927 no 3, with pictures of Roneo office furniture.

30 First page of V Shcherbakov's exhibition review in *The Construction of Moscow*, 1927 no 7, with pictures contrasting an ornate 'House of 1910–13' with the clean lines of 'A House by Andre Lurçat, France, from the Modern Architecture exhibition.'

## Notes

1  TsGAOR SSSR, f 5283, op 11, d 29, L 91.
2  TsGALI SSSR, f 681, op 3, d 27, L 24; and *Sovremennaia Arkhitektura* (Contemporary Architecture), Moscow (henceforth *SA*), 1927, no 3, p 96.
3  *Katalog 1-i vystavki sovremennoi arkhitektury* (Catalogue of the First Exhibition of Modern Architecture), Moscow, 1927; unpaginated.
4  See for example V Shcherbakov, 'Vystavka "Sovremennaia Arkhitektura"' (The exhibition 'Modern Architecture'), *Stroitel'stvo Moskvy* (The construction of Moscow), 1927, no 7 pp 8–11, which is republished below.
5  The main ones were: D Aronovich, 'Vystavka sovremennoi arkhitektury' (The exhibition of modern architecture), *Stroitel'naia Promyshlennost'* (The Building Industry), 1927, no 6/7, p 451, and V Shcherbakov, 'Vystavka "Sovremennaia Arkhitektura"'; see also Ia A Tugendkhol'd in *Izvestiia*, 1927, no 32 (12 June); N Markovnikov in *Izvestiia*, 1927, no 53 (8 July), and M Raikhenshtein in *Krasnaia Niva* (Red Field), 1927, no 31.
6  *SA*, 1927, no 4/5, p 133
7  TsGAOR SSSR, f 5283, op 11, d 29, L 91.
8  TsGALI SSSR, f 681, op 3, d 27, L 16, and TsGAOR SSSR, f 5283, op 11, d 29, L 265, 96, 98.
9  TsGALI SSSR, f 1923, op 1, d 978, L 6.
10 TsGALI SSSR, f 681.
11 Notice in *SA*, 1926, no 4, p ii.
12 These eight studies were published in full in: *SA*, 1927, no 4/5, pp 125–147.
13 D Aronovich, 'Vystavka sovremennoi arkhitektury'.
14 TsGAOR SSSR, f 5283, op 11, d 29, L 274–274a.
15 *Ibid*, L 92.
16 *SA*, 1927, no 6, p 163.
17 *SA*, 1927, no 6, p 169.
18 M Ginzburg, 'Novye metody arkhitekturnogo myshleniia' (New methods of architectural thinking), *SA*, 1926, no 1, p 4.
19 On their functional method, see the article by Catherine Cooke in this issue.
20 M Ginzburg, 'Itogi i perspektivy' (Results and perspectives), *SA*, 1927, no 4/5, p 118.
21 'Pis'mo v redaktsiiu' (A letter to the editor), signed by the President of ASNOVA, M Korzhev, and the Deputy President of the Moscow Circle of Architect-Artists, N Markovnikov, *Stroitel'naia Promyshlennost'*, 1927, no 6/7, p 454.
22 *Katalog 1-i vystvaki.*
23 *Stroitel'naia Promyshlennost'*, 1927, no 6/7, p 451.
24 Letter from ASNOVA to the Committee of the First Exhibition of Modern

Architecture; undated, but inscribed 'received 3 June 1927'; published in *SA*, 1928, no 6, p 176.
25 *SA*, 1926, no 4, p 108.
26 *Stroitel'naia Promyshlennost'*, 1927, no 6/7, p 454.
27 Letters of 9 April 1923 and 23 August 1924, TsGALI SSSR, f 2361, op 1, d 59, L 7, 3.
28 TsGAOR SSSR, f 5283, op 11, d 77, L 46, 55; d 71, L 8–9; d 27, L 106, 107; and d 28, L 131–133.
29 *Pechat' i Revolutsiia* (Press and Revolution), 1929, no 6, p 125.

Catherine Cooke

# MELNIKOV AND THE CONSTRUCTIVISTS: TWO APPROACHES TO CONSTRUCTION IN AVANT–GARDE ARCHITECTURE

High-Tech or Low-Tech? Modern building or traditional? A conventional technology or an 'appropriate' one? Since Peter the Great these alternatives had had connotations of 'Western' versus 'Russian'. That polarity itself had philosophical and political dimensions which ramified throughout Russian society in the eighteenth and nineteenth centuries, and ran through every issue it debated.

In the Soviet building industry after the Revolution the issue was as current as ever. Before the War, the peaks of sophistication in the metropolitan centres were on a level with comparable work abroad. Latest advances were displayed proudly across the whole range of architecture from industrial buildings to the domestic; from ever vaster Orthodox churches reasserting autocracy to the entirely new building types arising from the pressures to democratise. Men like Loleit, Kuznetsov, Shukhov had pioneered the introduction of techniques that were on the front line of current processes world-wide, with reinforced concrete as a prominent concern. Cast iron techniques had been a rallying point for the rationalist movement in design throughout the nineteenth century. But these pockets of modernity had existed within a sea of entirely traditional building technology that was still largely medieval.

On the one hand, and particularly Russian, there was timber building. Whole tree-trunks may appear the most primitive of construction materials, yet as practiced in Russia, even in the Middle Ages, the technique was sophisticated. Whole houses could be bought in knocked-down form as standardised pre-packages in the markets.[1] The fires that plagued Russia's timber-built towns would leave only the masonry churches and defensive structures standing when the overall matrix of building was razed, and that matrix would be reconstructed of these standardised, prefabricated units. In their thermal properties, as in much else, these log-built structures were ideally adjusted to the climatic extremes of continental Russia; many of them were very large.

At the same time there were techniques using sawn timber, and stuccoed lathe-and-plaster. A great deal of the masonry building in Russia-proper was massive brickwork stuccoed to a smooth surface, for stone is not indigenous here.

These mixed techniques stretched back to the very introduction of masonry architecture with the adoption of Christianity in the eleventh century, first manifested in the great Byzantine-inspired cathedrals like Chernigov. This was usually how the famous 'white' churches which spattered the blackened timber streets of Moscow had been constructed. The classical and neo-classical architecture of Russia was likewise rarely a stone architecture. Peter's insistence that all stone went to Petersburg was a factor in producing that situation, but established patterns were as strong. A major domestic complex like the Razumovskii Palace in Moscow, for example, of 1801–3, was grandly Westernised in its salons and composition, but the structure beneath its European costume was the age-old brickwork with lathe-and-plaster; hence the present, almost insuperable, problems of conserving this urbane city fabric.

Across Russia as a whole, it was the Civil War through which the Bolsheviks consolidated their control, rather than the initial Revolution, which destroyed the factories and plants of pre-War industry. By 1922–3, when specialists in the new State Planning Bureau, Gosplan, faced the problem of Russia's reconstruction, they encountered at the very foundations of their task a set of building materials industries that were the worst decimated of all industries in the country.

Building had effectively ceased with Russia's entry into the First World War, and that was already nearly ten years ago. At that date the major industrial cities like Moscow, or the textile centre of Ivanovo, were boom towns on the peak of a building explosion. From that period derived most of the middle-class apartment blocks in central Moscow, for example, into which the homeless working classes had now been resettled out of their grossly crowded and fetid basement 'corners'. In those intervening years, however, almost every brick-works in the country had become ruined; cement works likewise, but marginally better. Glass was nearly unobtainable. The production of steel was on its knees. Even skilled labour for felling and dressing timber was dispersed and depressed. Those planners in Gosplan's Building Sector fully understood that their industry must be the keystone on which Russia's whole industrial capital was reconstructed, and with it her economy. As ever, though, it was hard to persuade politicians of the urgency and logic of that priority. Those debates can be traced through Gosplan's journal *The Planned Economy* (*Plannovoe Khoziastvo*), where careful statistics alternate with near-despair.

This, like all other dimensions of their 'reality' was a central concern amongst practice-oriented members of the architectural avant-garde. Russian building had always been famous for its extravagance of materials: safety factors, if calculated at all, were several times higher than any in Western practice. How should they build now, when 'economy' and 'rationalisation' were central planks of the régime's survival campaign?

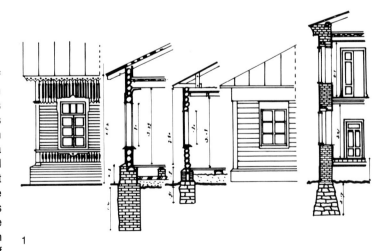

1

1 Markovnikov's approach to rationalising traditional timber and brick construction by reduced scantlings and storey heights (cf Map Guide no 2) RIGHT: Mel'nikov's house (Map Guide no 43). 2 Perforated cage of brickwork. 3 Double glazed window. 4 Framing of floors. 5 Bricklaying geometry. 6 Floor and ceiling details. 7 Site, with footings laid.

## Arguments by demonstration

By the time the avant-garde came on the scene actively, in the mid-twenties, Gosplan's Building Sector had grappled with this problem long enough to know that their whole edifice of plans for reducing building costs was fatally weakened by lack of data on the real possibilities of particular building techniques. They had no detailed figures about either the built area of each building type bought by a given sum of money, or about the quantities of each building material consumed in constructing it. Any 'normative consumption' data they could construct, through dividing areas output by gross materials input, was highly aggregated, and based on the archaic techniques habitual to the building industry from that half-affluent, half-medieval past when it last built anything.

In the end data bases, like their whole 'new world', could only be reconstructed from the bottom up, from attacking the grass roots.

Throughout all economic planning ran arguments on the relative merits of backing the 'high technology' or the labour intensive approach. The same argument ran through the Building Sector, and both sides of it found their most practical investigators amongst the avant-garde architects.

Konstantin Mel'nikov was never a man for rigid uniformity of principle. He used building techniques according to context. The great steel girders of his bus garage roofs were exploitations of a modern technique stretched near its maximum spans – and suitably poeticised in photography by Rodchenko. The bold cantilevers central to the formal idea of his Rusakov Club relied on the properties of reinforced concrete. Neither of these expanded the repertoire of proven construction techniques for early Soviet building. His own little house, however, was conceived as an experiment in updating traditional techniques that has been well justified by its underlying structural condition half a century later.

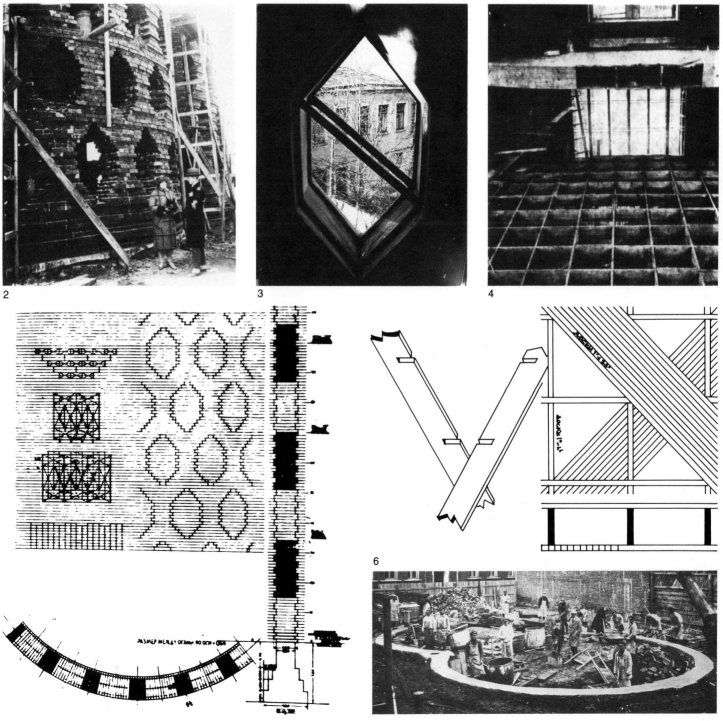

2

3

4

5

6

7

As Mel'nikov saw it, 'structural stability, heat insulation and daylight penetration' were the three basic problems to be 'unified through technology and architectural analysis'. He would explore here 'the materials most popular and widely available in our country', namely bricks and timber boarding. Most leading advocates of a rationalised traditional building since the Revolution had been adherents of the closely related Garden City or Housing Cooperative movements. Chief among them now was Nikolai Markovnikov (Map Guide no 2) who compacted space and reduced scantlings but still used brick and timber in the traditional ways. Mel'nikov sought a new approach: 'The fundamental principle of existing building is a concentrating of stresses into specific parts of the structure. My principle is the opposite, characterised by equal distribution; the dispersal of stresses over all parts of the structure.'[2] He saw this as the key to using low-grade, cheap materials. His 'opening up' of the medieval stuccoed-brick wall produced a load-spreading cage into which windows and insulation could be inserted as desired. His floors were entirely beamless: a two-way grille of notched planks stiffened by a 'structural' ceiling and floor, above and below, of diagonal tongued-and-grooved boarding, all notionally 'dropped in, like the top and bottom of a vast barrel.'[3]

Not for the Constructivists were such atavistic analogies. To them the progressive 'social task of architecture' was always paralleled by 'the technical task' of 'building rationally on the basis of the latest achievements of technology.'[4] With the Moscow Planetarium, the opportunity to demonstrate advanced technology came with the job.

In a newly atheistic state, this first planetarium had an ideological importance now hard to conceive. When foreign currency was extraordinarily scarce, Mossoviet were 'motivated by the possibility of promoting a wholesome scientific worldview in the population' that still clung to Genesis.[5] Aleksei Gan extolled it on the pages of *SA* as 'Our [Soviet] kind of theatre' where the individual 'extends his senses and perception . . . through a technological apparatus, allowing him to "see" 26 thousand years backwards and forwards.'[6] Given its prestige, any visitor will be struck by the awkwardly narrow site. This too resulted from deep, and indeed imaginative, educational principle. The young architects, Mikhail Barshch and Mikhail Siniavskii, explained in 1928: 'In the USSR, a planetarium must naturally be a place for popular dissemination of the theory of evolution.' Mossoviet and Glavnauk had therefore wanted it near the Moscow Zoo, 'in order to present as one whole the exhibition of non-organic evolution comprising the planetarium's astronomical museum, and the evolu-

Moscow Planetarium (Map Guide no 27): 8, 9 Netzwerk cupola details. 10 Concrete frame at ground level. 11 The Zeiss projection unit. 12 Section.

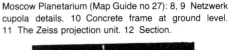

9

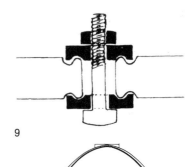

10        11        12

tionary sequences already planned in the Zoo Park directly alongside this site.'[7]

The 119-lamp optical unit from Carl Zeiss came as a package with Zeiss' hemispherical 'screen' and their patented anti-echo system of steel ribbons behind it. The architects commented on the extreme ease of erecting this Netzwerk hemisphere. The outer cupola was also a Netzwerk structure, with a thin concrete covering and insulation outside that, though its precise form was delineated 'for the Moscow skyline' by one of the founder-Constructivist artists, the Stenberg brothers. The architects were equally proud of their fine concrete frame below, and their neat flow diagrams of visitors' movement. An interesting, and sympathetic critique in Mossoviet's *Stroitel'stvo Moskvy*, however, criticised these for not maintaining the standards of 'logic and rationality' displayed by Zeiss: real 'economy' would have avoided taking heavy audiences up to the first floor at all, and saved much concrete thereby. The overall architectural treatment, though, was a model to its 'bourgeois predecessors abroad.'[8]

A planetarium would always be a one-off project, but Moisei Ginzburg's housing complex for fifty families of the Finance Ministry, NKFin, was treated programmatically as a test-bed for 'modern' techniques throughout state housing construction. Its social aspira-

tions, as the 'condenser' of a 'transitional' life-style, have been discussed elsewhere. Technically, it was 'an experiment in the possibilities of using concrete and reinforced concrete within an industrialised, mass-production system of housing construction'; in 'using new materials', and in 'examining the possibilities and cost-effectiveness of pre-casting components, by factory methods.'[9]

Totally new in Russia were the 'cold' (ie non-insulating) hollow blocks which his engineer, S L Prokhorov of Tekhbeton, applied for internal walls and the floor slabs. Blocks of identical form from 'slag concrete' used for outside walls were already known as the 'Peasant' system. Also new were the horizontal sliding windows, whose many space saving and draughtproofing advantages they advanced. They admitted learning much about the brittleness, heaviness and handling problems of precast elements; of exposure problems in stuccoed walls without protecting cornices. Here the long built-in window boxes had proved an unexpected if partial palliative.[10] In these discussions of their technical experiments, the avant-garde's engagement with their 'reality' is palpably real, whichever of the historic alternatives they see it pursuing.

Narkomfin Building (Map Guide no 28): 13 Period view. 14 Laying up hollow-block floors. 15 Parapet detail. 16 Sliding window details. 17 Pipework in internal walls.

13

14

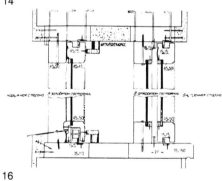

16

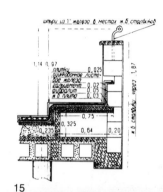

15

17

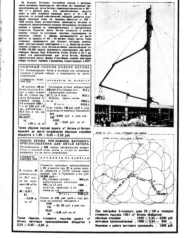

2 pages from *SA* 1926 no 3, deploring the building industry's 'WOODEN machinery from the age of Leonardo da Vinci', and expounding the economics and techniques of tower cranes.

**Notes**

1 George Heard Hamilton *The art and architecture of Russia* (Pelican History of Art, London, 1975), pp 114–5.
2 Mel'nikov, quoted in N Lukhmanov, 'Tsilindricheskii dom', *Stroitel'stvo Moskvy* 1929 no 4 pp 16–22.
3 Lukhmanov, ibid, p 18.
4 Slogans in *Sovremennaia arkhitektura* (*SA*), 1926 no 2 p 44.
5 M Barshch and M Siniavskii (presumed), 'Planetarii', *SA* 1927 no 3 p 80.
6 A Gan, 'Novomu teatru, novoe zdanie', *SA* 1927 no 3 p 81.
7 M Barshch and M Siniavskii, 'Planetarii v Moskve', *Stroitel'stvo Moskvy* 1928 no 8 pp 1–3.
8 A Zil'bert, 'Pervyi planetarii v SSSR', *Stroitel'stvo Moskvy* 1930 no 1 pp 30–32.
9 M Ia Ginzburg, *Zhilishche* (Moscow, 1934; written 1930–1), Chapter 5: 'Konstruktsiia, material, metody stroitel'nogo proizvodstva: opytny dom NKF', pp 98–102.
10 ibid.

# Andrei Chernikhov

# 'ARTIST SHOW US YOUR WORLD ...': IAKOV CHERNIKHOV 1889–1951[1]

*With this appreciation of his grandfather's work, Andrei Chernikhov opens a two-part feature on that well known but little read theorist and teacher, Iakov Chernikhov.*

*A year ago in AD (no 11–12 1982) I provided an introduction to Chernikhov's work in the context of the Royal College of Art exhibition, which 'reassembled', for the first time anywhere, his teaching curriculum and related theory of design, from the numerous books in which it was progressively expounded during the late twenties and early thirties. A few of the books are known in the West; others are virtually unknown items of antiquarian rarity.*

*The main components of that material are presented after this article, in a form derived directly from the exhibition. AD invited Andrei Chernikhov to complement that didactic distillation with a broader view.*

*In neither case are we concerned with Iakov Chernikhov's professional work, in the narrow sense, as a leader of major design offices for the chemical and other industries. A man of prodigious energy and output – assisted in execution of more mechanical works by the drafting team in his laboratory – he carried on several careers simultaneously, those of studio professor and author among them. Himself a team leader in a major Moscow design bureau, and well familiar with the thought processes of the computer age, Andrei Chernikhov shares his grandfather's view of the need for a symbiosis between speculative exploration of possible designs, and the day-to-day solution of design tasks in practice.*

*That principle assumed, he lays important stress on the nature of Suprematism, properly understood, as inspiration to his grandfather's work; on the underlying nature of the post-Classical formal revolution as Chernikhov perceived it, and on his view of history. Showing his fecundity as a creator of whole environments, he draws attention to the quantity of unpublished works that remain unknown. Two items are reproduced here from the numerous extraordinary series of 'invented architectures' of his later years – one retrospective, one forward-looking – which are published in the West for the first time.*

Catherine Cook

In Russia there are people, as there must be throughout the world, who either were born at the wrong time, or for whom time simply does not exist.

*Boris Pil'niak*

What now is proved was once only imagined.

*William Blake*

Thanks to the concreteness of building as an activity, and society's imperfect collective memory, architectural history hardly preserves even the names of those who created the great fictional architectures, of the architects whose destiny it was to be poetic visionaries of the future; whose ideas have a power independent of prevailing circumstances, but were not realised during their lifetimes.

In the short list of great architectural fantasists that has come down to us, the name of Iakov Chernikhov occupies a particular place, for he not only combined in his work functional, theoretical and aesthetic aspects of a future style, but he presented this style directly, on an artistic level, as a link in the organic chain of development running through the art of architecture. Behind the belated and somewhat hasty attention that he receives today lies a hidden feeling of the natural necessity for this recognition, combined with respect and slight awe for the creative artist who has already become an enigma.

On the one hand his achievement was a cosmopolitan one. On the other, he was inherently a phenomenon of post-Revolutionary Russia. It was a country where many of the ideas of twentieth-century art were being born out of a crucible of unprecedented shock, although art itself had till recently in Russia been a field that by no means reflected or expressed the general cultural level of the nation.

The Revolution transmitted its unique and blazing current to the pursuit of a new architecture, but in a country ruined and ravaged by fighting, architecture had no means of expression except the project and the declaration. This is certainly why Soviet architecture of the twenties now appears to many as a kind of *kunstkammer* of unrealised ideas.

In its whole and in its parts, the Russian avant-garde is a movement which tends to be viewed by the contemporary researcher through rose-coloured spectacles. At the same time, any attempt to understand this period must proceed from the fact that the majority of its innovators were creating their concepts in the name of the New Utopia which to them seemed already to have dawned, and precisely here lie the causes of the avant-garde's dramatic eclipse in the mid-thirties. They were the splendid, idealistic froth on the peak of a great historical wave, brilliantly identifying it yet having a short lifespan within it, and were retained in the subconscious of subsequent generations as a restless, tormented and beautiful past that was simultaneously unrepeatable.

Their activity embodied the playful spirit of renewal, hope and truth within the great transformation. At that level, which to them was real, Chernikhov's work may be seen as the embodiment of urges to express the collective will and the beautiful, to demonstrate the human gifts of forward-vision and fantasy. It embodies that same combination of knowledge with beauty whose energy we feel amongst the architects of Sumeria, Ancient Egypt and Greece, in the medieval Gothic and the High Renaissance. A fundamental difference between Chernikhov and the so-called 'leftists' is precisely his own feeling of belonging not only to the concrete, dynamic reality of the Revolution. He belonged not so much amongst the overturners of traditions and the iconoclasts as amongst those who recognised the real foundations, constantly aware of his own participation in the eternally valid rites of art. He was one of the few professionals of those years who, whilst understanding and accepting the historical necessity of the changes taking place, openly declared that innovation was not a bonfire of the old culture. For him the 'classics' which advocates of the new style, or more accurately the emergent style, were so zealously jettisoning from 'the ship of modernity', were important repositories of unchanging values.

Difficult as it is today, the twenties have to be understood, in the architectural context, not so much as an age of artists, as an age of inventors and discoverers, of ideologues and declamatory propagan-

66    Iakov Chernikhov, Memorial Museum to Revolutionary fighters, from *Fundamentals of Contemporary Architecture*, 1930.

Two 'coloured geometrical ornaments' by students of Chernikhov, from *Ornament*, 1930.

1 Iakov Chernikhov in the mid-thirties.

dists. This was not a period that history had designated to be a high point of architecture in the artistic sense. It merely delineated contours for the future. Neither poetry nor music had yet arrived at a new style, and there was still some time to go before 'modern architecture' would be raised to the level of art and stay there.

This does not at all mean that it lacked its own poets. Iakov Chernikhov was one of them: perhaps the most candid and sparkling representative of architectural futurology in Soviet Russia during the twenties and thirties. Today Chernikhov's architectural fantasies have become on the one hand synonymous with beautiful dreams, and on the other, a symbol of the real embodiment of research activities that were still, until quite recently, considered unnecessary and groundless.

*    *    *

Iakov Georgievich Chernikhov was born on December 17th 1889 in the quiet, patriarchal town of Pavlograd in the Ekaterinoslav gubernia of southern Little Russia, which is now the Dnepropetrovsk region of the Ukrainian Soviet Republic. Within the family, where there were ten children besides him, his parents had a love and understanding of art which they attempted to inculcate into the children. In 1906, Iakov Chernikhov left the parental home for Odessa, and entered the Odessa College of Art where he studied under two outstanding South-Russian artists and teachers of that period, Kariak K Kastandi and Gennadii A Lodyzhenskii. Of necessity his studies were frequently interrupted in pursuit of a livelihood. The benefits were a wide range of experience: at different times he worked as a stevedore in the port of Odessa, a retoucher, making cardboard boxes, doing photography and increasingly, as a teacher of drawing. As a result, by the time he left the College in 1914 he had already mastered many of the skills of graphics and their applications. This early teaching practice provided the impetus towards creating his own original pedagogical system in the future.

During the same year he moved to St Petersburg, where he enrolled simultaneously in the Painting Faculty of the Academy of Arts, and in the Academy's Higher Imperial Pedagogical Courses. In 1916 he

transferred from the Painting school to Architecture and entered the studio of Professor Leontii Nikolaevich Benua (Benois), whence he graduated in 1925 with the title of 'architect-artist', which distinguished the academically trained architect from those with a civil-engineering orientation. He then set up in Leningrad his own 'Research and Experimental Laboratory of Architectural Forms and Methods of Graphic Representation'.[2] Here, with the help of draughtsmen under his instruction, he prepared for publication the series of books that were to earn him the title of 'the Soviet Piranesi'.

At the same time he designed and built actively, most of his work being in industrial building and various areas of community architecture. He was constantly busy with teaching, first in a series of higher education establishments in Leningrad; then in Moscow, to which he moved in 1936, and where he died in 1951. He left behind him over fifty books, published and unpublished, in the fields of architecture, its methodology, and the various arts of drawing, and also more than seventeen thousand design drawings and works in various graphic media, covering an enormous range of genres.

He had first started to work in the field of graphic representation in 1912.[3] This work, concerned mainly with the development of Suprematist structures, was to become the foundation of his later highly original experiments in architecture, graphic work and teaching. His explorations in this field served as the basis for the method of teaching graphic representation which he developed during those years, and subsequently of the architectural disciplines rooted in non-objective principles which he called his 'Method of compositional invention'.[4]

Thus Chernikhov's starting point in advanced artistic issues was Suprematism, meaning, literally, at the level of the *highest* (Latin: *supremus*) and the *primary* simultaneously. More than once in its history, humanity has pursued a path of renewal, but each time art has marked this transition with its own 'suprematism', if we properly understand that term as meaning a graphically semantic conception of the world. But the level of knowledge, of 'intellect' of the preceding epoch determines the level and character of the 'suprematist revolution' at each successive stage up the spiral of human advance. Kazimir Malevich's *Black Square* was adjudged in its time to be the clean slate on which many of that period's ideas about art would be written. The basis of Suprematism – in other words non-objectivity – was the absence of any kind of utilitarian, 'meaning-loaded' burden in its compositions.

Chernikhov's main books of this period were the two unpublished volumes *Eksprimatika* and *Aristografiia*, and the *Course of Geometrical Drawing*.[5] They show him clearly as a theoretician of underlying philosophical aspects of Suprematism. They also show him anticipating by half a century certain graphic developments of our own times such as Op-art and computer graphics. Suprematism became an artistic phenomenon when it took possession of art, or, conversely, when art started to invade it. Up to that point, it was essentially an intellectual and speculative phenomenon.

Chernikhov communicated to his compositions that sensual colouration which brings these works properly into the category of art. But their essence is the result of another, higher level of creative energy. While Malevich in the last analysis created a philosophy of the non-objective, Chernikhov by his works reveals the nature of non-objectivity as an artistic principle and at the same time reveals the nature of Suprematism as art.

In working out the problems of Suprematism as a graphic ideology, Chernikhov saw it as something higher, and of a greater complexity, than just the organisation of space. Having approached them intuitively as an architect, it was natural that the further continuation of these experiments should be a system of purely architectural disciplines.

In 1929 he published his first major work, *Fundamentals of Contemporary Architecture*, which was a profound rethinking of such central architectural concepts as space, harmony, statics, functionality, construction (*konstruktsiia*), composition.[6] Being of the opinion that the classics had entered the twentieth century already static, and hence unable to manifest those 'life juices' that would allow them to grow and diversify creatively, Chernikhov expressed the idea that those *rhythms of repetition* which are the essence of most classical architecture must be replaced in twentieth century architecture by a *rhythm of relationships*. In its fullest implications, this would be the vital central factor of the architectural revolution.

*Fundamentals of Contemporary Architecture* contained models of abstract compositional work in the field of architectural forms. At the same time, Chernikhov's method of building up these compositions permitted him to obtain in each case a perfectly concrete, 'realistic', building form that expressed a quite specific set of architectural intentions and converted his underlying ideas into form with perfect clarity. In its publication *Fundamentals* was extremely timely, appearing as it did when investigations towards a new style had essentially only just begun, and methodological questions were still issues of primary importance, and great currency. It served not only as a declaration about the proper path of the new architecture; it was also a textbook for achieving it.

When he followed this up with *The Construction of Architectural and Machine Forms* in 1931, Chernikhov investigated the constructive approach as a natural phenomenon inherent to the organisation of life in its most diverse forms and conditions.[7] This in itself distinguished the work of this period from that of 'incorporeal', 'disembodied' Suprematism. He also formulated the fundamental laws of such an approach. Displaying them graphically in his drawings, he unfolded before the reader as it were a panorama of constructive situations, from the simplest cases of interaction between geometrical and physical bodies right up to complex combinations of forms at the architectural scale. A special place in his scheme of things belongs to the machine, which he saw as the embodiment of constructive principles in their purest form, and therefore accorded a central role as the 'symbol of faith' in the twentieth century. At the same time he was far from idolising it. Rather the opposite: unlike many architects, who had vulgarised the art of architecture in their passion for machinery, his way of glorifying the machine was a subordination of it to the laws of art, not the other way round.

Chernikhov believed that any building which imitated or decked itself out like a machine – or, incidentally, did the same with natural forms – was in its essence alien to architecture, since it is founded on a false conception of the main stimulus of construction (*stroitel'stvo*) itself.' He saw the asceticism of contemporary architectural forms as a temporary phenomenon; as no more than the submission to an economic obligation. He maintained that 'architecture becomes art at that moment when its created forms are perceived as something valuable at an aesthetic level, and the aesethetic definitions of the concepts of space and mass which we encounter throughout almost the entire history of the arts must be supplemented by an understanding of them as distinct artistic form and specifically artistic form-making.'

When the book *Architectural Fictions: 101 Compositions* was published in 1933, his cycle of treatises on contemporary architecture was effectively completed.[8] It was a cycle that contained numerous unpublished volumes too, most notably perhaps the richly illustrated volumes of *Architectural Miniatures, Tales of Industry* and *The Architecture of Industrial Buildings*.[9] Bringing together compositions of most diverse subject matter, ranging from individual industrial and public buildings to entire town-planning structures and architectural compositions of an abstract musical character, the *arkhitekturnye fantazii* constituted an original kind of poem to the scale, beauty and formal richness of the new architecture.

\*    \*    \*

From the published books of Iakov Chernikhov one imagines an architect of exclusively constructive preoccupation. In reality this was

2  Combination of extended ovals, *The Construction of Architectural and Machine Forms*, 1931, fig 80.
3  Asymmetry net, *Ornament*, 1931, fig 606.

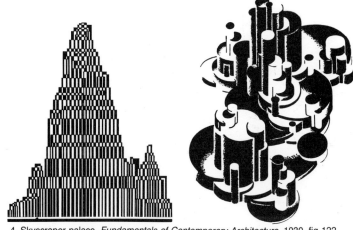

4  Skyscraper palace, *Fundamentals of Contemporary Architecture*, 1930, fig 122.
5  Chemical volumes, *The Construction*, fig 250.

6  Routes to the machine, *The Construction*, fig 210.
7  Machine architecture: a fiction, *The Construction*, fig 168.

8  Grandiose monolith, *The Construction*, fig 245.

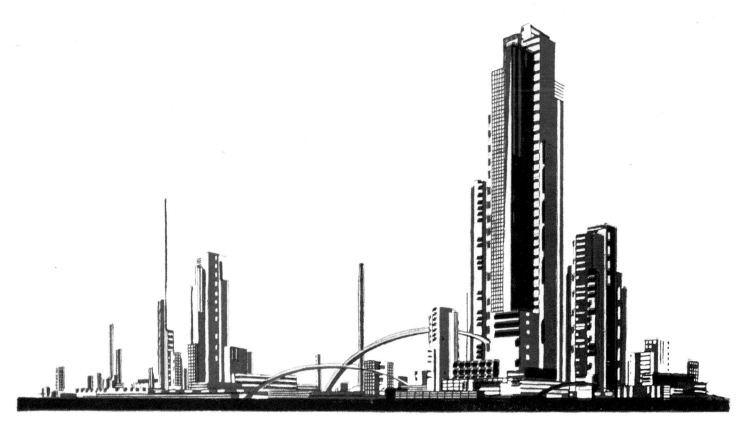

Above, from Chernikhov's series of drawings *City of the Future*. Below, 'Architectural invention of a complex type unifying rectilinear and curvilinear forms on constructive principles'. Opposite: two drawings from Chernikhov's series *Tales of Industry*. Above, 'Complex forms in a strict rhythmic perspective'. Below, 'Open girder structure of conveyors: a powerfully expressive construction in space.'

only one component of his creative output. Since a very large amount of his work was never published it is difficult for anyone interested in his oeuvre to judge the real scope of his talents.

At the same time as he was investigating problems of architecture in today's world, Chernikhov was producing cycles of numerous richly inventive compositions entitled *Painterly Architecture*, from which included the *Architectural Fairytales*, *Architectural Romances*, *Ancient Towns*, *The Architecture of Rural Buildings*, and a series of other experimental works.[10] Some of his *Fairytales* recreated the atmosphere of past styles that are familiar to us, like those of ancient Italy or medieval Russia. Others reconstructed whole worlds inhabited by peoples of whom no physical environments remain to us – environments of ancient Babylon and the Neolithic age. He offers us waking dreams here – the possibility to enter into the worlds of which we have no documentary record. Our knowledge of architecture since the Renaissance is inseparable from the architectural speculations of men like Leonardo da Vinci, Piranesi, Boullée, Mendelsohn, Sant Elia or the Russian Constructivists. Of earlier eras we know nothing except what we can learn from their actual structures. We do not know, and never can, what those ancient architects dreamed about, what worlds and compositions filled their imaginations. They may have thought only in terms of clearly established canons, but the very nature of architectural thinking contradicts that point of view. There can be no question that always, in all epochs, builders have dreamed and fantasised about structures and compositions unattainable to them. Chernikhov's ability to sublimate knowledge about the essence of the future attests to the fact that all temporal existence is relative.

This may be the explanation for the fact that right through the middle thirties and the forties Chernikhov maintained his capacity to invent and to demonstrate new directions of his talent as an architectural fantasist where many of the consistent Constructivists were not. From that period we have a series of works on *The Architecture of Palaces* which comprises extensive groups of studies for *The Architecture of the Future*, *Architectural Ensembles*, the *Architecture of Bridges* and *Palaces of Communism*.[11]

The years 1943–45 saw him producing a great suite of *Pantheons of the Second World War* which embodied and reflected the events, the shocks, the tragedies and grandeur of wartime consciousness in Russia.[12] Interspersed with these emotive subjects were simpler bits of research into 'Entasis and the shafts of columns', 'The anatomy of buildings', 'Methods of representation', 'The design of classical letter-forms' and much else.

Having developed the capacity to live amongst a myriad of ideas simultaneously, Chernikhov found the genre of the 'architectural fiction' to be his most powerful medium of expression, combining as it did the spatial and graphic elements of architecture. Works of this kind, with this coherence and power, have a life that is independent of the 'real', just as paintings or sculpture do. Not being part of a widespread movement, they are difficult to classify either internally or externally. Chernikhov determined his own goals and no part of his wide-ranging activity – except the purely professional design work – is a direct response to any particular external programme in the 'outside' world. In the end, his private worlds are an assertion that beauty is the highest aspiration of the architect when he builds in the real world, and that 'beauty' resides in a music and poetry of spaces. In his foreword to *Fundamentals of Contemporary Architecture* he himself expressed it thus:

> In its steadfast forward movement, the architecture of our time has made more than a few mistakes, but in the final result will be created a powerful embodiment of the human vision in spatial and volumetric forms. One must create; one must manifest one's own creative capacities and summon to creativity those who are inert, in order that life within the art of architecture should be in a state of maximum movement.

9 Ancient Russian townscape, from the series *Architectural Romances*, 1930.

10 Palace of the wonders of technology, from the series *Palaces of Communism*, 1934–41.

## Notes

1 Opening words of the inscription on the Darmstadt Architecture Exhibition main building: 'Seine welt zeige der Künstler die nie war und nie sein wirdl.'
2 *Nauchno-issledovatel'skaia laboratoriia arkhitekturnykh form i metodov graficheskikh iskusstv*
3 This refers to work in the field of *nachertaniia*, which has somewhat more technical connotations than *risovaniia*, or sketching.
4 *Metod kompozitsionnogo sochinitel'stva*
5 *Kurs geometricheskogo chercheniia* (Leningrad, 1928).
6 *Osnovy sovremennoi arkhitektury* (Leningrad, 1930)
7 *Konstruktsiia arkhitekturnykh i mashinykh form* (Leningrad, 1931)
8 *Arkhitekturnye fantasii: 101 kompozitsii* (Moscow-Leningrad, 1933)
9 *Arkhitekturnye miniatury; Skazki industrii; Arkhitektura promyshlennikh zdanii*
10 *Zhivopisnaia arkhitektura*, including *Arkhitekturnye skazki; Arkhitekturnaia romantika; Starye goroda; Arkhitekura dereviannykh stroenii*
11 *Arkhitektura dvortsov*, including *Arkhitekturnye ansembli; Arkhitektura budushchego; Arkhitektura mostov; Dvortsy kommunizma*
12 *Panteony Velikoi Otechestvennoi voiny*

CATHERINE COOKE

# ЧЕРНИХОВ ■ CHERNIKHOV
# The construction of architectural and ■ machine forms ■

Pages from Iakov Chernikhov's seven published books:
*The Art of Graphic Representation*, 1927
*A Course of Geometrical Drawing*, 1928
*Ornament: Classically Composed Structures*, 1930
*The Fundamentals of Contemporary Architecture*, 1930
*The Construction of Architectural & Machine Forms*, 1931
*Architectural Fictions 101 Compositions*, 1933
*The Construction of Letter Forms*, posthumously, 1958.

Architectural books are one of the themes of this issue. Russia's first, in Peter the Great's era, would have been broadly familiar to us in their content, being versions of established European texts. For Moisei Ginzburg's seminal work of Constructivist architectural theory two hundred years later, *Style and Epoch*, we now have a translation by Anatole Senkevitch from MIT Press. No practicing architect of the avant garde period, however, had a record of book publishing in architectural theory to compare in extent with that of Iakov Chernikhov.

Six substantial works appeared during the seven years 1927-33. Each one of them speaks of a rational and highly ordered approach to design and the education of students, yet each one, read in isolation, is confusing by its incompleteness. No one book presents the whole of what gradually emerges, on fuller examination, to be a detailed course of liberating, stimulating education in the fundamental disciplines of three-dimensional design as they are encountered in the complex functional and expressive tasks addressed by architecture.

Even the central ideas of his theory lie scattered amongst extreme specifics of pedagogy across the whole sequence of books. Yet the power and coherence of this Leningrad professor's approach is extraordinary, and extraordinarily relevant to the concerns of architecture today. On the one hand, it addresses the underlying disciplines required if architecture, as traditionally understood, is to profit from the form-generating power of computers. On the other, it analyses the means whereby architecture can re-equip itself aesthetically in response to demands that it be 'expressive'.

In an exhibition shown in London earlier this year, which took its title from his theoretically most powerful book of 1931, I presented for the first time a distillation of Chernikhov's programme, assembled from detailed study of his written oeuvre. Shortly to be published as an *AD* special profile is a book which brings together this detailed exposition assembled from his own scattered words in the exhibition, and a fully illustrated translation of that central theoretical treatise, *The Construction of Architectural and Machine Forms*. The book's title, *Fantasy and Construction*, encapsulates Chernikhov's great theme: that the capacity for fertile invention in architecture – the capacity to 'fantasise' – is only developed through progressive and systematic tasks in the 'construction' of ever more complex formal entities and compositions according to the fundamental laws governing the relationships of bodies in three-dimensional space.

Readers are refered to the article 'Iakov Chernikhov: what lies behind the *Fantasies*?' (*AD* 11-12 1983), where I discussed the relationship between Chernikhov's theory of a 'constructive' approach to formal composition, and the larger 'design method' of the Constructivist movement lead by Ginzburg and the Vesnin brothers from which Chernikhov was quite independent. That relationship should be clarified by the full exposition of the Constructivists' 'method' published here (pp 35-50 above), where Chernikhov's work may be seen as detailed elaboration of 'the 3rd object'.

The exhibition comprised the following sections.

1* Chernikhov's life. 2* His books. 3 Background (a)* The combinatorial approach in traditional Russian architecture (b) The machine as inspiration in the 1920s. 4 Underlying themes: Art and technology; Constructive principles; Teaching design. 5 The elements of form: elements on a plane (1) Linear elements (2) Planar elements. 6* The elements of form: elements in space (1) Planes (2) Surfaces (3) Volumes. 7* Types of constructive joint. 8* Force in constructions. 9* Constructiveness as a high level of creative energy. 10* Classes of constructive solution. 11 Classes of spatial idea. 12* Functionality and legitimacy. 13* Harmony: new anti-classical principles. 14* Rhythm in constructions. 15 Dynamics of static forms. 16 Constructive melodies. 17* The harmony of colours.

An asterisk indicates that the section is illustrated below, in views of the exhibition or as a text. *Fantasy and Construction* contains all sections fully footnoted to their sources in Chernikhov's various books.

Typographical aspects of the original show, based on Chernikhov's own style, were designed by Gillian Crampton Smith. Models were made by Cyril Hughes.

## Fantasy and Construction: Iakov Chernikhov's Approach to Architectural Design Catherine Cooke

Includes the first English translation of Chernikhov's *Construction of Architectural and Machine Forms*, 1931. Academy Editions, St Martin's Press 27.8 x 22.2 cm, 80 pages, over 200 illustrations including many in colour. ISBN 0 85670 841 0  Paperback  £ 7.50  $ 16.95  This *AD* special profile will be dispatched as soon as available: to reserve your copy send £ 7.50 + £ 2. p&p to: *Architectural Design*, 7 Holland Street, London W8.

'The Construction of Architectural and Machine Forms', Royal College of Art, London, March 1983: Entrance wall. Chernikhov's life and books.

Background section, The combinatorial approach in traditional Russian architecture, based on studies of volumetric structure by V I Pluzhnikov.

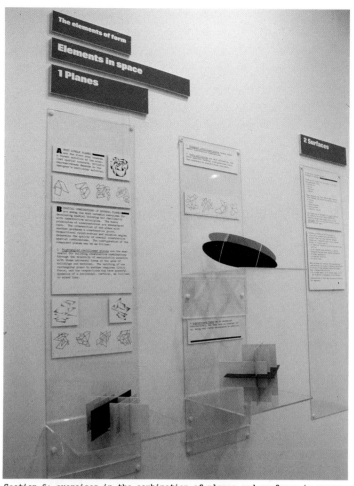

Section 6: exercises in the combination of planes and surfaces in space

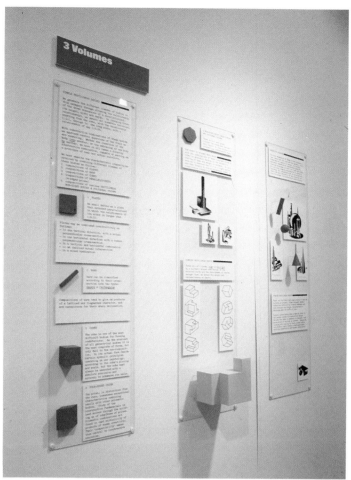

Section 6: exercises in the combination of simple volumes

Detail of section 7, Types of constructive joint: models from Chernikhov's compositions exemplifying 'penetration', 'embracing', 'mounting' and others coloured in the traditional white, gold and green of rural churches.

# Harmony: new anti-classical principles

Lev Tolstoi regarded art as that activity through which one person consciously transmits, through certain eternal signs, the feelings he has experienced, and other people are infected by those feelings, which influence their lives. In this definition there is already a clear conception of the great social mission of art. Art socialises human feelings, unifies the vast multitude of consumers of it on the basis of a collaborative living experience, on the basis of the 'infectiousness' of the beautiful.

Equally important to a correct understanding of of the nature of art and the essence of the beautiful are the views developed by Marx, as the first to see art as part of the superstructure of the economic base, and those others who endorsed the materialist analysis of the history of art.

The conception of beauty in our time is not determined by the cost of materials, not by their richness and variety, but by the compositional and constructive appropriateness, or by the expressiveness, level of resolution and formal consistency with which the final object manifests its function and social purpose.

Even an industrial building must attempt to be beautiful, as well as pleasant, convenient, light and joyful.
   Any worker can work better amidst the very best combination of surrounding walls and ceilings. Coming to the factory, or leaving it, the worker must perceive an interaction of exterior forms that helps raise his mood, and stimulate him to life, work and creativity.
   The enjoyment of beauty will become an inalienable property and condition of existence of the individual.

Thus the architect is required to create an object that answers aesthetic concerns and the requirements of convenience to an identical degree, and gives a clear visual answer to both.

Classical aesthetics as historically developed were based upon:

1  enforced symmetry of structure ▆▆▆▆

2  the rhythm of simple repetition ▆▆▆▆

3  combination of different component elements on universally 'beautiful' principles ▆▆▆

The first two of these compositional principles are too partial to serve as a basis for us. We have to look to other sources of formal harmony. Many such principles were present in classical work, but hidden. Their elucidation is amongst the most interesting of our present tasks, the main ones being:

1  free assymetries in the assembly of the elements on functional principles ▆▆▆▆

2  The minimum use of simple repetitive rhythms and their replacement by the rhythm of dynamic diversified combinations▆

3  the harmonic interrelationship of the component elements by the subtle proportions of their vertical and horizontal dimensions ▆▆▆▆

4  adjustment of the tonal force of component elements in accordance with the impressions sought of the viewer ▆▆▆▆

5  maximally expressive use of colour effects to manifest the constructive and other characteristics of the planes and surfaces being treated. ▆▆▆▆

These are the rules which must be the basis of the new harmonies.

Through appropriate training in these compositional fundamentals we must nurture in ourselves the most precisely tuned feelings for combining all the component elements of a form.

# Force in constructions

The two concepts of **Force** and **Construction** are inseparably connected.

Construction is inconceivable without the presence of force. They complement eachother functionally, but in various different ways.

**1** Force expended in the jointing process ▆▆

Certain forms of constructive joint cannot occur without the application of a specific level of force being applied. Thus, in the COUPLING of parts we exert the LOWEST level of force. The PENETRATION of one element into another requires a SECOND LEVEL of force to be applied. In EMBRACING and the CLAMPING of one part by another we see the THIRD LEVEL of force. ▆▆▆▆

**2** Force as the action of weight ▆▆▆▆

Force is present in constructive compositions when we observe the action of weight or heaviness in a specific part of the whole assembled object. ▆▆▆▆

**3** The force of influence ▆▆▆▆

This force is measured by the strength of the impression which the constructive product makes upon each of us. The longer that impression remains in our consciousness, the stronger the force of influence. ▆▆▆▆

**4** The force of dynamics ▆▆▆▆

The dynamics manifested as movement in a constructive composition represent a subtle but powerful union of complex phenomena, operating in a coordinated way upon our psyche and giving us the possibility to feel a higher form of emotional sensation. ▆▆▆▆

# Constructiveness as a high level of creative energy

Every person is endowed with the feeling for the CONSTRUCTIVE. But that feeling expresses itself in the most diverse ways and in different intensities. ▆▆▆▆

There are sudden moments of constructive inspiration, when new solutions and new ideas flow extremely rapidly in our creations. The force of the energy in these valuable moments can be measured only by the real results that follow.

In contrast, there are depressive moments, when we lack any feeling for construction, and when the desire to resolve a problem constructively has atrophied. Then we desire to create more PEACEFUL compositions - compositions that are less demanding to formulate, than a constructive composition. In such cases we enter into the stream of as-it-were 'minimum consumption' of constructive principles, and we ignore the constructive possibilities.
This coincides with a LOWERING OF CREATIVE ENERGY but it can also be an appropriate creative response in certain situations.

It is necessary therefore to recognise the unarguable fact that the act of CONSTRUCTION must be regarded as a complex and powerful experience. ▆▆▆▆

On the basis of what has been said above, we can propose the following hierarchy of feelings for the constructive:

**1** Higher moments of individual inspiration with its maximum tension.

**2** Commonplace, everyday experiences, in accordance with the given requirements and solutions.

**3** The depressive condition, as a result of which other approaches to designing ones object will be pursued.

**4** An indifferent attitude to the questions of constructivism and as a result an atrophying of the feeling for constructiveness.

**5** Absolute non-comprehension of the very nature of constructive principles and, as a result, a complete ignoring of this approach to design in all situations regardless of their characteristics.

Not every task can be solved constructively,▪ and we must never ARTIFICIALLY IMPOSE ▪▪▪ constructive forms in our creative work. ▪▪▪

# Functionality and legitimacy

The things that can be unified on the basis of constructive principles may be both material and non-material, but they are always subject to the recording action of our brain by means of SIGHT, HEARING and TOUCH.

Every new construction is a result of a human being's INVESTIGATIONS, and of his requirement to be inventive and creative. ▪▪▪

## Functionality
funktsional'nost'
means that every aspect of the real forms and their interconnections derives from the actions which have given birth to that form. ▪▪▪

Every constructive solution must have a MOTIVE on the basis of which the construction is made

Every constructive composition must fulfill its IDEOLOGY and reflect the TOTALITY of the idea underlying it.

Every construction is a construction ONLY when the unification of those elements in that way can be rationally JUSTIFIED.

The greater the RATIONALITY in a construction, the more valuable it is; in other words, the significance of constructivism lies in its RATIONALITY. ▪▪▪

## Legitimacy
opravdannost'
in all constructive structures depends upon our being simultaneously able to prove the TRUTH and CORRECTNESS of the chosen solution BY ANALYTICAL MEANS.
The form we have devised is LEGITIMATE to the extent that it is JUSTIFIABLE. ▪▪▪

In all design we face the necessity of giving foundations to, and thereby as it were legitimising the construction that we have finally adopted.
We must prove that the construction which we are proposing is correct and fits the case concerned. ▪▪▪

# Classes of constructive solution

The wealth of forms in general and the diversity of possible combinations of different elements make the range of possible constructive solutions infinitely great. This does not at all ease the task of classifying constructions by types, given the lack of precision pervading this whole issue. However, we can classify constructive solutions according to their generally dominating properties. On this basis, we can distinguish the following general types:

## 1 Amalgamation ▪▪▪
ob"edinenie

Amalgamation of forms can occur by bringing together either identical elements, or different variants of the same element.

Amalgamation also includes the case when we receive the impression of a constructive solution simply by skillfully 'putting together' components without making any real constructive connections.

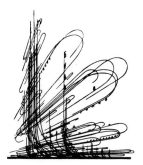

## 2 Combination ▪▪▪
soedinenie

A combination usually comprises elements which can come together without violating each other. In combining one body with another we study the particular characteristics of each, and if there are factors impeding their combination, these will represent a serious obstacle to executing the combination at all. The form and configuration of the elements themselves may provide obstacles. So too may their positions in relation to the surrounding space. In combining one element to another we are pursuing harmony. The very unity of the composition depends upon the fact that no antipathetic elements are present. 'Combination' often requires 'third parties', elements that serve to unify the rest.

## 3 Assemblage ▪▪▪
sochlenenie

Assemblage can be characterised by the constructive look which finds particular reflection in the machine. The elements maintain their separate identities whilst being grouped into one whole. The principle of assemblage also implies that only a certain combination of specific parts is capable of creating the required solution; the absence of any one part may prevent the task being solved. As a result, the structure of the composition is often visually evident. Each component part in such an assemblage requires careful attention since only the absolute fit of parts is capable of producing the required effect. The designer has to give formal coherence to the parts of an assemblage as well as functional cohesion.

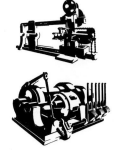

## 4 Conjugation ▪▪▪
sopriazhenie

Conjugation is the phenomenon which permits a transition from one condition of a form to another; or from one variant of a form into another. When the forms are lines, the task is fairly simple, though still interesting. When we conjugate complex objects, the task is both richer and more complicated. The integrity and constructive properties of the composition must be preserved in the transition.

Conjugation of elements is one of the most powerful tools the designer possesses, since it permits him to achieve those complex transformations which his inventive capacity dictates. By conjugation we can move freely from a configuration of one kind to a new configuration of quite another type, moving not only painlessly, but also rationally and meaningfully. The conjugation of elements occupies a large place in the life of every individual in his various forms of creativity, and we must pay it the maximum of attention.

A composition successfully derived by conjugation acquires dynamic properties from the fluency of the transitions.

# The harmony of colours

Rhythmic movements of space and volumes can be augmented by colour harmonies. The coordination of colour with the formal rhythm, and the use of colour itself as a rhythmic device, are always important, but especially so in interiors, and in large urban ensembles. The colour impression produced by a given building may be influenced by

1 the factural treatment of natural materials, whose diversity can be further enriched by skillful selection of surface treatments

2 applied colours, such as paints, where an infinite diversity of colour combinations are possible for strengthening the architect's concept

3 selected combinations of technologically produced materials such as concrete, glass, steel. These are giving the contemporary designer new tools for formal composition and expression and hence creating whole new types of rhythm and harmony.

Different colour harmonies produce radically different effects. Examples show that dark brown, dark red, dark grey and black will produce the impression of a dirty heavy building that is dirty and heavy. They give 'weight' and monumentality, where green, yellow, sky-blue, light-grey, and white, give a building a cheerful, light and invigorating look. By fragmentation of colours we approach that polychrome decorativeness characteristic of architecture in the East, the Ancient World and the Middle Ages.

Harmonic planning of a building's colours may do the following:

- convey lightness or heaviness

- create a gloomy or cheerful atmosphere

- give unity or fragmentedness

- underline or distract from selected formal characteristics of the building or its components

- surpress dominating or protruding masses or bring forward recessive ones

- enhance the illumination of internal accommodation

- create some particular atmosphere through decorative effects on the planes and volumes of the mass.

In order to learn the mastery of combining colours in architectural constructions, it is necessary to develop a familiarity with the fundamentals of harmonic colour composition in spatial structures through colouring constructive, non-objective compositions.

Thus we execute a series of special exercises in so-called 'coloured ornaments', each requiring the student to obtain a specific effect of colour on some geometrical figure or a graphic construction he has already created in his study of form.

The simple name of a colour says nothing about what tones or 'gradations' of hue it possesses. 'Red' may mean vermillion, red ochre, carmine and all the other so-called 'red' colours. We know equally many 'yellow' colours: light ochre, ochre, cadmium, lemon yellow, light and dark chrome and so on. We have to study a colour in all its various gradations and tones.

Thus we take for example a series of planes in a compact constructive composition and fully harmonic relationship. The planes are to be coloured either with different gradations of a single colour, or in multi-coloured combinations. The colouring itself can be applied in different ways, overall, 'from the corners'; as dense or transparent colour.

Then we make it a rule that every architectural fantasy must be turned into a coloured image, given perhaps a minimum number of colours or paints, creating harmony by the selection of the actual colours, their strength and their tonality.

2

1

3

4

5

● *Geometry and colour in Russian historical architecture of pre-classical periods.*

*ABOVE:* Experimental composition from the series 'Principles of architecture': an architectural fantasy on the theme 'City of the East'.

*RIGHT:* Compositions numbers 61 & 91 from Chernikhov's *Architectural Fictions 101 Compositions* published 1933.
*Above:* An architectural composition of wooden towers demonstrating lightness through a constructive amalgamation of components. These are articulated by a manifestly 'artificial' colour scheme.
*Below:* Axonometric view of an integrated industrial complex. Saturated colouring of the architectural elements in non-bright tones against a brilliantly coloured partial background.

*LEFT: Geometry and colour in Russian historical architecture of pre-classical periods.*

These examples have a triple purpose. FIRSTLY, they illustrate the evolution taking place over the period preceding Peter the Great's programmatic introduction of classicism, discussed by Lindsey Hughes in opening sections of her article, above. SECONDLY, they indicate the kinds of architecture to which Chernikhov is refering when he speaks here of 'the polychrome decorativeness characteristic of architecture in the Middle Ages' in Russia, as a starting point for his reintroduction of colour harmonies into Soviet architecture. THIRDLY, they further elaborate themes of the exhibition's background section on 'The combinatorial approach in traditional Russian architecture' (p 74 above).

That section illustrated the diversity of compositions constructed according to the established rules of Russian church design in vernacular examples of the limited period 1695–1730. Figures 1–5 here illustrate innovative changes in the rule-system itself under the influence of an 'avant garde' amongst aristocratic patrons.

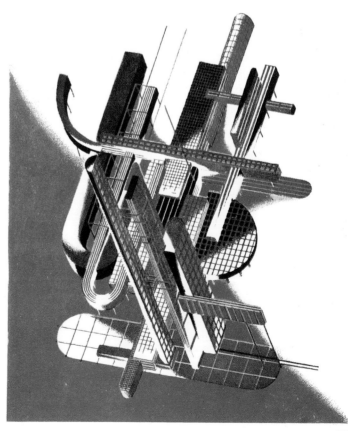

● 1  St Basil's Cathedral, Moscow, built to the orders of Ivan III in 1555: one of the high points of Russian medieval architecture, in both its diversity of form and its rich polychrome.
2  Domestic architecture of the Russian upper classes in the 16th and early 17th centuries: a particularly fine example of the large urban mansion recently revealed under a neo-classical remodelling in central Moscow. Proto-classical elements around windows and in banding derive in fact from timber architecture at this date.
3  Church of the Birth of Christ in the village of Izmailovo, near Moscow, in the estate of Peter's father Tsar Aleksei Mikhailovich, 1676. A conservative use of the traditional Russian forms and details for its date (gateway later), under a highly conservative patron.
4  A high point of the Moscow or Naryshkin Baroque of the late 17th century: church of the Intercession at Fili, one of the Naryshkin family estates in SW Moscow, 1693–4. The typical dynamic imposition of different plan forms into a single pyramidal composition, with elements of classical detailing.
5  Church of the Archangel Gabriel built and designed by Ivan Zarudy for Peter's favourite, A D Menshikov, in Moscow in 1701–7 (the so-called Menshikov Tower). A turning point in Russian architecture for its overtly classical detailing and vertical composition. Its successor, in St Petersburg, was the Cathedral of the Peter and Paul Fortress. (phs Catherine Cooke)

# Rhythm in constructions

In the old aesthetics, rhythm was any periodic movement or regular repetition of elements.

The new aesthetic uses rhythm of a different kind, 'of a higher order', rooted in subtler harmonies constructed from:

1 - relations of overall masses

2 - mutual interlinking of weight of parts

3 - appropriate 'percussiveness' of individual contiguous parts

4 - general coordination of elements of a highly colouredness

5 - generalised advancement of general dominating impression

6 - tonal deviations, (above and below the general base) of the component elements

7 - regular shifts in the whole side (forward, back, left, right etc.) of component elements

The rhythm inherent to music is kinetic, and clearly manifest. By contrast, rhythm is embodied in depictive art through principles of latent dynamics. These must operate at the level of the art-work's basic properties, which are of 4 types:

● Spatial

● Motor

● Compositional

● Formal

Rhythm must therefore be examined in relation to each of these, through the following questions:

1 How is rhythm <u>distributed in space</u>?

2 What <u>motor character</u> does the movement have?

The motor characteristics of rhythm are:

Height     Extension (width and depth)

Direction  Form  Impression

Movement   Consistency or sequentialness

Speed  Force  Reaction

The 4 directions of rhythmic movement communicate the following ideas:

(a) horizontal movement forward expresses <u>feeling</u>

(b) horizontal movement sideways expresses <u>will</u> and <u>influence</u>

(c) vertical movement upwards represents <u>thought</u>

(d) vertical movement in depth represents <u>confidence</u>

3 By what <u>compositional means</u> is the result being sought?

4 How are <u>formal means</u> applied to obtain the required effect?

In constructive design, rhythm will be a property of the composition's <u>constructive</u> elements, not its decorative ones.

Many perceptual aspects of constructive rhythm do not submit to speculative analysis.

Our task is to elucidate relevant factors empirically.

**Without pretending to be exhaustive, we can identify the following types of constructive rhythm:**

1 Percussive rhythm ▊▊▊▊▊▊▊▊

in which either: identical forms repeat themselves regularly

or: regular gestures involve different forms, configurations or displacements

2 Rhythm of vertical or horizontal transitions▊

in which non-identical, variously spaced elements create a harmonic pattern of either: ascending and descending

or: advancing and distancing

3 Rhythm of stable linkages ▊▊▊▊▊▊▊

in which constructively linked parts move in coordination against a fixed and stable base.

4 Rhythm of heaviness ▊▊▊▊▊▊▊▊

in which constructively combined masses are piled up so that they overwhelm their bearing. The totality may be stable or unstable, according to the psychological effect desired. This rythm is often the basis of monumentality.

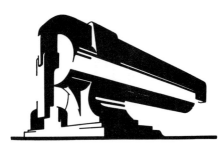

5 Rhythm of stratification ▊▊▊▊▊▊

created when we are assembling elements that are all either horizontally recumbent or vertically standing, within certain extended ratios of height to length

6 Rhythm of expansive curvature ▊▊▊▊▊

when the aspirational character of individual curvilinear forms is cordinated into a single dynamic

7 Rhythm of load-bearing moments ▊▊▊▊

through a harmonic relationship of the loads being carried by constructive bearing members and the spatial configuration in which they act.

# Catherine Cooke
# MOSCOW MAP GUIDE 1900–1930

This Map Guide owes its inspiration to the exhibition *Moscow-Paris 1900–1930*, shown in the Pushkin Fine Arts Museum, Moscow, in the summer of 1981 (*AD* 1981 no 10–11), and it has likewise extended its period on either side of those dates.

The architectural climax of the exhibition was provided by two major competitions, for the Palace of Soviets and the Commissariat of Heavy Industry, which extended the period up to 1934. In the present context these are represented by identification of their sites. The listed buildings end with four major complexes whose construction extended (in the case of two Clubs and the *Pravda* building) well into the thirties, and in one case (the Lenin Library) through the whole decade.

At the beginning of the period, there are twenty representatives of the late 1890s. Some were still under construction, of course, well into the 1900s, but their purpose here is to give some background on sources and precursors of the movements which dominate the pre-War years, in particular to the most complex and most easily misunderstood movement of the *Moderne*. This was both synthetic, and highly original. The elements and sources of its synthesis were extremely varied; what they shared in the eyes of their analysts and adherents was a certain constructive honesty and integrity. They included elements of European Art Nouveau and Arts-and-Crafts work and of Rationalism in the late nineteenth-century and Wagnerian mould. To a certain extent they included as well elements of the European Gothic (which is why the listing goes back, as the exhibition did, to Shekhtel's no 24, of 1893), but most particularly, the *Moderne* was influenced by the freely constructive aesthetic of the Russian vernacular in various periods that re-emerged as the Neo-Russian movement (which is why the listing goes back finally to no 132, and Viktor Vasnetsov's house of 1892).

There are problems in presenting this material when the paucity of the literature makes it difficult for the Western architecural tourist to know what he is looking at. Rather than append a background essay I have enlarged individual building notes beyond what is normal in *AD* Map Guides. Covering as this one does two very different and innovative periods that bridge a major revolution in social attitudes and economic structures, no short introduction can be adequate in the face of the architecture's astonishing diversity. It is hoped that careful reading and cross-connecting of these notes on the buildings themselves will build up that background and context around them more appropriately.

Since time is always short in the Soviet Union, notes on preliminary reading may be useful, though without Russian language much of it can only offer visual material.

For a brief discussion of the nature of the *Moderne*, of its leading architect and one of his best works, see my own 'Fedor Shekhtel': Derozhinskaia's Mansion 1901' in *AD* 1980 1/2 ('New Free Style') pp 82–3. Also relevant to this Guide are my 'Russian Perspectives' in *AD* 1980 3/4 ('Viollet-le-Duc') pp 60–3, and the latter part of Evgeniia Kirichenko's 'Theoretical Attitudes to Architecture in Russia 1830–1910s' in *AAQ* vol 11 no 2 1979 (Russian issue) pp 9–23, where five important buildings on the present pre-1917 list are illustrated. The same issue also contains a good account of the Palace of Soviets competition; an article of current relevance on early Vesnin work from neo-classicism to Constructivism in the context of the Palace of Labour, and a review article referring to recent Soviet and Western publications on the present period.

All the following items by Kirichenko have been available in the West (some are still available at time of writing): *Moscow. Architectural Monuments 1830s–1910s* (Iskusstvo, Moscow, 1977; superb b+w photos; background essay in English); *Russkaia Arkhitektura 1830–1910x gg* (Iskusstvo, Moscow, 1978; covers all Russia in this period; some thirty listed buildings illustrated; only the index to illustrations is in English); *Moskva na rubezhe stoletii* (*Moscow at the Turn of the Century*; Stroiizdat, Moscow, 1977; Russian text only, but some good pictures with plans); *Fedor Shekhtel'* (Stroiizdat, Moscow, 1973; the authoritative biography; as previous item). For Russian speakers another first-class text is: E A Borisova & T P Kazhdan *Russkaia Arkhitektura kontsa XIX – nachala XX veka* (Nauka, Moscow, 1971) and there is interesting material in: V V Kirillov *Arkhitektura Russkogo Moderna* (Moscow University Press, 1979). Both contain useful photos and plans.

Two sources in particular should not be overlooked in any preparatory survey of the 1920s buildings. Outstanding in this context is the illustration section of El Lissitzky's *Russia: An Architecture for World Revolution* (1930, republished MIT/Lund Humphries 1970) because the photographs are contemporaneous ones, showing numerous *Modernist* items of the Guide in their original condition and context. Still not replaced for its biographies, as well as useful illustrations, is the *AD* special issue of February 1970 edited by O A Shvidkovsky, republished as *Building in the USSR 1917–32* (Studio Vista, London, 1971). Indispensable to Russian speakers interested in the background and provenance of these twenties works are the two volumes of archival and documentary materials *Iz Istorii Sovetskoi Arkhitektury* compiled and annotated by Vigdaria Khazanova (*vol 1, 1917–25* & *vol 2, 1926–32*; Nauka, Moscow, 1963 & 1970). A dozen listed buildings are illustrated in Chapter 5 of Kathleen

Berton's *Moscow, An Architectural History* (Studio Vista, London, 1977), but the narrative on this period is schematic.

## Organisation and use of the Map Guide

Two things must be clearly understood in the Soviet context. First, that any *accurate* map is a secret document. Second, that certain kinds of buildings are seen as having security connections where none would exist in the West, and these may not be photographed freely.

The Map Guide is based upon the two, near-identical, tourist maps published (by *Falk* and *Hallwag*) in the West, which combine reasonable *topological* accuracy with acceptability from the Soviet point of view. It is essential to realise, however, that distances are greatly (and in some areas, randomly) distorted, in particular by a compression towards the outer areas that gives a wholly illusory sense of what is walkable. On the axis of ulitsa Gorkogo (Gorkii Street) for example, the distance from the Hotel Natsional (no 98) to the Boulevard is about 15 minutes walk. From the Boulevard to the Sadovaia Ring Road is similar, though it appears to be half. Anywhere beyond that definitely needs public transport, and to Sokol (no 2) the only sensible transport is the Metro. Maps published in the Soviet Union are only schematic diagrams. The *Falk*, *Hallwag* or equivalent is the essential complement to this Map Guide, and these cannot be bought inside the USSR.

For a general guidebook that gives serious (if eratic) attention to architecture, the *Blue Guide to Moscow and Leningrad* (Ernest Benn, London) is highly recommended.

Tour agents' notes for the Soviet Union will provide guidance on those categories of building and installation which it is forbidden to photograph. In general these prohibitions provide no problems for the architectural photographer. A problem arises in this case, however, through the fact that some of the finest buildings of the *Moderne* period, in particular certain great private mansions, are now foreign embassies; a few others house Party organisations (eg nos 24, 84, 132), and certain major buildings of the 1920s, most notably the Corbusier (no 123), house 'sensitive' official agencies. *These are indicated by 'X' at the end of the note, after present use. In the case of embassies, never attempt photography without prior consent from the Militia officer in the brown guard box.* (This applies to any building having such a guard post.) *For other buildings marked 'X' you should refrain from photography.* In practice this does not represent a serious constraint: there is plenty else to photograph. *As in any country, however, consequences of disregarding the Law can range from unpleasant to serious.* Except in the case of buildings formally open to the public, interiors will not normally be accessible.

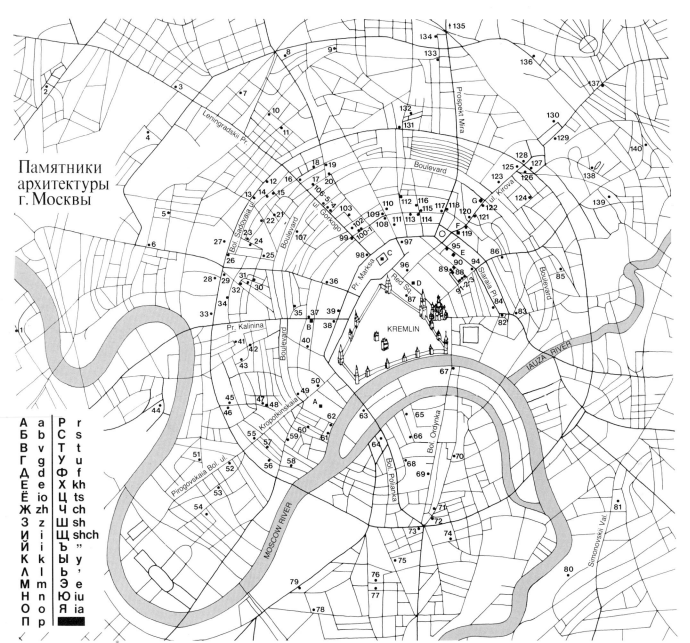

Памятники
архитектуры
г. Москвы

| А | a | Р | r |
|---|---|---|---|
| Б | b | С | s |
| В | v | Т | t |
| Г | g | У | u |
| Д | d | Ф | f |
| Е | e | Х | kh |
| Ё | io | Ц | ts |
| Ж | zh | Ч | ch |
| З | z | Ш | sh |
| И | i | Щ | shch |
| Й | i | Ъ | " |
| К | k | Ы | y |
| Л | l | Ь | ' |
| М | m | Э | e |
| Н | n | Ю | iu |
| О | o | Я | ia |
| П | p | | |

**ON THE MAP**, *dots* mark the 140 listed buildings. They are given by their original function, with present usage in brackets. Seven *square dots* A – G, mark relevant competition sites and museums. Numbering generally reads across the map from L to R.

In the **INDEX BY ARCHITECTS**, each man's works are in *chronological* order, to convey some sense of biography and development of individual oeuvres. (Where forenames, dates of birth etc are missing, these have not been traceable.) Bracketed numbers without dates indicate references in other notes. In the **INDEX BY DESIGN DATES**, the clustering of works emerges as a quite accurate reflection of changing overall levels of building activity in relation to the changing economic fate of Russia. The scanty activity of immediately post-Revolutionary years, for example, clearly gives way to a rising curve of major works starting in 1925 – when building revived – which peaks with the inauguration of the First Five Year Plan in 1928–9. It should be noted that most construction activity within the Plan itself went, as a matter of principle, outside established centres, and therefore outside Moscow. It should also be noted that the rising curve of the pre-First World War years is depressed here below its true peak, of phenomenal building activity during 1911–13, by the fact that much of that boom was speculative housing (cf no 42) that did not employ the best architects.

In the **INDEX BY BUILDING TYPES**, examples are again *chronological* within the type. Careful reading here will indicate the extent to which the immediately pre-Revolutionary years saw a wave of building types new to Russia that was quite as significant in its time as that of the early Soviet years, where this phenomenon has been much more widely discussed. Among them were the vast new educational institutions, the Western-style hotels, the office and commercial buildings that reflected growing entrepreneurial activity and the vast one-off mansions manifesting the fortunes made thereby, as well as apartment housing for the growing professional and middle classes and the big department stores and printing houses. Amongst 'Clubs', there is an apposite reflection of the changing social emphasis brought by the Revolution. At the same time, there are elements of real continuity in prototypes across this divide, for example between philanthropic housing, and the communal houses of the Soviet years.

Twenty-five buildings and one museum have been *starred*. This is intended to represent a balanced selection of the most interesting works, rather than an absolute judgement of architectural quality. Individuals with specific interests may select otherwise: the notes are intended to aid that selection.

I am grateful to Eugenie Markesinis for her assistance in the preliminary literature search, and to Sally Sharpey-Schafer for drawing the map. I am particularly indebted to Sergei Romaniuk for bringing his profound knowledge of Moscow architecture to the criticism of my last draft, and leading me to some further important buildings.

A *Map Guide* to Moscow architecture of all other periods will appear in due course. This one is dedicated to Elena Borisova, Vigdaria Khazanova and Evgeniia Kirichenko, in the hope that this architecture which they have pioneeringly researched may be more widely enjoyed.

Catherine Cooke

**1  Club named for S P Gorbunov  1930–8**
Ia A KORNFEL'D
Novozavodskaia ulitsa, 27  *Metro: Fili*
A fine piece of late Constructivism by one of OSA's
founder members. A large and complex composition
whose main block, R, contains a full theatrical auditorium with free-standing entrance vestibule and three
floors of glazed foyers. Three-storeyed linear block, L,
with wings to front and rear, contains smaller facilities
including a sports-hall.

**2  Sokol Garden Suburb  1923–30\***
N V MARVKOVNIKOV, A V SHCHUSEV et al
Between ulitsy Alabiana and Vrubelia  *Metro: Sokol*
First cooperative housing settlement of the Soviet
period inspired and with numerous types of ex-
perimental cottage housing – by Garden City supporter
Markovnikov, though the lay-out is now attributed to
Shchusev, who was then leading the planning commis-
sion for a 'New Moscow'. From the S end of Alabiana, ul
Surikova and Levitana intersect with the original central
boulevard, Polenova. Vrubelia, intersecting this, was
originally the secondary boulevard focused on the
Serebrianyi Bor suburban railway station. Houses are
of timber, brick and experimental blockwork.

**3  Dinamo Stadium  1928**
A Ia LANGMAN & L Z CHERIKOVER
Leningradskii prospekt, 36  *Metro: Dinamo*
Pioneering structure in its scale, if visually crude, that
belonged originally to a major electrical engineering
works; arena substantially reconstructed later.

**4  Soldatienkovskii Hospital  1908–10**
I A IVANOV-SHITS
2-i Botkinskii proezd, 5  *Metro: Dinamo*
Built as a 245-bed free hospital for all classes of the
population by rich merchant K T Soldatienkov. Spacious planning typical of medical thinking at that date,
on wooded site. Simple 2 and 3-storeyed blocks of
varying but generous fenestration according to function, some now yellow, some red, with white detailing.
Administrative buildings generally more decorated than
the ward blocks, and some good details remain in
places (wrought iron etc). Fenestration, broken roof-
lines etc typical of *Moderne*, achieved with simple
means; muted verticality typical of the architect. (cf
Morozov Children's Hospital, no 78) (Part of the vast
Botkin Hospital complex)

**5  P I Shchukin's House  1898**  B V FREIDENBERG
Malaia Gruzinskaia ulitsa, 15  *Metro: Ulitsa 1905 goda*
Expansion of house by A E ERIKHSON, 1892, to house
Shchukin's collection of Russian antiquities and handi-
crafts; in a glorious Pseudo-Russian style, red brick and
white stone, in a free composition with high-pitched
roofs and bold cornices.
(State Biological Museum named for K A Timiriazev.)

**6  Mostorg Department Store  1927\***
L A VESNIN, with A A & V A VESNIN
ulitsa Krasnaia Presnia, 48/2  *Metro: Ulitsa 1905 goda*
Second Vesnin design built in Moscow after the
Revolution (cf no 68), and best indicates what their
early competition projects (ARCOS, Central Telegraph
etc) might have represented. Fluent, symmetrical plan
on a cramped corner site; three-storeyed, with a fully
(and double) glazed elevation played against bold but
perforated horizontals of attic and solid enclosing
corners. Conceived as a demonstration building for
economical modern construction techniques in its
calculated concrete frame, slender steel glazing frames
and as a model of proletarian retailing. Much original

detailing remains especially on the facade, though the
attic typography has been replaced by three new
windows. (Moskovsko-Krasnopresnenskii Department
Store.)

**7  Headquarters and Production Complex of Pravda
newspaper  1930–5**  P A GOLOSOV
ulitsa Pravdy, 24  *Metro: Belorusskaia*
Large and handsome masterpiece of the elder and
more convincedly Constructivist Golosov, Pan-
teleimon, comprising a seven-storeyed editorial block
with a low-rise printing building behind. Finely propor-
tioned and detailed building by one whose pursuit of a
modern synthesis pre-dated the Revolution.

**8  Shatskii's Experimental Kindergarten  1907**
A U ZELENKO
Vadkovskii pereulok, 3  *Metro: Novoslobodskaia*
The first children's 'work and leisure community' in
Russia: a pedagogical experiment by future Soviet
educational pioneer Stanislav T Shatskii to teach poor
children the elements of science, the arts and collective
endeavour, funded by subscriptions from the liberal
intelligentsia. Internal complexity of plan and diversity
of levels expressed in a bold but somewhat grotesque
exterior. Remarkable interiors originally included workshops, theatre, observatory. (Imaginative proposals for
reuse as young people's centre currently under
consideration by local education authority.)

**9  Bakhemt'evskii Bus Garage  1926**
K S MEL'NIKOV
ulitsa Obraztsova, 12A  *Metro: Novoslobodskaia*
The first of Mel'nikov's garages, for 104 buses parked
*en echelon* in a long parallelogram behind five
staggered entrances. A low structure of brick walls and
steel trusses with the rear, exit wall more characteristically handled to include circular windows over each
door.

**10  Club named for S M Zuev  1927–9**
I A GOLOSOV
Lesnaia ulitsa, 18  *Metro: Belorusskaia*
A vigorous if not very rigorous object of unhappy
proportions, but highly evocative of the 'experimental'
nature of its period and in that respect expressive of the
approach of this younger, more romantic Golosov.
Inside the glazed cylinder on the street corner a
staircase links two levels of foyers to the auditorium in
the centre of the side elevation, with other accommodation at ground level and the S end.

**11  Shaniavskii People's University  1910–13**
I A IVANOV-SHITS

Miusskaia ploshchad, 6  *Metro: Belorusskaia*
A refined synthesis of classicism and *Moderne*
achieved with modest means. A typical balance of long
horizontals and thrusting verticals with delicate decorative accents sometimes highly geometricised. Occupies the whole length of a block. Built as an 'open'
higher education institution giving evening tuition at
secondary and university levels to the otherwise
unqualified, on an initiative from the Moscow liberal
intelligentsia with funds from AL Shaniavskii.
(Academy of Social Sciences of the Central Committee
of the CPSU.)

**12  Pigit's apartment house  1903**  A N MILKOV
Bol'shaia Sadovaia ulitsa, 10  *Metro: Maiakovskaia*
A bold and handsome example of the *Moderne* with
elevational details well preserved. Five storeys; three
strongly vertical accents formed by linked sequences of
balconies and bay windows that break through the
cornice in a manner typical of the style; equally bold
first-floor bay windows balance the composition L and
R. Fine gradation of rhythmic geometrical decoration
around windows. Originally had a front garden, as did
everything on this Sadovaia (Garden) Ring Road.

**13  Shekhtel's second house  1909–10**
F O SHEKHTEL'
Bol'shaia Sadovaia ulitsa, 4  *Metro: Maiakovskaia*
Built for himself at the height of the pre-Revolutionary
Neo-classical revival. Spare classical detailing of the
central Doric portico and decorative relief panels, all in
stucco, refer directly at this scale to comparably sized
private houses of early 19th-century Moscow. But the
plan and volumetric organisation are typical of that
medievally inspired asymmetry based on domestic
convenience which Shekhtel' himself pioneered in the
*Moderne*. Three internal staircases link the two stories
of accommodation that embrace the great double-
height hall behind the portico. Free-standing studio
building in the yard. (Kindergarten.)

**14  Shekhtel's first house  1896**  F O SHEKHTEL'
ulitsa Zholtovskogo, 28  *Metro: Maiakovskaia*
Interesting for its evocation of the European medieval
influences which parallel the Russian in the *Moderne*
(cf no 24). A free plan with the gabled wall of one wing
cut off at the street line and a domestic, privacy-seeking
relationship to its site. Its pointed towers somewhat
redolent of the French; the craftsmanship of its
brickwork and immaculate dressed stone detailing,
especially of the window head on the gable wall,
particularly English. (Embassy of Uraguay; X)

**15  A A Levenson's Printing Works  1900**
F O SHEKHTEL'
Triokhprudnyi pereulok, 11  *Metro: Pushkinskaia-
Gorkovskaia*
Most evocative in its massing and corner towers of
late-medieval provincial France, though more super-
ficial decorative detailing in doors, windows, ironwork
etc has Art Nouveau characteristics.

**16  I D Sytin's Printing Works of the Russkoe Slovo
newspaper  1905–7**  A E ERIKHSON
ulitsa Gorkogo  *Metro: Pushkinskaia-Gorkovskaia*

A pyramidal build-up on the main elevation of 5, 4 and 3 storeys with circular and half-circular top windows giving vigour to the descending roofline. Glazed facing brick, stylised floral polychrome tile work and relief decoration; fluid fenestration and iron-work within strong structurally based overall grid.
(Part of *Trud* newspaper complex; moved bodily in 1979 from its original location 50 yards S of here.)

**17 Headquarters building of Izvestiia newspaper 1925–7** G B BARKHIN
Pushkinskaia ploshchad', 5 *Metro: Pushkinskaia-Gorkovskaia*
Sober but handsome seven-storeyed framed structure by one of Moscow's leading but non-partisan modernists, whose considerable pre-Revolutionary experience (cf no 50) tells here in a quality and hence longevity of components and details that is exceptional in buildings of the mid-twenties. This scheme with its distinctive circular windows resulted when an original twelve-storey scheme fell foul of new planning controls.

**18 Credit Bank building 1913–16**
V A POKROVSKII & B M NILUS
Nastas'inskii pereulok *Metro: Pushkinskaia-Gorkovskaia*
A single symmetrical elevation on the street, with protruding porch and tower above pitched roof; a classically constrained essay with medieval elements compared to Pokrovskii's earlier work in Petersburg. Basic forms of church and domestic architecture applied to a consciously planar facade of glazed blocks, stone trim and *eau-de-nil* stucco. Elements of the Moscow Baroque in the upper windows; rippling 5-bayed central 'pediment', and free-standing porch; elements of *Moderne* in the slender spire, play of surface textures and general mood.

**19 Merchants Club 1907–8** I A IVANOV-SHITS
ulitsa Chekhova, 6 *Metro: Pushkinskaia – Gorkovskaia*

Built as the new headquarters of an old-established Moscow club for leading industrialists, bankers and businessmen. The central colonnade of six engaged Corinthian columns gives this long street elevation a more strongly classical character than that of the later no 11, but the interiors were originally amongst Moscow's finest examples of the *Moderne* at its most rectilinear, and at its closest to Art Deco. (Theatre of the Leninist Youth Movement, Komsomol)

**20 Printing House of SP Riabushinskii's newspaper Utro Rossii 1907** F O SHEKHTEL'
proezd Skvortsova-Stepanova, 3 *Metro: Pushkinskaia – Gorkovskaia*
Shekhtel' at his most austerely simple. The long three storeyed printing shop behind becomes two broad and fully glazed office bays on the street, clad in brown glazed tiles with arched lintels and a string-course in cream stone. Boldly rounded corners and set-back bays, L & R, with pedestrian and vehicular entrances under enormous plate-glass windows above. The attic band was originally plain with a stone panel bearing the paper's name, but four attic windows and another balustrade element have been added.

**21 ulitsa Ostuzheva 1900s**
*Metro: Pushkinskaia-Gorkovskaia*
An unusually complete example of a typical street of apartment houses developed in the 1900s.

**22 Gosstrakh apartment block 1926–7**
M Ia GINZBURG
Malaia Bronnaia, 21 *Metro: Pushkinskaia-Gorkovskaia*

First post-Revolutionary building by the principal theoretician of Constructivism. Five-storeyed 'L' shaped plan on corner site for employees of State Insurance Office. Shop and amenities at ground level, 4 conventional but 'model' flats on floors 1–3 and 12-roomed communal apartment with shared kitchen etc on the 4th. The Corbusian roof-garden of original development characterised its role as demonstration of 'the new architecture' that is less powerful in its present condition and with equally high buildings on the rest of Spiridonovka.

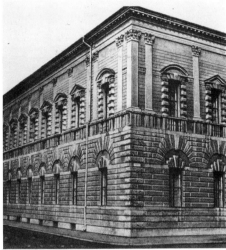

**23 Tarasov's Mansion 1909–1912\***
I V ZHOLTOVSKII
ulitsa Aleksis Tolstogo, 30 *Metro: Pushkinskaia-Gorkovskaia*
Best example of Zholtovskii's most slavishly Renaissance period of the early 1910s: a virtually exact copy of Palladio's Palazzo Thiene with only a subtle change of proportions between the floors, to that ratio used in the Doge's Palace, which shifts the visual emphasis onto the heavier, rusticated ground floor. Superbly constructed: an example of the Russian building industry's potential on prestige projects at that date.

**24 Z G Morozova's Mansion 1893–8**
F O SHEKHTEL'
ulitsa Aleksis Tolstogo, 17 *Metro: Pushkinskaia-Gorkovskaia*
A mansion of monumental proportions for a branch of the millionaire textile family that was particularly involved in the arts. The exterior demonstrates a scholarly use of European Gothic quite different from the Romantic Gothic of the earlier 19th century in Russia, but its relative restraint belies a richness of decorative and structural detailing inside, and of materials, light effects and colours, that is quite astonishing, and manifests Shekhtel's early ability to orchestrate these architectural elements, as well as his pioneering use of the free plan in domestic architecture. (Government building for official entertaining etc; X)

**25 S P Riabushinskii's Mansion 1900–2\***
F O SHEKHTEL'
ulitsa Kachalova, 6/2 *Metro: Arbatskaia*
Sunny and lyrical house for one of the eight brothers forming the second generation of this conservative industrial and banking family, who ran the newspaper *Utro Rossii* (cf no 20) as their political mouthpiece. One of Shekhtel's masterpieces, on a compact but free plan of genuinely domestic scale that opens in several

directions onto its garden. Mainly two-storeyed, around a central staircase daylit from above. Around the exterior, of creamy glazed brick and pinkish stucco, run deep eaves and a broad frieze with polychrome mosaics of exotic flowers into which the smaller windows are set and edged with gold leaf. The interior is a feast of natural materials, where marble, various fine hardwoods, brass and leather are celebrated in superb craftsmanship and organically expressive, but always functionally disciplined forms. When open to the public this should not be missed.
(House Museum of Maxim Gorkii – lived here 1931–6)

**26 Kan's House 1901** F O SHEKHTEL'
ulitsa Kachalova's corner with Sadovaia-Kudrinskaia *Metro: Krasnopresnenskaia-Barikadnaia*
A three-storeyed box of traditionally classical form, but detailed and articulated with Shekhtel's typical subtlety. Each floor has a different surface texture and treatment of the deep window embrasures, which are picked out, like the strong string-courses and garlanded frieze, in white.

**27 Moscow Planetarium 1928–9***
M O BARSHCH & M I SINIAVSKII
Sadovaia-Kudrinskaia ulitsa, 5 *Metro: Krasnopres-nenskaia-Barikadnaia*
A socially and technically pioneering work by leading young Constructivist architects; a symbol and centre of popular access to 'scientific and atheistic knowledge' under Socialism. The dome is a lightweight steel frame and the auditorium floor is carried on radial concrete beams from a single central column. External stairs, and external walls and windows of the lower floor are of Corbusian geometry and simplicity, though the original cantilevered concrete entrance canopy has been unsympathetically replaced.

**28 Narkomfin housing building 1928–30***
M Ia GINZBURG, I F MILINIS & engineer S PROKHOR-OV
ulitsa Chaikovskogo, 25 korpus B. *Metro: Krasnop-resnenskaia-Barikadnaia*
Most important and sophisticated of the experimental buildings 'of transitional type' commissioned to apply dwelling plans and principles developed by Construc-tivist architects who worked under Ginzburg as the Type-planning Sector of Stroikom RSFSR during 1928 (see also no 49 & 135). Here the six-storeyed main

block contains the two-storeyed, studio types 'F' and 'K' with their minimal kitchens etc. Technically, a demon-stration building for economical concrete framing with hollow-pot floors etc. Elements of the roof-garden structures remain but the ground floor is no longer open around the pilotis. The linked three-storeyed block of dining and recreational facilities is also much altered; likewise the two-storeyed former laundry and crèche etc across the garden. A once elegant building whose original aesthetic class still speaks powerfully despite dreadful physical delapidation.

**29 Club for the Society of Pre-Revolutionary Political Deportees**
ulitsa Vorovskogo, 33 *Metro: Krasnopresnenskaia-Barikadnaia*
Designed 1929: construction 1931–4 A A, V A & L A VESNIN
Penultimate Constructivist building to start construction in Moscow. A large and spreading complex of typical internal lucidity of which only the R side was built due to abolition of the Society during the building period and redundancy of the museum element of the plan. The part built comprises an auditorium and the usual supplementary club facilities.
(Studio Theatre of Film Actors)

**30 Solov'iov's Mansion 1901** S U SOLOV'IOV
ulitsa Paliashvili, 6 *Metro: Arbatskaia*
A compact but highly articulated little corner house on three storeys, built to the high standards common in this period. Great diversity of fenestration; glazed brick in pale ochre and stone trim, with some exotic detailing especially in the decorative ceramic plaques. (Geor-gian Republic's Mission in Moscow)

**31 V N Gribov Mansion 1909** AN MILIUKOV
Khlebnyi pereulok, 15 *Metro: Arbatskaia*
Fine 3-storeyed essay in the free neo-classicism characteristic of this date (cf nos 13 & 48). Typically bold forms and clear cutting of sill-less windows etc into consciously smooth stucco surfaces. Powerful central porch leads up steps from the street; arch in simple pediment and 2 rather baroque protruding bays, 4 Ionic columns each, on rusticated bases. Clipped dome gives daylight into central hall behind. Free classical relief on string-course between windows, L & R; crisp, half-round Doric porch onto garden at the end typically modernises a common 19th-century neo-classical motif.

**32 Mindovskii's Mansion 1903*** L N KEKUSHEV
ulitsa Vorovskogo, 44 *Metro: Arbatskaia*
Perhaps the best extant work by this leading architect of the *Moderne*. A cubic house, entered via fine period iron gates from Skaternyi pereulok into the forecourt, with stable block, L. Typically *Moderne*, the strong eaves rippling outwards round one bay and arching upwards over the grand triple window and balcony on Vorovskogo, where S-facing corner is curved with a 5-window, faceted belvedere. Private accommodation on the garden side rises to 3 storeys. Bold volumes; enormous windows with deep reveals; square propor-

tions and full, semicircular curves; luxuriant, often figurative sculpted decoration which articulates but remains subordinate: these add up to Kekushev's typical style, and are superbly orchestrated here.
(Embassy of New Zealand; X)

**33 Prince SS Shcherbatov's apartment house 1911–13** A O TAMANIAN
ulitsa Chaikovskogo, 11 *Metro: Krasnopresnenskaia-Barikadnaia*
One of the best examples of the pre-War neo-classical revival. A new synthesis of Renaissance palazzo mótifs for the new problem of apartment housing that prefigures the 1930s. U-shaped in plan. Top, colon-naded floor of the main 5-storeyed block was the Prince's own luxurious home. The rest, including the 3-storeyed wings that create the open formal court, was apartments he rented. Forty years later he described the conception of the house in his autobiography. The passage conveys vividly the flavour of this Moscow artistic élite in the pre-War period. Particularly charac-teristic is the combination of grand long-term planning for one's own place in history with great pragmatism and inventiveness about immediate practicalities. Parts are worth quoting as a vignette on the background of many building operations in this period.

> *Having settled down firmly in Moscow, and greatly loving the city, I decided to build a large house and to leave some kind of artistic monument to myself: I would do this by making the building something of aesthetic value and giving it a special function after my death. At the same time I wanted to create living conditions for myself and my wife that were attuned to my aesthetic needs and tastes. . . .*
> *I decided to build something on the lines of the palaces of Catherine's time . . . and reckoned it feasible to do this if the fine edifice also answered the practical, rational needs of an apartment house. At the same time, I myself did not want to live in a numbered apartment, but would have a one-off mansion within this building. According to my conception, the mansion would be raised on a pedestal of apartments, like a luxuriant flower, nourished by the roots of the plant. High up like that it would fulfill my dream of a view into the broad distance . . .*
> *When I built the house it was my intention to bequeath it to the city to become 'The Moscow Museum of Private Collections'. Collections must be arranged just as they had been by their owners, to preserve their 'spirit' . . . Apartments would be reached by broad staircases, each one so planned internally that it could readily be rearranged by demolishing walls. Thus the whole distribution of accommodation could be altered as necessary to receive collections of varying size and character. I dedicated my own home, at the top of the building, to becoming some kind of cultural and artistic centre for bringing together artists, actors and men of letters . . .*
> *Having made a special study of English, Swed-ish and Norwegian interiors, as being the most comfortably arranged, I sought to plan the apart-ments so that the inhabitants should feel 'at home' and relaxed in them. On the front of my own house were statues; at the entrance were vast stone lions, and on the gateposts were highly decorated iron torcheres.*

(Prince S A Shcherbatov, *Khoduzhnik v ushedshei Rossii* (An artist in the departed Russia) New York, 1955.)
Urbanity at a human scale; painted deep red.

**34 Neo-classical house 1909–12** P P MALINOVSKII
Trubnikovskii pereulok, 19 *Metro: Arbatskaia*
A further example of the pre-War neo-classical revival by a prolific housebuilder of the period.

**35 Mossel'prom building 1923–4** D KOGAN
Kalashnyi pereulok, 2/10 *Metro: Arbatskaia*
One of the first multi-storeyed buildings erected after the Revolution; at 8 storeys with a tower of 11, then described as a 'skyscraper'. Housed coordinating agency for processing of agricultural products. With repetitive, vertical fenestration now appears gaunt in plain white, but originally picked out with horizontal banding of sill and balcony elements, and verticals between alternate windows, to stress the frame structure, and with strong typography and a clock in the top of the tower, to produce an articulation redolent of the *Moderne*. It was on the end wall of this building,

facing down Kislovskii Nizhnyi pereulok, that Rodchenko painted the colourful supergraphics for Mosselprom products, in 1924–5, which he recorded in photos and of which his wife Stepanova painted a picture.

## 36 Zoological Museum of Moscow University 1898–1902  K M BYKOVSKII
ulitsa Gertsena, 6  *Metro: Biblioteka imeni Lenina-Kalininskaia*
One of the last buildings of the President, since 1894, of MAO, which was founded by his father the radical theoretician and reformer of architectural education M D Bykovskii. Free and vigorous classicism symbolic of scientific enquiry – as distinct from the stifling classicism of the early 19th-century autocracy fought by his father. A two-storeyed colonnade of engaged Corinthian columns on a richly worked wall surface with bold rustication below, in cool pale green and white.

## 37 Department Store of the Moscow Guards Officers' Society 1911–13  S B ZALESSKII
prospekt Kalinina, 10  *Metro: Biblioteka imeni Leninina-Kalininskaia*
Last of the pre-Revolutionary department stores. Half the size of the slightly earlier 'Army & Navy stores' in the capital, but of similar and equally spacious plan with grand staircase giving access to galleries round a broad, top-lit hall. Strong vertical emphasis and suitably military asceticism of detailing in the elevation into which only a few distinctly *Moderne* elements have crept, notably at the roofline, but the dense small-scale fenestration belies the bold structural frame inside.
(Voentorg Department Store.)

## 38 State Library named for V I Lenin 1928–41
V A SHCHUKO & V G GEL'FREIKH
prospekt Kalinina, 3  *Metro: Biblioteka imeni Lenina-Kalininskaia*
Large, mainly three-storeyed complex around two courtyards that spans from the 20s into the 30s. Asymmetrical cubic massing and generally non-academic planning reflect the debt of this final design to premiated entries in the original competition, of 1928–9, by the Vesnins et al. But detailing, of square, matchstick-like granite and marble columns, and the heroic double frieze, are typical of 'socialist classicism' in the 30s.

## 39 Moscow University Library 1901
K M BYKOVSKII
Prospekt Marksa, 20  *Metro: Biblioteka imeni Lenina*
L-shaped building with bold corner rotunda, forming LHS of an open courtyard of Moscow University's 'New site' (mid-19C – the 'Old site' of 18 and early 19C being E of Gertsena ulitsa). Bykovskii was here making a radical reconstruction of the mid-19C structure. Bold modelling characteristic of his work (cf no 36). Here too a powerfully rusticated 1st floor over semi-basement, which unifies the variously treated 2nd floor elements in this conversion job: some quietly pilastered, the rotunda and extreme LH block have giant order and bold fenestration of double-height spaces akin to 36.
(Part of Moscow State University's city-centre accommodation).

## 40 Shamshin's apartment house 1909
F O SHEKHTEL'
ulitsa Frunze, 8  *Metro: Biblioteka imeni Lenina*
The residential building of Shekhtel's most Rationalist period, comparable in austerity with his preceding newspaper building (no 20) and the contemporaneous commercial building (no 95). Decorativeness derived from the rhythm of constructive elements, the balance of flatness and curves, choice and distribution of facing materials (glazed brick and stone, in cream; glazing). Applied decoration of earlier *Moderne* confined to bas-relief accents at cornice and doorway. The 'soft' corner developed into a rotunda hinting at his new sympathy with neo-classicism (cf no 13).

## 41 NA Vtorov's Mansion 1913
V M MAIAT & V D ADAMOVICH
Spasopeskovskaia ploshchadka, 10  *Metro: Smolenskaia*
Large, mainly two-storeyed house typical of that branch of pre-War neo-classicism which sought to emulate the Russian *Empire* style of late 18th and early 19th century, and found opportunities to apply the maximum number of its motifs on the new, free plan forms introduced by the *Moderne*.
(Residence of the American Ambassador; X)

## 42 ulitsa Arbat 1900s–1910s
Metros: Arbatskaia, at NE end, or Smolensksaia, at SW.
Central axis of a district populated originally by the aristocracy and then by the intelligentsia. Where no 21 represents the townscape created by developers of the 1900s, the cliff-like, eight-storeyed apartment blocks of Arbat Street typify the townscape arising in the building boom that preceded World War I. Nothing is by the best architects, but of the earlier, lower-rise buildings several are well known including, on the S side, No 23 (1903) by N G LAZAREV, and No 29 (1904), 5–6 storeys, by N G LAZAREV, and on the N side, No 28 (1901), 3-storeys, by A A OSTROGRADSKII and No 30 (1904), 5 storeys, by N N BOBRYKIN. Architects of the biggest blocks, a decade later, on eve of War, are generally undistinguished. That of Mr Tryndin's apartment house at No 27 (1911–12), 6 storeys, is one S F KULAGIN; A T Filatova's block at No 35 (1913–14), 8 storeys, is by V E DUBOVSKII & N A ARKHIPOV; V P Paniushev's block at No 51 (1911–12) is by V A KAZAKOV.

## 43 K S Mel'nikov's House 1927–9*  K S MEL'NIKOV
Krivoarbatskii pereulok, 10  *Metro: Smolenskaia*
Fascinating demonstration by one of the twenties' leading modernists, of the rich functional and daylighting possibilities of the medieval cylindrical form, and of traditional peasant construction methods (stuccoed brick; two-way timber flooring). Two such cylinders interlock. Perforated N-facing one at the rear contains utilities, bedrooms and architect's studio (visible from backyard of adjacent housing); Entrance, dining room, 1½-storeyed living room and roof terrace in the S-facing solid cylinder on the street side.

## 44 Briansk Station 1912–17  I I RERBERG & V K OLTARZHEVSKII; engineer for the platform vaults V G SHUKHOV.
ploshchad' Kievskogo Vokzala  *Metro: Kievskaia*
Fine example of neo-classicism applied to a new building type. Pedantically accurate historical details are freely composed to solve a new volumetric problem. L-shaped concourse and administrative building, rusticated below with Ionic colonnade above on a reinforced concrete frame and dominated by a bold clocktower; embraces magnificent train-shed of rivetted steel with semicircular arches that rise directly from hinged bearings at platform level.
(Kievskii Mainline Railway Terminus; suburban and metro entrances, L, are of 1940–5).

## 45 Kekushev's first house 1898–9  L N KEKUSHEV
ulitsa Lunacharskogo, 8  *Metro: Smolenskaia*

Early essay in the *Moderne* by one of its most prolific adherents, for himself. Even a relatively modest house appears complex in massing through vigorous cutting and emphases on the external walls. The geometrical 'carved' banding and dumpy column of the corner verandah in particular are redolent of heavy folklorique furniture still in production at Abramtsevo and Talashkino. Warm golden-brown glazed bricks with natural stone bay and detailing. Fine ceramic panels in string-course and over main door. Celebration of the semicircle, square and cube are typical Kekushev.
(Argentine Embassy; X)

## 46 Neo-classical mansion 1914  P P MALINOVSKII
ulitsa Lunacharskogo, 7  *Metro: Smolenskaia*
See no. 33.

## 47 Villas for the Moscow Trading and Construction Company 1900–1902  V F VAL'KOT (WILLIAM WALCOT)
pereulok N A Ostrovskogo, 8 & 10  *Metro: Kropotkinskaia*
Interesting examples of villas for the upper-middle class or intelligentsia built by this Moscow housebuilding company, presumably speculatively (see also next item, no 48). No 8, known as Gutkheil's house, of 1900, is a low development on the street, whose formal symmetries link it to the neo-classical 19C precursors of this type, though the styling is an eclectic mixture typical of the early *Moderne*. Fine central doorway. (Embassy of Morocco; X). No 10, known as Iakunchikova's house, of 1902, is a genuinely 'modern' villa with very European relationship to the street and garden. Planning dictated by internal domestic convenience in a manner Shekhtel' was now emulating, but the simplicity of rectangular volumes and windows (notice bare RSJ's exposed as lintels, inter alia), and of the iron and tile work, give it a relaxedly unrhetorical and international air characteristic of its author. Original fine gateposts and other external features gone; some conversion, L. Born in Russia of English father and Russian mother, Walcot had his early education in France before studying architecture in St Petersburg. (Embassy and Residence of Zaire; X)

## 48 Villa for the Moscow Trading and Construction Company 1906  N G LAZAREV
pereulok N A Ostrovskogo, 6  *Metro: Kropotkinskaia*
Cf no 47 above, for same company. Owner was N I Mindovskii. Awkward site on sharp corner handled informally, by free composition of volumes in the newly revived neo-classical idiom.Corner turned with a highly stylised 'portico' element running back to form main volume of house, a polygonal entrance porch, L. and curved colonnade with bold Doric columns, R Restrained decorative panels incised into wall surface; numerous details lost. Interesting comparison with Shekhtel's own second house, 1907 (no 13) and Miliukov 1909 (no 31).

## 49 Housing Complex of the Workers' House-Building Cooperative (RZhSKT) 'Model Construction' 1929  M O BARSHCH, V N VLADIMIROV, I F MILINIS, L S SLAVINA, A L PASTERNAK & engineer S V ORLOVSKII
Gogolevskii bulevard, 8  *Metro: Kropotkinskaia*
Another experimental building 'of transitional type' by Constructivist architects (see no 28). Stroikom types used here are the relatively conventional, but mini-kitchened, 3 & 5 person flats 'A2' & 'A3', and studio type 'F'. Site constraints caused the two to be separated into different blocks. Some communal facilities are in the base of one block, others are free-standing. Structures are reinforced concrete frames with special two-skin timber flooring for maximum sound insulation. Certain

experimental materials used here gave trouble quickly so that this complex is much more altered, but in a better state, than no 27.

**50 Aleksandr III Museum of Fine Arts 1898–1912** on the basis of a design by R I KLEIN & P BOITSOV
ulitsa Volkhonka, 12 *Metro: Kropotkinskaia*
A vast classical art gallery in delicate Ionic order derived, especially in its 6-columned main portico, from the Erechtheum, with an accuracy typical of the period. Behind these on the main elevation, 8-columned colonnades to each side. The overall plan is some 70m × 80m, with four internal courts, two covered; a series of long galleries and a fine Corinthian basilica on the main axis upstairs. The museum was built to house Moscow University's collection of classical casts. Klein executed the design with which Boitsov won the initial competition. Among his assistants were Zholtovskii, who designed the grand staircase hall, and G B Barkhin. External sculptural frieze of the Olympic Games by G Zaleman.
(State Museum of Fine Arts named for A S Pushkin.)

**51 Club of the Kauchuk factory 1927**
K S MEL'NIKOV
ulitsa Pliushchikha, 64 *Metro: Park Kul'tury*
A very unassertive building in comparison with the contemporaneous no 1. A quadrant in plan, whose four-storeyed bands of alternating wall and window, and formal double staircases to the first floor entrance give it a neo-classical air. Inside dominated by the raked auditorium; a sports-hall extends to the R.

**52 City Primary School 1909**
A A OSTROGRADSKII
Bol'shaia Pirogovskaia ulitsa, 9 *Metro: Park Kul'tury*
Educational complex typical of these pre-War years in its enormous scale and the cliff-like main elevation. Basically a simple and symmetrical building of four very high storeys of well-lit classrooms, superficially Russified by *kokoshniki* over the rhythmic round-headed windows. Mosaic panel at the roofline typical of the *Moderne*, depicting St George, by S S Cherkhonin. Interesting as a new building type. (Research Institute).

**53 Building of the Higher Courses for Women 1910–13** S U SOLOV'IOV
Malaia Pirogovskaia ulitsa, 1 *Metro: Park Kul'tury*
Pioneering private institution to give women higher education. Closed in 1888 as over-represented in the revolutionary movement but reopened 1900, and by completion of this new building had become effectively the women's half of Moscow University. Perhaps as reassurance of its loyalties, Solov'iov builds here in a neo-classicism that reproduces late 18th- early 19th-century Russian *Empire*, increasing the surface femininity with light decorative friezes, slender fluting of the Doric columns etc. Domed and colonnaded corner rotunda is the entrance, on the axis of the quadrant-shaped plan whose heart is the great raked auditorium for lectures. Urbane solution to accommodating that

large internal volume.
(Moscow State Pedagogical Institute named for V I Lenin).

**54 Housing district on Usacheva Street 1925–7**
A I MESHKOV & engineer G A MASLENNIKOV
Usacheva ulitsa and Kooperativnaia to Saveleva ulitsy *Metro: Sportivnaia*
One of the very first integrated workers' housing developments in Moscow after the Revolution. A model in its time, erected by the municipality. 25 hectares developed as a community with crèches, play areas, school, shops, dining room, bath house and green planting between crisp and simple 4–5-storeyed blocks. Walk-up access to clusters of 2–3 roomed family apartments of newly designed Mossoviet standard types.

**55 I P Isakov's apartment house 1906\***
L N KEKUSHEV
Kropotkinskaia ulitsa, 28 *Metro: Park Kul'tury*
Moscow's most feminine essay in the *Moderne*; still a building of almost bridal quality when sunshine restores its sparkle. Five high storeys. Dark, deep eaves ripple round the outer bay windows of fine original glazing and up over the circular window above the central, recessed sequence of 4 very fine wrought iron balconies. Rich play of flat and curve, soft against strong, is typical Kekushev (cf no 32). Perfect balance of top and bottom as of L & R (where ground level is asymmetrical). Plain ground level of dark hammered stone; floors 1–3 in grey-green glazed brick with pinky-cream stone details; 4th floor under dark eaves covered in delicate geometricised leaf pattern that develops into purely figurative sculpture in a *Moderne* version of the pediment. A masterly work.

**56 Derozhinskaia's Mansion 1901\***
F O SHEKHTEL'
Kropotkinskii pereulok, 13 *Metro: Park Kul'tury*
Competes with no 25 as Shekhtel's domestic masterpiece, but of different scale and conception. Built for Aleksandra, daughter of textile millionaire Ivan Butikov, whose mills were nearby, just before she married a Director of his company, V V Derozhinskii. Domestic spaces, on two floors, are large, but are wrapped around a double-height Great Hall of medieval charac-

ter and scale, half panelled, with vast fireplace axially opposite the full-height window dominating the street elevation. Free planning of the rest (like its proportional system) is partly medieval in inspiration; also bourgeois 'modern' from Europe, as is the high standard of technical comfort throughout. Complete theme of decorative motifs throughout from iron railings to furnishing fabrics, with tree-based secondary theme (especially in library gallery; fireplace). Exterior and most intimate interiors (main bed and bathroom) nakedly simple, between Art Deco and Purism (as exterior of half-round stair at rear). Exterior glazed brick in palest *eau-de-nil* with cream stone detailing. The building with which Shekhtel' really breaks through from the *Moderne*'s sources to a 'new style'.
(Australian Embassy; X; see *AD* 1980 1/2)

**57 N N Medyntsev's Mansion 1907**
F V VOSKRESENSKII
Pomerantsev pereulok, 6 *Metro: Park Kul'tury*
Eclectic but disciplined house whose whole relationship to the street, its porch and bay window are very English. Its masculinity; its urbane verticality, delineated in grey-brown stone against cream glazed brick; its railings (and its fine panels of carved thistles), however, have a Scottish air. Roofline emphasis is a blue-green tiled frieze linked to a gable panel with coat of arms. Highly individual. (Embassy of Guinea; X)

**58 Old Believers' Church 1908–10**
V M MAIAT & V D ADAMOVICH
Turchaninov pereulok, 4 *Metro: Park Kul'tury*
Charming little street church built with money from the Riabushinskii family (cf nos 20, 25) who all belonged to the Old Believer sect. The main volume is a simple cube, 3 arched windows on each elevation, topped by a single drum-and-cupola ('head') of traditionally correct proportions (contrast, for example, contemporaneous Neo-Russian churches by Shchusev and Bondarenko, nos 69 & 140). To the L a tall gabled doorway in a more *Moderne* wall feature leads up into a porch and bell-tower with pitched roof topped by slender single head. An essay in the Neo-Russian that uses traditional elements flexibly, but with the classicists' respect for their traditional functions and proportions.

**59 L N Kekushev's Second House and adjacent hospital 1902–3** L N KEKUSHEV
Metrostroevskaia ulitsa, 25 *Metro: Kropotkinskaia*
Relatively ordinary 3-storeyed, L-shaped house plan given flavour of the National Romantic by separation of 3 rooms into a hexagonal tower with the tall tent-shaped (*shatior*) roof of Russian vernacular timber architecture; also by panels of all-over floral carving, which only have Art Nouveau stylisation at the front gable head. Bold cream stone trim against matt brown brickwork has the boldness but not the consistent proportions or the depth characterising his other work (cf. nos 32, 45). Alongside, L, of 1902, a small 3-storeyed district hospital building, a simple box which already displays essential elements of his mature *Moderne* work (contrast no 96) but is very flat. Grey and cream.
(House is an Embassy; X)

**60 Varvarin Company's Apartment Block 1898**
A V IVANOV
Savel'evskii pereulok, 10 *Metro: Kropotkinskaia*
Very large 5-storeyed apartment block refined by a carefully balanced hierarchy of classical treatments for each floor of identical fenestration. A late example of the 'models of good taste' for which Ivanov had been appreciated over 20 years in Petersburg and Moscow,

from five years before he became President of MAO. Terra cotta and cream.

**61 I E Tsvetkov's Mansion 1897** V M VASNETSOV
Kropotkinskaia naberezhnaia, 29 *Metro: Kropotkinskaia*
Important example of scholarly Neo-Russian (as opposed to Pseudo-Russian) work, from an artist-designer-architect of impeccable pedigree: former member of 'Wanderers' group; central activist and practitioner in vernacular design research and revival at Abramtsevo arts-and-crafts colony (see no 132). Buildings use carefully researched volumetric and compositional systems of the medieval (Vasnetsov was Shekhtel's mentor here: see no 56). The model here is mid-17th century. For brick detailing, window forms, polychrome tilework, compare the church of Grigorii Neokesariiskogo, B Polianka ulitsa, 1662–9. Square tiles inset into red brick here are undoubtedly from Abramtsevo workshops, possibly made by Vasnetsov himself.
(Military Section, French Embassy; X)

**62 P N Pertsov's Apartment House 1905–7**
S V MALIUTIN & N K ZHUKOV
Soimonovskii proezd, 1 *Metro: Kropotkinskaia*
An apposite comparison with the nearby no 61. Maliutin moved in similar circles to Vasnetsov, but was eleven years younger. He directed the workshops at the other arts-and-crafts colony, Talashkino. This is his largest architectural work, but typically little more than an application of his 'applied arts' at architectural scale. A decorative treatment of the 4–5-storeyed red-brick block by engineer Zhukov, which seeks to suggest that additive characteristic of medieval Russian building, and provides occasions for 'medieval' window shapes and his many vast panels of folklorique polychrome tilework and carved animals. One entire apartment was originally decorated and furnished in the claustrophobic Talashkino manner. Cosmetic, where Vasnetsov's interest is genuinely architectural.
(Bureau for Services to the Diplomatic Corps; X)

**63 Housing complex on ulitsa Serafimovicha 1928–31**
B M IOFAN & D M IOFAN
ulitsa Serafimovicha, 2/20 *Metro: Kropotkinskaia*
First realisation of the concept of the 'living combine' prevalent during this First Five Year Plan period. Spans the whole island width, in 3 interconnecting courtyards of mainly ten storey concrete framed housing on concrete piles. Five hundred family apartments are supplied a full range of services (childrens' establishments, laundry, library, sports-hall, dining hall, post-office; club-cum-theatre on the River embankment; 1600 seat cinema on the canal side; department store on Serafimovicha ulitsa; gardens and play areas in the courtyards); also with internal conveniences (built-in cupboards, garbage chutes, central heating and hot water from district heating plant on site). The totally undecorated architecture of the twenties on a monumental scale belonging to the thirties, by the winning architect of the Palace of Soviets competition.

**64 Church of the Iverskaia Nurses Community 1896** I E BONDARENKO, attrib
Bol'shaia Polianka ulitsa, 20 *Metro: Novokuznetskaia*
Important example of the academic Neo-Russian revival of late 1890s, attributed, very plausibly, to one of its leading propagandists. Features from 16–17th-century brick churches on the classic Moscow-region form of early 15th century (compare Cathedral of Trinity, Zagorsk, 1422–3). Square plan; 3×3 bays making cubic volume; 3 half-cylindrical apses to the E with blind arcading; tall slit cylindrical drum, ditto, with clipped half-spherical dome; in pink brick with stone infill to all nine elevational bays. Interesting comparison

with Bondarenko's National-Romantic essay no 139, and in slightly better condition.
(Located in yard of Children's Hospital No 20).

**65 The Tretlakov Refuge (Ubezhishche) for Widows and Orphans of Russian Painters 1912–1919**
N S KUDRIUKOV
Lavrushinskii pereulok, 3 *Metro: Novokuznetskaia*
A benefaction named in memory of the same P M Tretiakov whose house and collection became the gallery (no 66). Two simple, almost industrial blocks in red brick, with pitched roofs, in T-shaped plan, 2 & 3-storeyed. Entered by small porch, LHS of street elevation, into head of T, where very large arched windows at 1st floor illuminate public rooms. Accommodation in tail of T, with regular, more domestic fenestration, in 2 floors. All has economical, indeed austere air; only ceramic decoration at eaves of main elevation, including arms of Moscow city, mainly lost. Interesting as a type. Construction completed after Revolution, but plain design original.

**66 Tretiakov Gallery 1900–5*** V M VASNETSOV
Lavrushinskii pereulok, 10 *Metro: Novokuznetskaia*
Reconstruction of P M Tretiakov's mansion of 1873, after his death in 1898, to house his collection of Russian art, for which Vasnetsov (see no 61) produced perhaps the finest National-Romantic facade in Moscow. Two-fifths of the main rectangular elevation is dominated by a rich floral frieze of polychrome tilework from Abramtsevo, and the medievalised typographical band in black and white below it, all on a deep red stuccoed wall. Central bay of carved triple windows, black, set slightly R, breaks cornice with a tall *kokoshnik* (blind ogee gable) containing bas-relief of St George. Three porches, white brick with gilded gables, stand forward. With the glazing of two N-light gables above, the whole is a feast of colour, craftsmanship, natural materials and subtle proportions that genuinely re-creates the Russian 'spirit' which Vasnetsov pursued.

**67 Hotel Novomoskovskaia 1897** A V IVANOV
ulitsa Balchug, 1 *Metro: Novokuznetskaia*
Classic Ivanov (see no 60) applied to a large hotel. Elevation to street, with its corner tower, is original hotel; riverside block was originally apartment house. Storeys added.
(Hotel Bucharest, 1–i korpus.)

**68 Central Institute of Mineral Raw Materials 1925–9**
V A VESNIN
Staromonetnyi pereulok, 29 *Metro: Dobryninskaia*
First building erected by any of the Vesnins after the Revolution, and first such new Institute of the Soviet period. Commissioned, after unfruitful open competition. Executant team drawn from Viktor Vesnin's diploma class at Moscow Tech (MVTU), included later well-known members of OSA. Open green courtyard some 85 metres square is enclosed by four asymmetrical blocks, the main building 4-storeyed, others 3. Planning worked out in close collaboration with Institute staff concerned, and on basis of latest comparable Western practice. Concrete framed construction; otherwise plain elevations articulated by the fenestration that reflects diversity of accommodation inside (labs; auditoria; study rooms; library; museum etc). Described by Bruno Taut after his visit as 'a very rational building, beautifully thought out in all its details'. Nonetheless has an overwhelming atmosphere of mid-twenties austerity, when building activity was only just reviving again.
(All Union Research Institute of the Ministry of Geology USSR.)

**69 Church of the Martha and Mary Mission (obshchina) 1908–12** A V SHCHUSEV
Bol'shaia Ordynka ulitsa, 34a *Metro: Dobryninskaia*
Neo-Russian work akin to the later Bondarenkos in spirit (nos 139, 140) by an equally dedicated though younger student of the Russian heritage. Models here are early 16th-century churches of Pskov and Novgorod, given tension and theatricality characteristic of the *Moderne* by exaggeration of certain details and overblowing of key elements (central cupola; triple apses), also by bas-relief panels in contrasting materials. New convent (all by Shchusev) founded by the Empress's sister; nuns' habits designed in spirit with Shchusev's architecture by painter Mikhail Nesterov, who also did internal murals. Entrance wall with gateway on street. (Central Artistic Restoration Workshops.)

**70 Korobkov Mansion late 1890s** L N KEKUSHEV
Piatnitskaia ulitsa, 33 *Metro: Novokuznetskaia*
Two-storeyed house that combines the scale and form of a 19C neo-classical mansion with the emergent dynamism of the *Moderne*. Ten massive undivided plate-glass windows, plus bay window and corner tower at first floor of asymmetrical street elevation; long wing to side yard less glazed, and more classically composed. Heavy rustication with squat windows at street level, smoother surfaces above, all in pale green. Richly eclectic detailing in white. Bold semi-circles, rich modelling and figurative details typical of Kekushev. An interesting transitional work.
(Embassy of Tanzania; X)

**71 M I Rekk's Mansion 1897** S V SHERVUD
Piatnitskaia ulitsa, 64 *Metro: Dobryninskaia*
Luxuriant and freely composed confection of classical elements on a relatively small L-shaped house by son of the academic Russianist architect of the Historical Museum, in the year of his death. Domed hexagonal corner tower set back behind temple front on street with paired columns of a rich composite order and ornate sculptural decoration. Ostentation handled with confidence, in pale green and white; 2-3 storeys, but of Russian scale.
(Mosproekt-3.)

**72 I D Sytin's Printing Works 1912** I A GERMAN
Piatnitskaia ulitsa, 71 *Metro: Dobryninskaia*
One of German's several examples of this new building type, for a man of peasant origins who was one of Russia's most prolific publishers, producing cheap mass editions of Russian and foreign classics, popular encyclopedias etc (cf newspaper activities, no 16). Long, framed building of 5 high storeys, in cream, with maximum simple but well-proportioned fenestration. *Moderne* features include simple but elegant gridding of glazing frames; contrast of textures between brick piers and rendered infill panels; grouping of end and entrance bays into threes under simple, industrial version of the *Moderne* gable in corbelled brick.
(First Model Printing Works named for A A Zhdanov.)

**73 Department Store on Serpukhovskaia Ploshchad' 1928–9** K IAKOVLIOV
Dobryninskaia ulitsa, 1/3 *Metro: Dobryninskaia*
Moscow's first Post-Revolutionary department store of a comparable scale to the old ones, and significantly located out of the centre, towards industrial housing areas. Six storeys, the top two being administration and thus having paired windows rather than floor-to-floor glazing. A rational and not inelegant building for its period.
(Moskovsko-Leninskii Department Store.)

**74 Men's and Women's Commercial Institute 1911–12** S U SOLOV'IOV & A V SHCHUSEV
Stremiannyi pereulok, 28 *Metro: Dobryninskaia*
Another progressive higher educational establishment (cf no 52). Founded 1907, this in its time also had strong revolutionary connections and again he used a variant of the patriotic Empire style of the early 19th century, though here with touches of *Moderne*. The young Shchusev was his assistant. This was Russia's first establishment for higher education in the economic and technical aspects of trade and manufacture.
(Moscow Institute of the National Economy named for G V Plekhanov.)

**75 Morozov Children's Hospital early 1900s***
I A IVANOV-SHITS
Liusinovskii 3–i pereulok *Metro: Oktiabrskaia*
In the tradition of large philanthropic foundations for

medicine by leading families, stretching back to the late 18C – this was built by Old-Believer textile millionares. An extensive complex of dispersed, mainly 3-storeyed blocks among trees. Very similar in planning to the architect's slightly later Soldatienkovskii complex (no 4) in N of the city. Here too, entrance and administrative building are given more external 'finish' architecturally than the ward blocks, and the elements of *Moderne* decoration are more florid here, picked out white against deep red walls. Fine iron railings. Altogether a very fine example of the type at this date.
(Moscow Clinical Hospital for Children Number 1)

**76 Shabolovka Radio Mast 1922** V G SHUKHOV, engineer
Shabolovka ulitsa, 53 *Metro: Shabolovskaia*
An inspirational structure in its time, though not strictly architectural, as one of the very first 'modern' erections of post-Revolutionary years. Very light, 160 metre high circular, tapered lattice in steel by the designer of the similarly spectacular steel vault of Briansk (Kiev) station (no 44) a decade before. Shukhov had proposed a 350 metre tower, but the steel shortage made it impossible.

**77 Shabolovka Communal Housing complex 1926–30** G Ia VOL'FENSON
ulitsa Lesteva, 18 *Metro: Shabolovskaia*
Design submitted to Mossoviet's *dom-kommuna* competition of 1926; built 1928–30. U-shaped complex of five 5-storeyed interconnected blocks of living accommodation on corridor plan forming open, S-facing court. Originally entered at inside bottom of 'U' with communal dining room to the N and crèche, kindergarten etc at ground level in adjoining wings, E & W. (No longer housing.) Across the street, S, lies Shabolovka Housing District, by N Travin, 1927–8; 22, 5-storeyed 'model' blocks of family apartments, with 3-storeyed school etc, arranged on zig-zag forming grassed courtyards.

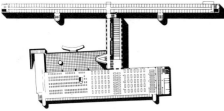

**78 Communal House for students of the Textile Institute 1929–30** I S NIKOLAEV
ulitsa Ordzhonikidze, 8/9 *Metro: Leninskii Prospekt*
Only Moscow example of this concept being realised by a distinguished architect – in this case a leading member of the Constructivist group OSA. To accommodate apprentices, technical personnel etc of the industry undergoing training courses in Moscow. The long eight-storeyed block with two stair towers and horizontally banded windows contains 1,000 two-bedded cabins of 6m² intended only for sleeping. The linked three-storeyed building contains all other facilities: dining rooms; large library; sports-hall; 1000-seat auditorium; activity rooms, including some for individual use; crèche and laundry. The two blocks and their link, of Corbusian stylistic inspiration, form a slightly wedge-shaped entrance court where a sweeping curved *porte cochère* identifies the community entrance.

**79 Medvednikov Poorhouse 1902–3**
S U SOLOV'IOV
Leninskii prospekt, 27 *Metro: Leninskii Prospekt*
Quite extensive 2-storeyed complex in a smoothed and somewhat routine Neo-Russian style, with forms and details of Pskov-Novgorod origin reduced to an agreeable form of domestic decoration.
(Part of City Hospital No 5)

**80 Palace of Culture of the Proletarskii District 1931–7\*** A A, L A, & V A VESNIN
Vostochnaia ulitsa, 4 *Metro: Avtozavodskaia*
The last Constructivist building to start construction in Moscow. A very large workers' club of which the biggest single element, a 4000-seat free-standing theatre building to enclose the entrance court, was never started. The Vesnins did not enter the 1930 competition but were commissioned when it proved unfruitful, and building started in 1932. Behind a flat curve of 1st and 2nd floor glazing, L, lie the foyers of a 1000-seat, single galleried, daylit auditorium with full and varied theatrical and other facilities. Over a colonnade this is linked by a double sided exhibition hall convertable to dance-hall. This is the stem of a T-shaped complex of club facilities which also contains club rooms, library, restaurant, astronomical observatory, and central semicircular 'winter garden' in marble and glass that looks to the nearby Moscow river. Practical planning and the Vesnins' typical 'free-flowing' internal space, with rich and subtle daylighting, make this a masterly and happy work. They gave its interior details more attention than normally, with finishes and colour being done by the Stenberg brothers, P Likin & A Kolodnyi.
(Palace of Culture of the Likhachev Automobile Factory, ZIL)

**81 Dubrovka Housing District 1925–8**
M I MOTYLEV & N MOLOKOV
Between ulitsy Krutitskii Val, Dubrovskaia I-aia & Sharikopodshipnikovskaia *Metro: Proletarskaia*
Model public housing development of the very early Soviet period comparable to no 54. Twenty-five, 5-storeyed blocks of small family apartments with 'all conveniences' and communal facilities which form open, planted courts. Considerable reconstruction in the late 1970s.

**82 The Trade Centre (Delovyi Dvor) 1912–13\***
I S KUZNETSOV
Ploshchad' Nogina, 5 *Metro: Ploshchad' Nogina*
A 5-storeyed complex of accommodation conceived as the latest thing in efficient wholesale trading. Main building, R, is a concrete frame structure with uninterrupted floors for warehousing, glazed floor-to-ceiling, with large areas set aside for demonstration of goods and equipment etc, and special accommodation in the front block for negotiating, formal signing of contracts etc. This forms a complete courtyard with vehicle access through 2-storeyed corner archway. The linear building, L, with main entrance in the rotunda behind the church, was the businessmen's hotel on a simple corridor plan. Appropriate glazing and slightly more refined elevational treatment distinguish it visually. Classicist gestures of the high-level portico over the archway, and end windows, are the only compromises with an otherwise almost Constructivist simplicity best seen within the yards.
(Offices etc of various establishments.)

**83 Moscow Trading Company's apartment housing development 1912–15**
V V SHERVUD, I A GERMAN & A E SERGEEV
ulitsa Solianka, 1 *Metro: Ploshchad' Nogina*
Perhaps the finest remaining example of maximum density site development in middle-class housing for rent from 1910s. (For 1900s, see nos 117, 121) Awkward corner site bisected by an L-shaped alley. Rectangular island piece has six storeys of 2, 3, 4 and 5-bedroomed apartments wrapped around two light-wells; living spaces generally outside, services inside. Outside the alley, a single layer of building with wings forms lightwells with the Monastery wall on ulitsa Zabelina and encloses a triangular well at the Solianka end. Density made civilised by the quality of architecture: relaxed and gentle classicism of giant pilasters and fine relief panels in a free composition of the surface whose curved corners, bay window shafts and roofline have the *Moderne*'s softness. Grey now, where it should be white.

**84 Moscow Insurance Company's Building 1901** F O SHEKHTEL'

Staraia Ploshchad', 5 *Metro: Ploshchad' Nogina*
Later well known as the *Boyarskii Dvor Hotel*. A 5-storeyed framed building which occupies almost the entire block between ulitsy Razina and Kuibysheva belongs to the Rationalist current of the *Moderne* with all the top-emphasis and tense curves of the latter, half-way in Shekhtel's *oeuvre* between the still heavily decorated and slightly classicised no 89 of two years before, and the subtle simplicity of no 95. Piers in pale blue-green glazed brick; spandrels and upper storey in cream stone.
(Central Committee of the Communist Party of the Soviet Union; X)

**85 Apartment House 1903** Prince G I MAKAEV
Podsosenskii pereulok, 18 *Metro: Kurskaia*
Exotic, somewhat Gaudiesque elevational, and particularly corner, treatment of an otherwise fairly ordinary block of *Moderne* housing, in rough grey rendering and smooth cream stone. Deep-cut curves give a fleshy quality to the stone bays that break up through the roofline with fanciful *Moderne* 'pediments'. Vertical strips of flat, geometrical floral decoration against the rendering of circular corner tower and long elevation give a vegetable air.

**86 Headquarters of the Triangle Company 1914** M S LIALEVICH
ulitsa Bogdana Khmel'nitskogo, 12 *Metro: Ploshchad' Nogina*
Immediately pre-Revolutionary work by a leading Petersburg architect of this period who took a firmly principled stand on the technological and aesthetic novelties of the *Moderne* as 'historically necessary', but only as a revitalising, modernising stimulus to the more 'deeply founded' principles of classicism. Clean-cut arcaded elevation is typical; here with paired Ionic columns embracing floor-to-ceiling glazing of the 3 upper storeys over nicely scaled rusticated base.
(Ministry of the Chemical Industry)

**87 Mausoleum of V I Lenin 1924–30\***
A V SHCHUSEV
Red Square *Metro: Ploshchad' Revoliutsii*
A stepped, cubic structure in granite and red marble which merges masterfully with the Kremlin Wall behind. This third and permanent structure was designed in 1929. The first, on Lenin's death in January 1924, was a timber box with two outlying guard-huts; the second, that spring, also timber, was closer to the present form, (both by Shchusev). A sequence of ideas-competitions followed in 1925.

**88 Riabushinskii Brothers Banking House 1903–4** F O SHEKHTEL'
Ploshchad' Kuibysheva, 2 *Metro: Ploshchad' Nogina*
Important work in Shekhtel's career, though much altered since. Though a conversion, thus of traditional internal construction, it was his first rigorous elevational expression of the frame idea, in a 3-bayed front almost wholly glazed in the 4 lower floors of banking halls. Original top floor with small windows was administrative offices, and was topped by strong cornice. For the first time all was in neutral cream and white, and no decoration except typography in the stuccoed spandrels. In 1908 Shekhtel' himself removed cornice and added certain decorative elements; in 1913 AV Kuznetsov added top and penthouse stories; recent renovation has moved the entrance from R to centre.

### 89 Arshinov Company Building 1899
F O SHEKHTEL'

Staropanskii pereulok, 5 *Metro: Ploshchad' Nogina*
Very much a transitional building, that combines clear statement of a daringly simple structure with rich eclectic detailing in strong colour. The centre of the elevation is effectively a single broad arched window rising 3 floors, divided by spandrels that originally carried typography and topped by bold scrollwork with a woman's head looking down. Behind were 3 floors of warehousing and display, whose only interruptions were a long cast-iron staircase, R, two central cast-iron columns and a cast-iron balustraded hole at the rear allowing goods to be hoisted to all floors. The top floor, presumably administrative, is expressed as a deep cornice with narrow rhythmic fenestration. Facing material deep blue-green glazed brick, with bold and florid detailing in cream stone.

### 90 Commercial Building 1898–9* A V IVANOV
Staropanskii pereulok, 6/8 *Metro: Ploshchad' Nogina*
Four-storeyed frame building of great sophistication, especially for its date. L-shaped, on a corner site, with yard through double-height archway. Cream, with metalwork in dark brown. Chicago-like refinement, especially in technical quality of fenestration which remains almost entirely original; in set-back of street level glazing, and in spareness of the slightly classicised detailing overall. Makes the contemporaneous Shekhtel' next door seem a very emotional exercise.

### 91 International Commercial Bank Building 1910–11 A E ERIKHSON
ulitsa Kuibysheva, 9 (left hand building) *Metro: Ploshchad' Nogina*
One of the most imposing, and well constructed, of pre-War office buildings. Five high storeys, roughly square elevation, under strong cornice surmounted by flat, stylised 'pediment' over central bay. A concrete frame construction, almost completely glazed, so that dark grey granite facing belies the obviously very light quality of space inside. Rusticated piers at street level; giant order of 4 engaged, Ionic columns in centre, and pilasters, L & R, on 1st and 2nd floors; 3rd & 4th, in centre, derive somewhat Egyptian character from flat 'columns' and stylised figurative 'capitals'. Finest extant building by Erikhson, for obviously powerful clients.
(Ministry of Finance of the USSR; X)

### 92 Azovsko-Donskoi Bank Building 1912
A N ZILIGSON
ulitsa Kuibysheva, 9 (right hand building) *Metro: Ploshchad' Nogina*
Five-storeyed, but considerably lower overall than its LH neighbour no 91, and narrower site. 5-bayed, framed elevation, also fully glazed, between broad granite piers at street level which step back into a giant

order of rusticated engaged columns of a token 'order' running through floors 1–3. Attic storey above an absolutely plain frieze (probably originally carrying company name etc), and simple unbroken cornice. Robust but not pretentious work by an otherwise unknown architect.
(Ministry of Finance of the USSR; X)

### 93 Office Building 1927–28 V M MAIAT
ulitsa Kuibysheva, 11 *Metro: Ploshchad' Nogina*
Corner site, whose narrowness is stressed by the verticality of elevational treatment. 6–7 storeys, reaching the same height as the 5 of no 91. 5-bayed main elevation, of which outer bays have conventional solid spandrels and fashionable circular windows in blind walls of the 6th floor. 3 central bays have curtain wall of 3 faceted bay windows rising unbroken through 1st–4th floors. Sensitive bit of infill into this predominantly late 19-century and early 20th-century street at the heart of the pre-Revolutionary business district, by an architect who was himself active in that period.
(Administrative building)

### 94 Northern Insurance Company Buildings
1909–12 I I RERBERG, M M PERETIATKOVICH & V K OLTARZHEVSKII
ulitsa Kuibysheva, 21 & 23 *Metro: Ploshchad' Nogina*
An extensive complex, built over a basement undercroft of broad, low concrete arches typical of Rerberg's early structural virtuosity. L-shaped site above split by a through route with cul-de-sacs off, which gets maximum daylit accommodation though it is fragmented. Elegant five-storeyed frame buildings, with leading Petersburg architect Peretiatkovich, are similar to no 95 in conception, but retain a classical static stability. There is free classical detailing, in particular on the seven-storeyed circular tower identifying the way in, but it is far lighter than most work by either of the main architects.
(Committee for National Control of the USSR and other government organs; X)

### 95 Moscow Trading Company Building 1909*
F O SHEKHTEL'
Novaia Ploshchad', 2 and Malyi Cherkasskii pereulok, 6 *Metro: Dzerzhinskaia*
One of the masterpieces of pre-Revolutionary commercial architecture. A building of dazzling modernity and sparkle in its time, when the softly curved glazed-brick piers and the smooth-rendered spandrels were fresh

off-white and the enormous windows were almost uninterrupted plate glass in the slenderest steel frames. Five-storeyed, with the bold square geometry of the frame given sensual plasticity by bold and subtle curves in the outer form of the piers and the rippling 'cornice' below the top, office floor; in the niches above which are the only overtly decorative motif; in the rounded corner of Malyi and Bol'shoi Cherkasskii streets, and in the fleshy curve of the archway on Novaia Ploshchad'. Spandrel panels originally carried delicate typography, with names and specialisms of the trading group's component companies.

### 96 Nikolskie Trading Rows 1899–1900
L N KEKUSHEV
ulitsa 25 Oktiabria, 5 *Metro: Ploshchad' Revoliutsii*
Boldly composed retail shopping building of the kind that preceded unified department stores in Russia (in this respect similar to the Upper Trading Rows, now GUM). Symmetrical facade expressing a frame structure within. Diversity of elements, top emphasis, rippling cornice and broken roofline are typical early *Moderne* though many decorative motifs are still classical. All the vigour and fluidity characteristic of Kekushev with his usual delight in the semicircle and the square.

### 97 Hotel Metropol' 1899–1903
V F VAL'KOT (WILLIAM WALCOT) with others
prospekt Marksa, 1 *Metro: Ploshchad' Sverdlova*
Largest of the great international hotels of pre-Revolutionary Russia with over 400 bedrooms, banqueting-hall, numerous restaurants etc. Occupies an entire square block. Five storeys, with floor-to-ceiling arched windows of restaurants, small shops etc around the granite-faced ground floor. Two lines of fine Art Nouveau iron balconies divide the rest into two equal strips whose relatively simple basic fenestration is interrupted below by flat, round-cornered bay windows, and above by triple windows over which rise banner-like curved ceramic panels; the central one by Mikhail Vrubel', from Abramtsevo workshops, depicting the Princess of Dreams, the rest by Diaghilev associate and Talashkino habitué Aleksandr Golovin. Above the upper balconies runs a plaster relief of human figures round the whole building, part of a rich play of textures and materials typical of the *Moderne*; these by the former Wanderers group artist, Nikolai Andreev. History: the original Metropol' hotel, a classical building of similar form, was bought in the late 1890s by the St Petersburg Insurance Society for radical remodelling. In a competition, Kekushev's richly eclectic design won, but the Society's artistic adviser, Savva Mamontov, founder-owner of the Abramtsevo colony, selected as the basis for building Val'kot's fourth-prize design, because it offered the best opportunities for incorporating artists' work. Kekushev supervised much of the construction; Erikhson did interior work, also Viktor Vesnin, who did the hairdresser's salon in mirrors and white. Little of interest remains inside, since it had a long period of use as offices.

### 98 Hotel Natsional' 1903 A I IVANOV
ulitsa Gorkogo, 1 *Metro: Prospekt Marksa*
Another prestigious turn-of-the-century hotel. Magni-

ficent fenestration of restaurant spaces at street and first-floor levels with some fine *Moderne* detailing in red marble against matching stucco. Above a cornice, uniform fenestration of rooms on 3 storeys is freely decorated overall with a rich eclecticism, in ochre. Above a continuous iron balcony, the upper storey's corner bay, boldly rounded, rises to a figurative polychrome panel, the original design replaced in the 1920s by an industrial theme. A fine building, but far more traditional in elevational conception than no 97.

**99 Central Telegraph Building 1925–7**
I I RERBERG
ulitsa Gorkogo, 7   *Metro: Prospekt Marksa*
Subject of a competition in 1925 after which the six premiated designs were rejected in favour of Rerberg's. Four storeys, with five-storeyed polygonal corner tower. Concrete frame, fully glazed and virtually undecorated, on a granite base. Piloried by Constructivists as example of 'How not to build', for its planning inside and out; for its extravagantly heavy cladding to a concrete frame when materials were scarce; for 'haberdashery' at the roofline of the tower 'reminiscent of the Morozov mansion' (in Moorish style by Mazyrin, 1894, nearby); for 'half-baked' connection of pilasters and cornice on the elevation; in short, for 'a futile attempt at genuinely modern architecture'.

**100 Moscow Arts Theatre 1902   F O SHEKHTEL'**
proezd Khudozhestvennogo Teatra, 3   *Metro: Prospekt Marksa*
Reconstruction of the old Lianozovskii Theatre which produced one of Shekhtel's finest sequences of coordinated interiors. Through his own early theatrical work and personal closeness to Chekhov it was a job highly sympathetic to him that was executed within 3 months, with Shekhtel' often drawing on site. A comprehensive design schema in its organisation of space, light, brown and beige colours, brass and glass details, and in its graphics, which builds to that emotional and intellectually charged climax so beloved of the *Moderne*, in the simple and intimate 1300-seat auditorium. Public accommodation towards the street, performers behind, all with a convenience unprecedented in that period. Shekhtel's facade design of 1903 was never executed through lack of funds, except for the sculptured panel over the door, R, by World-of-Art sculptress Anna Golubkina, and the doors, light-fittings etc. Golubkina's *Wave* reflects same theme of restless, creative searching intended by Shekhtel's graphic motif of the *Seagull*, which the theatre still uses.

**101 Exhibition and commercial building 1914**
F O SHEKHTEL'
proezd Khudozhestvennogo Teatra, 5   *Metro: Prospekt Marksa*
The small building on RHS of the Theatre, above, was designed to accommodate exhibitions, offices and shops. Simple elevation divided horizontally into two parts, four square piers reflecting the frame structure above, 4 engaged columns below, glazed between. Simple and mature.

**102 Savvinskoe Hostelry 1905–7**   I S KUZNETSOV
ulitsa Gorkogo, 6 (in the yard through archway)   *Metro: Prospekt Marksa*

A vigorous hierarchy of arcades and friezes decorated with the freedom and diverse materials characteristic of early, eclectic *Moderne*. Polychrome tile work with much pastel colour gives a rather confectionary character; combined with the bold underlying structure (cf his no 82) and rhythm of semicircles the building is undemandingly pleasurable in a manner appropriate to its function.

**103 Institute of V I Lenin 1925–7**
S E CHERNYSHEV
Sovetskaia ploshchad', 1/3   *Metro: Prospekt Marksa*
One of the first new official buildings of the Soviet period; winning entry in a competition of 1925, the year after Lenin's death, and building finished by January 1927. Extremely simple square building in pink-grey rendering. Four storeys of seven slightly differentiated windows, circular over side doors. Given monumentality by developing piers into a pilaster-like grid, and by stepped profile of rooftop.
(Central Party Archive of the Institute of Marxism-Leninism under the Central Committee of the Soviet Communist Party.)

**104 Hotel Liuks 1911   N A EIKHENVAL'D**
ulitsa Gorkogo, 10   *Metro: Pushkinskaia-Gorkovskaia*
Five floors of grand rooms over high ground floor, between nos 97 & 98 in size. Like them, has floor-to-ceiling, arched plate-glass windows giving direct views into the ornate restaurant, R, from the pavement. Long, horizontally banded elevation with strong 4th-floor cornice and fine eclectic decoration. 'Good taste' in the manner of the pre-War *haute bourgeoisie* (cf nos 60, 67) as symbolised in the name 'Luxe'.
(Hotel Tsentral'naia.)

**105 Bakhrushin's Apartment House 1901–2**
K K GIPPIUS
ulitsa Gorkogo, 12   *Metro: Pushkinakaia-Gorkovskaia*
Rare remaining example in Russia of work so close in spirit to European, and here particularly Parisian, Art Nouveau. Ironwork of balconies is close in style and quality to Guimard. Slightly more formalised, but equally florid, are the capitals of free-standing columns under first-floor balconies, R & L, and upper balcony brackets, comprising heads and flowing hair of young women intertwined with ribbons and flowers. Five-storeyed, symmetrical, with the three balcony bays breaking the roofline. Ground floor obliterated by modern shop fronts.

**106 Eliseev's Food Halls 1898–1901***
G V BARANOVSKII
ulitsa Gorkogo, 14   *Metro: Pushkinskaia-Gorkovskaia*

G G Eliseev ran the St Petersburg equivalent of Harrod's Food Halls, and opened his Moscow branch here in 1901. Brought Baranovskii from the capital to convert a long, 3-storeyed neo-classical building of late 18th century, already much altered, before erecting his externally more spectacular premises on Petersburg's Nevskii Prospekt during 1902–3. Insides very similar, and leave Harrod's in the shade with their grandiose mixture of coloured marbles, gold, chandeliers, mirrors and palms. Eclectic street facades, on Gorkogo and Kozitskii, R, have very fine plate-glass windows.
(Food Store, Gastronom No 1.)

**107 Smirnov Mansion   early 1900s**
F O SHEKHTEL'
Tverskoi bulevard, 18   *Metro: Pushkinskaia-Gorkovskaia*
A 3-storeyed neo-classical house of the early 19C that was radically reconstructed to the tastes of this millionaire family of vodka distillers. As considerable patrons of the arts, they needed major reception rooms for their frequent exhibitions, soirees etc. Rather as in the contemporaneous Arts Theatre conversion (no 100), Shekhtel' imposes a gentle asymmetry of emergent *Moderne* onto the framework of classical fenestration through developing a large elevational feature around the entrance, reinforcing it here on the skyline. Over entrance, triple-arched window within a giant arched panel, with relief decoration, gives onto magnificent double-height interior. All with a mixture of eclectic detailing (cf 70, of earlier date, by Kekushev). Most luxuriantly *Moderne* feature is very finely scrolled wrought iron balcony below 3 central first-floor windows. Yellow stucco, like neighbours on boulevard.

**108 Khomiakov's Office Building 1899–1900**
I A IVANOV-SHITS
Petrovka ulitsa, 3/6 & Kuznetskii Most, 6/3   *Metro: Ploshchad' Sverdlova*
A relatively early work which shows the architect already replacing classical motifs with a free eclecticism characteristic of this early *Moderne* period, embracing the bold glazing possibilities offered by framed structures and developing themes of rhythmic, close-spaced verticals that were a particular feature of his mature work. The top two floors are a much later addition.
(Ministry of River Shipping of the RSFSR.)

**109 'Sokol' Apartment House 1902–3**
I P MASHKOV
Kuznetskii Most, 3   *Metro: Ploshchad' Sverdlova*
A long, 5-storeyed block whose subtle plays of planes, curves, and slight compositional asymmetries, as well as its decoration, make it a fine example of *Moderne* work. Cream stucco, with polychrome tile work predominantly in blues. Complete tiled frieze under the cornice rises in the centre between intertwined verticals and scrolls, patterned with rhythmic, Art Nouveau plants and a falcon (*sokol*) soaring among clouds above. These by well-known painter, contributor to World of Art, Blue Rose etc, Nikolai Sapunov. Geometrical relief decoration and blue-green banded tilework lower down, with some metallic copper glazes. Scrollwork filling outer profile of 'pediment' is lost, also shop fascia, R, which resolved the narrow verticals there; some ironwork preserved.

**110 Petrovskii Passazh 1903**
S M KALUGIN & B V FREIDENBERG
Petrovka ulitsa, 10   *Metro: Ploshchad' Sverdlova*
The only remaining example in Moscow of the shopping galleria, of which there were eight in this fashionable shopping district before the First War, five of them running, like this one, from Petrovka to Neglinnaia. The first was built in 1835; this was the last. (GUM, the Upper Trading Rows, of course has a similar form, but is far more extensive.) Three shopping floors, middle one

linked across with slightly curved bridges; eclectic detailing, under a fine glass barrel vault.
(Operated as a branch of the nearby Central Department Store, TsUM.)

### 111 Muir & Merilees' Department Store
**1908–10** R I KLEIN
Petrovka ulitsa, 2 *Metro: Ploshchad' Sverdlova*
First of the modern, integrated department stores in Moscow, on the galleried plan around a central space that was to become typical in Russia (cf no 37) and unlike the galleria, maximally exposed goods to casual view from a single central staircase. A thoroughly progressive concrete framed structure is clad in a belated essay in European Gothic that has features of the *Moderne*. Messrs Muir and Merilees seem obscure; the styling may originate with them.
(The Central Department Store, TsUM.)

### 112 State Bank Building, new wings 1927–9
I V ZHOLTOVSKII
Neglinnaia ulitsa, 12 *Metro: Kuznetskii Most*
Two six-storeyed wings added outside K M Bykovskii's handsome and vigorous 2- & 3-storeyed eclectic building of 1893–5 for the Imperial Bank. A piece of restrained, indeed reticent Neo-Renaissance work whose extreme flatness offers no competition to Bykovskii, speaks of the austerity of its time, and probably seemed to Zholtovskii suitably 'modern'. Constructivists recognised it to be 'qualitatively different . . . from the ideologically empty Rerberg' (cf no 99) but 'far more dangerous to our society' as 'the practical propagation of the ideology of passeists and eclectics' by someone 'who does not believe in the truths of his epoch and has not the creative capacity to create its new values.'
(Moscow City Office of the State Bank USSR; X)

### 113 J W Junker & Co's Bank Building 1913
A E ERIKHSON; facade by L A, V A & A A VESNIN
Kuznetskii Most, 18 *Metro: Kuznetskii Most*
A fine six-storeyed building in grey stone; 3-arched arcade on a colossal Ionic order embraces 4 floors of floor-to-ceiling glazing. Heavily rusticated ground floor, and three colonnaded windows above with dumpy, convex-sided columns which are the most *Moderne* decorative motif used. As a very bright trio of young architects, the Vesnins did elevational work for several leading Moscow offices at this time (cf 120, 122). Here the final design is a development from the published sketch which suggests influence from Lialevich's Mertens Building in Petersburg of 1910–12.
(Offices and Fashion House.)

### 114 Commercial offices of the Zharkov Company
**1913** A V KUZNETSOV
Kuznetskii most, 16 *Metro: Kuznetskii Most*
Kuznetsov at his most austere (cf nos 116, 124). Direct expression of the reinforced concrete frame, stressed by 'exposure' of columns at roofline, and almost entirely glazed infill. Elevations given touches of *Moderne* composition by extending end bays and central, curved corner bay upwards, to break the strongly horizontal cantilevered 'cornice', and by slight change of grid in the entrance bays to L & R of corner. Interesting development from no 124, through 116, to this complete absence of decoration.
(Administrative offices)

### 115 International Trading Bank Building 1898
S S EIBUSHETS
Kuznetskii Most, 15/8 *Metro: Kuznetskii Most*
A fine piece of banker's architecture that could be in any European city. Constructed to the highest pre-Revolutionary standards in a sober but inventive classical mode with gestures towards the extensive fenestration then becoming fashionable.
(International Bank for Economic Collaboration).

### 116 Studio Building for the Stroganov College of Applied Arts 1913–14 A V KUZNETSOV
ulitsa Zhdanova, 11 *Metro: Kuznetskii Most*
Grey, L-shaped building which encloses back RH corner of courtyard, as extension of classical main building of college. Two wings, framed construction, meet in stepped-back tower element with vertical circulation, with entrance on diagonal at GL. On Kuznetsov's work on concrete, see no 124. Here, beamless floors and full exploitation of the resultant freedoms used for free-planning of large simple interiors, flat roofs with top-lighting for painting studios, and very fine reinforced concrete spiral staircase. Pioneering study of daylighting work environments had been his doctoral dissertation in 1907. Here, the first use of horizontal strip windows in an r.c. frame in Russian architecture. Superb technical quality of detailing and construction typical of Kuznetsov. A good demonstration of his statement at this time to the 5th Congress of Russian Architects in Moscow (1913), that: 'In reinforced concrete we have not only a new material, but what is more important, new forms of construction and a new method of designing buildings. Therefore in using it, it is necessary to abandon old traditions and devote ourselves to solving new tasks.' This thoroughly modern building shows clearly how he became a close mentor and ally to the Vesnins and other Constructivists after the Revolution. In 1918, Kuznetsov was founder of the Architectural Faculty in Moscow Higher Technical College (MVTU), to which he later brought them and Ginzburg as teachers.
(Ministry of Higher and Middle Specialised Education of the USSR; X)

### 117 Apartment Building of the First Russian Insurance Company 1905–7 L N BENUA (BENOIS) & A I GUNST
Kuznetskii Most, 5/21 & ulitsa Dzerzhinskogo, 5
*Metro: Kuznetskii Most*
The unique Moscow work, it seems, by this generation's most influential teacher of architecture at the Empire's leading school, the Academy of Arts in Petersburg. Central figure in architectural and town planning aspects of the movement for a Russian cultural revival spearheaded on other fronts by his brother Aleksandr. His free-thinking, anti-Academic education, in the Academy and Institute of Civil Engineers, nurtured leading architects of the next generation as varied in persuasion as the Vesnins, Shchuko, Fomin, Shchusev. This large six-storeyed building in grey stone forms a cul-de-sac and two closed courts around a square that was then occupied by a church. Typical site-filling of the period, but executed in a restrained and urbane eclecticism that he considered appropriately unassertive for private homes. A convinced exponent of the unity and discipline represented by classicism, but always with innovative interpretation.
(Ministry building)

### 118 Dinamo Building 1928–9
I A FOMIN & A Ia LANGMAN
ulitsa Dzerzhinskogo, 12 *Metro: Dzerzhinskaia*
Among the few built examples of Fomin's pursuit during the twenties of 'a reconstruction of the classic'. Won a competition, with project for two such buildings, symmetrical about Furkasovskii pereulok. It is hard to know whether two would have been built. His attempt to preserve classicism's 'strict discipline and order' whilst discarding its stylistic details has produced a gross, almost grotesque administrative and services building on the corner with seven storeys of paired, rounded piers, circular attic windows and jutting balconies. The latter are the only connection made to the adjoining housing, seven-storeyed with a tower of fourteen. The more positive claim to novelty was its still then unusual combination into one block of housing, servicing and work functions for the employees of one single enterprise. Rendered concrete.
(State Security Building; X)

### 119 Offices and shop of the M S Kuznetsov Porcelain and Faience Company 1898 F O SHEKHTEL'
ulitsa Kirova, 8/2 *Metro: Dzerzhinskaia*
A transitional building between eclecticism and *Moderne*. Many features in common with the smaller no 89, including full exploitation of the framed construction to liberate interior trading space; wholehearted use of plate-glass for enormous areas of glazing, and the use of this to generate principal elevational rhythm; figurative decorative motifs alongside the near-abstract derivations from classicism, with the young woman's head and floating hair common at this time, setting up strange dissonances in the scale. Four large arched bays form a polygonal street corner, closed L with tower, and extended R with two arched and two narrow bays. Proportions of rustication at street level nicely transmitted through arch rustication at 1st and 2nd to the vertical rhythm of the top.
(Branch of the glass and china shop *Dom Farfora*.)

### 120 I E Kuznetsov's Apartment Building 1910
B M VELIKOVSKII & A N MILIUKOV with facade by A A & V A VESNIN
ulitsa Kirova, 15 *Metro: Dzerzhinskaia*
Aleksandr and Viktor Vesnin worked in this office from 1908–10, though technically still students. Execution corresponds to the published drawings here (cf no 113) except for the unifying giant order used on bay and central windows at 2nd and 3rd floors. Ground and first floors are large-windowed shops; three floors of apartments above, whose simple fenestration at the sides is developed into a finely judged play of projection and recession, trabeated and curved elements, in the centre. A confident synthesis of neo-classical and *Moderne* elements.
(*Instrumenty* and other shops.)

### 121 Apartment Building of the Stroganov College 1904–7 F O SHEKHTEL'
ulitsa Kirova, 24 *Metro: Kirovskaia*
A very advanced piece of middle class housing in Russia for its date. Occupies a whole block with C-shaped, perimeter development of 5 storeys with one almost free-standing 'wing' protruding into the central court. Courtyard entered from the side street, for a privacy then unusual. One of the very first schemes to use a concrete frame for commercial accommodation at ground level and first floor, with brick-built housing above. Convenience of the 4–7-roomed apartments quite exceptional. Paired around 'front' entrance stairs but each also shares a back, service stair at the other end, their plans being linear with rooms to court and street about a central corridor-hall. The development also contained its own boiler house and electricity generation, garages, laundry, basement storage rooms, a dispensary, and shopping and office accommodation on the 3 main street fronts. Elevations are austerely simple in grey-brown matt glazed brick with cream stone spandrels and string-courses. Vestigial acanthus-leaf frieze-cum-capitals at first floor, other-

wise the only decoration is ceramic panels in blue and cream on the housing floors whose superbly delicate sweeps of Art Nouveau garlanding are still visible, though decayed.

**122 Central Post Office 1911–12** O R MUNTS, engineer L I NOVIKOV, elevational treatment V A, L A & A A VESNIN.
ulitsa Kirova, 26a *Metro: Kirovskaia*
Building design and basic schema of three-storeyed facade by Munts. Outer wings stand forward to the building line from the main flat-arcaded facade, from whose centre protrudes a cubic block with large central arched window, that rises to a blind 4th storey. Over that, a flat dome on a tall drum with 12 arched windows. Form of dome, relation to blind walling, arcaded corbelled detailing at eaves and long horizontals give the building an early-Byzantine air with which the almost Brunelleschian delicacy of the triple-arched central porch cannot compete. Reads like a somewhat literal and immature essay on the theme of his well-known 1916 discussion of the classic, or 'architecture as art' and medieval, or 'architecture as construction', entitled 'The Parthenon or Sta Sophia?'. Vesnins merely detailed and executed. Now smoothly rendered and a gloomy grey.

**123 Tsentrosoiuz Building 1928–35\***
LE CORBUSIER & P JEANNERET with executive architect N Ia KOLLI
ulitsa Kirova, 39 *Metro: Kirovskaia*
Administrative centre of the Cooperatives network, to accommodate 2,500 office workers in 3 rectangular blocks of 8 storeys, in an extended H-form with free-standing auditorium building at the rear. Formal entrance intended to be at LH end, not on Kirova. Open sections of the ground floor have been filled in, and certain other changes made. Dark pinkish-grey sandstone facing is dreary amidst Moscow's coloured stuccoes by now.
(Central Statistical Administration of the USSR: X)

**124 Polytechnical Society Building 1904–6**
A V KUZNETSOV
ulitsa Griboedova, 4 and Kharitonevskii pereulok *Metro: Lermontovskaia*
Early Moscow work by the principal turn-of-the-century pioneer and publicist of concrete in Russian architecture, then making his name mainly in large and environmentally advanced factory buildings, especially for the textile industry, in provincial industrial cities, after post-graduate technical studies in Germany and Italy. A tall building in a form of Perpendicular Gothic, with corbelled tower features emphasising skyline; 4 storeys over 5-arched arcade at ground level; bay elements and close mullions give dramatic verticality. Demonstrates Kuznetsov's early concern to find 'a truthful union of technology and art'. He was technically interested in the Gothic as 'the best and most truthful epoch of architecture, with a highly developed technology, . . . that depicted a building's structure, and the static forces operating in it, through its external forms.'
(Academy of Sciences of the USSR, House of Technology; X)

**125 Gostorg Building 1925–7\*** B M VELIKOVSKII with M O BARSHCH, G VEGMAN & M GAKEN.
ulitsa Kirova, 47 *Metro: Lermontovskaia*
A dramatically bold gesture in its time by this established architect and engineer (cf no 120) with his young Constructivist assistants. One of the very few that took off where the best rationalist *Moderne* had stopped at the Revolution, with aesthetic rooted in direct use of materials and expression of structure; quality of light, which early photos show to have been dramatic

internally, especially in such areas as the staircases; and of proportions, which are not unhappy. A concrete frame with 100% glazed infill, rendered and white painted. Square but tapering plan with two internal courts; mainly 6 storeys but recessed central bay rises to seven. Original project was far higher, but this, like no 17, was a victim of the 1925 height restriction. Exhibition and operations spaces on the higher ground level and first floor, offices above. Roof-terraces edged in simplest steel railings.
(Ministry of Trade of the RSFSR.)

**126 M M Levin's Apartment House 1909–10**
A K GOTMAN
Kirovskii proezd *Metro: Lermontovskaia*
Four storeys of apartments over one commercial floor, rising to stepped towers at each side whose form and simple grid of close-spaced mullions are of Art Deco flavour. Vestigially classical engaged columns frame ground-level windows, L & R, with some delicately geometrical period glazing, whilst half the height of the two columns supporting the entrance comprises bold and square-cut women's heads whose hanging hair is matched with upright acanthus leaves above, into a device evocative of Red Indians. Other flat and stylised decorative motifs have the air of 1930s Sweden. Strangely original building, though not in the best condition.

**127 F I Afremov's Apartment House 1904\***
O O SHISHKOVSKII
Sadovaia-Spasskaia ulitsa, 19 *Metro: Lermontovskaia*
Moscow's first eight-storeyed building, thus regarded as a 'wonder' and called a 'skyscraper' in its time. Also enormously long, with a cliff-like street elevation comprising an almost undifferentiated grid, forty windows long by seven over the higher ground floor of shops. With single and double protrusions of elevational bays however, over three of which broad and handsome Art Nouveau panels break the roofline through the very deep curving cornice, and with subtly rhythmic patterning of different portions of the facade, the whole effect is delicate. Glazed brick and stucco, in cream.

**128 Narkomzem Building 1928–33**
A V SHCHUSEV
Orlikov pereulok, 1/11 *Metro: Lermontovskaia*
An essay in the asymmetries and 'stylessness' of modernism by one who had already practiced several styles, but spent much of the twenties doing planning. Eight storeys, mainly of offices on corridors, around a square courtyard entered at the rear corner; numerous personnel entrances around the street perimeter. Horizontally banded fenestration runs around all elevations with local variations, the strongest elevational element being a half-round full height bay on the main corner with Sadovaia-Spasskaia. Rendered exterior, in warm pink.
(Ministry of Agriculture of the USSR, successor to the People's Commissariat of Agriculture, Narkomzem; X).

**129 Kazan Railway Station 1913–26**
A V SHCHUSEV
Komsomolskaia ploshchad', SE side *Metro: Komsomolskaia*
An extensive complex whose scale and fragmentation belie the simplicities of the railway sheds behind. The whole scheme a plagiarisation of an earlier Shekhtel' project for this site, of greater coherence. Shchusev's

tower derives from the Kazan Kremlin and other monuments of that region, but many details, eg round windows, are from the Moscow, Naryshkin, Baroque of pre-Petrine years. Originally faced in red brick and white stone true to that same period, but unhistorically refaced in pure stone in 1940. Mural paintings and other elements of the ornate interior decoration (eg of restaurant) contributed by three great realist painters of the pre-Revolutionary World of Art and Union of Russian Artists groups Boris Kustodiev, Evgenii Lansere and Nikolai Rerikh. L of the station itself is one of the very first purpose-built workers' clubs, for railway workers, built within the complex by Shchusev during 1925–6.

**130 Iaroslavl' Railway Station 1902\***
F O SHEKHTEL'
Komsomolskaia ploshchad', N corner. *Metro: Komsomolskaia*
The *Moderne* at its closest to National Romanticism. A larger-than-life essay in the forms of North Russian architecture to celebrate the first direct railway line up to the Arctic coast. Particularly interesting comparison with no 129 for the light touch with which Shekhtel' selects essentials of the architectural language (roof forms, certain defensive details, general compositional relationships) so that a thoroughly functional building results and the scalar conflict between medieval and modern is dissolved. Warm wooden architecture of the N has become evocatively cold white and blue: relief panels and polychrome tilework are set in the dominating stonework of the upper walls. Ceramic work to Shekhtel's designs was made in Abramtsevo workshops just up the line. Mural paintings of N Russian landscape by World-of-Art member and Abramtsevo habitué Konstantin Korovin originally formed friezes to the austerely *Moderne* Waiting Room and Main Hall.

**131 V Pravdina's House 1908** Architect Unknown
Sadovo-Samotechnaia ulitsa, 5 *Metro: Kolkhoznaia*
Rare remaining example of the relatively modest middle class house with strongly Art Nouveau features of the *Moderne*. Two-storeyed, in three bays. Attractive but not too coherent styling of the large windows in the two R-hand ones, but splendid bulbously curved arch window embraces the front door, L, beside which vertical elements thrust up through cornice to a typical roofline feature. Delicately detailed, in pinkish tile and plasterwork.
(Party building; X)

**132 Viktor Vasnetsov's House 1892\***
V M VASNETSOV

pereulok Vasnetsova, 13 *Metro: Kolkhoznaia*
Purist's model of that particular brand of Russianism most characteristic of the fin-de-siècle period, by one of its pioneers. In his early period at Abramtsevo colony (1880–5), had been one of the first to investigate the Russian vernacular tradition seriously from a constructive and spirit-seeking point of view akin to that of the Western Arts-and-Crafts Movement. Through later friendship with the younger Shekhtel', transmitted that view of the Russian heritage into the *Moderne*. A modest L-shaped house 1-, 2- and 3-storeyed elements entered in Russian fashion through a gated yard (*dvor*). At junction of rectangular elements, of cream stuccoed brick, rises 3-storeyed log-built tower with stairs and landings, with ogee-gabled roof. Entire construction and details in the vernacular. Superb Russian Arts-and-Crafts furniture and fittings internally.
(House-Museum of Viktor Vasnetsov; open to public.)

**133 Solodovnikov Cheap Housing Block 1906**
T I BARDT
ulitsa Giliarovskogo, 57 & 65 *Metro: Rizhskaia*
First significant initiative of private capital to provide cheap 'modern' housing for the Moscow poor. Imperial Philanthropic Society had some accommodation; City Council had done nothing. Six million ruble bequest by well-known businessman Solodovnikov lead eventually to design competition in 1906 run by Institute of Civil Engineers for single-person and family housing. Former not extant. Here one room for each of 185 families, with kitchens and toilets etc shared in groups, all to exact standards of daylighting, area, construction and especially ventilation. Communal dining room, child-minding, reading and recreation rooms. Solidly built 5-storeyed block of triangular plan on corner site; brick with stone dressings and touches of ceramic and textured friezes, round tower at corner, *Moderne* features at the roofline which relieve the dominant austerity.

**134 Vindavskii Railway Station 1899**
Iu F DIDERIKHS
Rizhskaia ploshchad' *Metro: Rizhskaia*
Confection of Russian medieval motifs, mainly 16th and 17th century, assembled with such vigour, and boldly enough executed, to be more enjoyable than most of the contemporary and very routine Pseudo-Russian public buildings. Brick, painted pale green and white. One and two-storeyed, with high-pitched roofs and ogee gables, all of Russian solidity.
(Rizhskii, or Riga, Mainline Railway Terminus.)

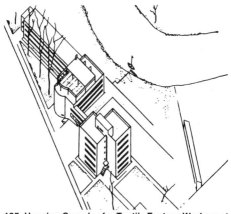

**135 Housing Complex for Textile Factory Workers at Rostokino 1929–31** M Ia GINZBURG & S A LISAGOR
LOCATION: This building is located just N of the VDNKh (Exhibition of Economic Achievements), among trees on the S bank of the Moskva River at the bend, N of Galushkina ulitsa. *Metro: VDNKh, then walk or 2 stops on tram.*
Another experimental building 'of transitional type' by Constructivist architects (see nos 28 and 49). Planned as three elements; 2 of living units, 1 of communal facilities between. Nearest road, a 5-storeyed block, brick built, 4 identical 2-roomed apartments on each floor, with micro-kitchen and shower etc, for family workers (extant). Second, hostel-type block comprising 2 layers of 10 type 'F' units, timber frame with pressed-board cladding, parallel to River to the W (gone). Communal block between, on E end of latter, linked with bridge (gone) to former, containing dining room, laundry, meeting rooms etc (extant). Evocative, even though incomplete, and somewhat modified; white, with distinctive strip-windows etc.

**136 Workers' Club of the Burevestnik Shoe Factory 1929** K S MEL'NIKOV
3-ia Rybinskaia ulitsa *Metro: Krasnosel'skaia*
A dramatic little building thanks to the 5-petalled plan of its fully glazed and nearly free-standing block on the street front. Linked by a stair to the long rectangular block behind, this could be variously subdivided on each floor by radial partitions, into sunny little meeting rooms etc. Otherwise very simple, in plain cream stucco or brick. Most significant change visually is insertion of two further horizontal glazing bars into each rounded window panel, which makes a fretfull, horizontal emphasis here.

**137 Club of the Union of Municipal Employees named for IV Rusakov 1927–8\*** K S MEL'NIKOV

Stromynskaia ploshchad', 10 *Metro: Sokolniki*
Most dramatic of Mel'nikov's workers' clubs and aesthetically perhaps the most satisfactory, even now the original articulation of the rear part, as brick with rendered trim has been eliminated. Plan is a 60° segment with stage, flytower and some services at its focus. Upper levels of the raked and galleried 1200-seat auditorium are split by two triangular staircases (vertical glazing on facade) so that mechanically moved partitions can form several small auditoria here, where rear walls emerge onto the street elevation as soaring cantilevered segments, which originally carried bold typography. In this club other accommodation is relatively limited.

**138 Mossoviet Truck Garage 1929** K S MEL'NIKOV
Novo-Riazanskaia ulitsa *Metro: Lermontovskaia*
Ingenious and effective plan for the efficient garaging and maintenance of Mossoviet's fleet of goods and servicing vehicles. Two ends of a half-annular shed join the road as entrance and exit to the 110 parking bays around its interior perimeters. In the centre of the street elevation, equally accessible to all vehicle spaces, are a block of maintenance shops. Bold industrial glazing throughout, plus circular windows marking entry and exit; red brick, with radial steel trusses roofing the curved shed.
(Now used for buses.)

**139 Church of the Second Community of Old Believers 1907–8** I E BONDARENKO
Tokmakov pereulok, behind flats at 13/15 *Metro: Baumanskaia*
A free composition with the full expressiveness characteristic of the *Moderne* by an earlier leading propagandist of the Neo-Russian (cf no 64). For the purist, Old Believer sect. High bell-tower over porch is a steeply-pitched gable, borne with full sense of its weight upon squat columns. Ceramic work depicting angels and plants on this and the ogee side gables (*kokoshniki*). Solemnity of its planar surfaces and massive geometry formerly lightened by slender ogee-cupolas astride bell-tower gable and main body of church. Half ruined but remains recognisable. (Workshop/garage).

**140 Church of the Virgin's Shroud (Pokrova Pres-'iatoi Bogoroditsy) 1911** I E BONDARENKO
Gavrikov pereulok, 29, between ulitsy *Metro: Baumanskaia*
F Engels and B Pochtovaia.
Large, bulky church built for the Uspenskii-Pokrovskii Mission (obshchina) of Old Believers in a Neo-Russian style of mixed origins. Main cubic volume topped by a short drum and flat cupola; half-cylindrical apse one end; dumpy octagonal tower over bell and porch at the other; flat, 'cut-out' gables of free silhouette 'applied' to the other two elevations, breaking roofline of cube. Some ceramic and relief decoration. Otherwise white walls under dark slate roofs. Strange distorted proportions, flat curves and massive scale typical of what the *Moderne* brought to revivalism.

## COMPETITION SITES AND RELEVANT MUSEUMS ■

A *Site for the Palace of Soviets competition, 1931–3*
Metro: Kropotkinskaia
(Open air heated swimming pool, built in the Palace's circular foundations.)

B *Museum of Architecture named for A V Shchusev**
Prospekt Kalinina, 5 *Metro: Biblioteka imeni Lenina – Kalininskaia*
*Closed Mon & Fri; otherwise 11–7 daily.*
The first group of rooms, on the first floor, has a permanent display of original drawings etc by leading architects of the 1920s including Shchusev, Ginzburg, Mel'nikov, Ladovskii etc. Highly recommended.

C *Site for the Palace of Labour competition, 1922–3*
Metro: Prospekt Marksa – Ploshchad' Sverdlova
(Hotel Moskva, built early 1930s.)

D *Site for the Commissariat of Heavy Industry (Narkomtiazhprom) competition, 1934*
East side of Red Square *Metro: Prospekt Marksa*
(Site was never cleared. Still GUM etc.)

E *Museum of the History and Reconstruction of Moscow*
Novaia Ploshchad', 12 *Metro: Dzerzhinskaia*
*Closed Tues & last day of month; otherwise Mon 10–4; Wed & Fri 2–9; Thurs, Sat & Sun 10–6.*
Originally founded in 1896. Reorganised after the Revolution by Apollinarii Vasnetsov, historical-topographical painter brother of V M Vasnetsov (see nos 54, 58, 114). Now housed in 19th-century neo-classical church. All aspects of the city's physical and architectural evolution are displayed with archival materials, models, drawings etc.

F *Vladimir Maiakovskii Museum*
Proezd Serova, 3/6 *Metro: Dzerzhinskaia*
*Closed Wed; otherwise Mon & Thurs 12–10; Sun, Tues, Fri & Sat 10–6.*
Modern insertion into a building where he lived. Lively and well displayed collection on several floors, of materials relating to his early life, pre-Revolutionary activity in the Russian Futurist movement, and agitational, advertising and theatrical work in the 1920s. Recommended, for background and atmosphere of this section of the 1900–1930 avant-garde.

G *Main building of the VhUTEMAS-VKhTEIN, 1920–30*
ulitsa Kirova, 21b *Metro: Kirovskaia – Turgenevskaia*
Taken over from the pre-Revolutionary Moscow College of Painting, Sculpture and Architecture, but originally built around 1790 by Bazhenov, as the neo-classical mansion of the merchant Iushkov.

## INDEX BY DESIGN OR STARTING DATES ▬▬▬